DYLAN THOMAS: THE
LEGEND AND THE POET

Dylan Thomas: The Legend and the Poet

Dylan Thomas: The Legend and the Poet

A COLLECTION OF BIOGRAPHICAL AND CRITICAL ESSAYS

EDITED BY

E. W. TEDLOCK

GREENWOOD PRESS, PUBLISHERS
WESTPORT, CONNECTICUT

Library of Congress Cataloging in Publication Data

Tedlock, Ernest Warnock, 1910- ed.
Dylan Thomas: the legend and the poet.

Reprint of the ed. published by Heinemann, London.
1. Thomas, Dylan, 1914-1953.
PR6039.H52Z855 1974 821'.9'12 [B] 72-9050
ISBN 0-8371-6564

Originally published in 1960 by William Heinemann, Ltd., London

Reprinted in 1975 by Greenwood Press
A division of Congressional Information Service
88 Post Road West, Westport, Connecticut 06881

Library of Congress Catalog Card Number 72-9050

ISBN 0-8371-6564-4

Printed in the United States of America

10 9 8 7 6 5 4 3

Contents

PART TWO

THE POET

Acknowledgments

The editor and publishers are grateful to the following for permission to include copyright material: *Accent* (for an essay by Cid Corman); *Adam International Review* (for essays by Philip Burton, David Daiches, Augustus John, Pamela Hansford Johnson, John Lehmann, Mario Luzi, W. S. Merwin, Cecil Price, Suzanne Roussillat and Ralph Wishart); Mrs Mary Campbell (for an essay by Roy Campbell); J. M. Dent & Sons Ltd (for extracts from the poetry of Dylan Thomas); *Encounter* (for essays by Marjorie Adix, George Barker, Lawrence Durrell, Daniel Jones, Louis MacNeice and Theodore Roethke); Mr Lawrence Durrell (for his essay 'The Shades of Dylan Thomas'); Mr Geoffrey Grigson (for his essay 'How Much Me Now Your Acrobatics Amaze'); the *Hudson Review* (for an essay by David Aivaz); the *Kenyon Review* (for essays by Robert Horan and Geoffrey Moore); Mr E. Glyn Lewis (for his essay 'Dylan Thomas'); the *New Republic* (for an essay by D. S. Savage); the *New Statesman* (for an essay by G. S. Fraser); Mr Elder Olson (for his essay 'The Poetry of Dylan Thomas'); *Poetry* (for essays by Roy Campbell and Karl Shapiro); the *Poetry Review* (for essays by John Graddon and Geoffrey Johnson); Mr Hugh Gordon Porteus (for his essay 'Map of Llareggub'); Routledge & Kegan Paul Ltd (for essays by Geoffrey Grigson and Francis Scarfe); Mr Francis Scarfe (for his essay 'Dylan Thomas: A Pioneer'); *Sewanee Review* (for an essay by Marshall Stearns); Dame Edith Sitwell (for her essay 'Comment on Dylan Thomas'); the Trustees of the Dylan Thomas Estate (for use of copyright material by Dylan Thomas); *Vogue* (for an essay by John Davenport); and *Yale Literary Magazine* (for essays by William Jay Smith, Alastair Reid and Richard Eberhart). The editor also wishes to acknowledge the help of Robert Brain of the Editorial Department of William Heinemann Ltd.

Introduction

When Dylan Thomas died a few years ago, many people felt a personal loss. It was not necessary to have known him to feel this way, though a surprising number had – he was hardly an isolate, unconvivial poet, and could be met in pubs and American bars and at low and highbrow parties, where his unconventional behaviour had already become legendary. For many it was enough to have heard his reading voice, over the B.B.C., in lecture halls, and in recordings. The voice was powerfully and unashamedly emotional and dramatic, giving the illusion of endless vitality while it celebrated, as one of its keynotes, the agony of inevitable death. Through it other men's poetry as well as his own found a large audience at a time when poetry seemed to have retreated altogether to coteries of varied seriousness and philosophical and social position, to the little magazines, and to the lecture halls of the universities. So at his death there was an expression of regret, grief, and even anger unprecedented in our time. It was said that he was a slow suicide through his legendary beer-drinking, and that the hidden cause was a milieu increasingly unsympathetic to man as man. As raconteur and good drinking-companion, he represented, to some, the survival of an apparently vanished species – the Villonesque king of the vagabonds, taking 'vagabonds' to mean what we all essentially are in our loves, laughter, suffering, and eventual deaths. He had struck a blow for basic humanity, and died of the fight.

This personal aspect of the man, with its truths, its exaggerations, and its apocryphal anecdotes – anyone in touch with literature can repeat stories about him – should not be neglected, and is well represented in this book. But, though it recedes with the man, it threatens to draw attention from his essential claim to permanent significance – his poetry. My hope, in gathering material for this book, is to restore the focus. Beyond the stories, plays, and film scripts, his poems are his most serious and crafted work, and it is on their quality he must stand or fall. In the second part of this book I have presented the kinds of attack made – charges of Celtic loquacity, mere verbal cleverness, wilful obscurity, physiological obsessions, ethical and religious immaturity – and the responses by Thomas's defenders. The reader can make up his own mind where the weight of the evidence lies. To me it falls on Thomas's side, particularly when the critics attempt to understand the special nature of his language, and seriously read the poems – hard, but it seems to me, rewarding work. As for limited themes, after all, whatever our civilised occupations and preoccupations, procreation and death are basic in our existences; it can be strengthening and even exalting to be reminded; and Thomas may range further than was thought.

In making this book I have tried to look at everything written about Thomas. Because of duplication it was necessary to omit some otherwise good things. Coverage of the important aspects was the controlling criterion. William H. Huff's bibliography was very useful, and he was kind enough to look over the final list of selections. Rare periodicals, and some others not in my own university's library, were secured with the help of our reference librarians, and I thank them. I owe thanks to the University research committee for financial aid in assembling the manuscript. I am especially grateful for the generosity of the authors and periodicals represented.

University of New Mexico,
August 5, 1959.

PART ONE

The Man

Suzanne Roussillat

TO WRITE A BIOGRAPHY of Dylan Thomas is premature but the role played by his past years in the formation of his personality cannot be ignored. This is not a psychoanalysis of Dylan Thomas; it is only a sketch based on the details which were given to me by the poet himself. However, as his works are a lyrical inquiry into the springs of his own being, an attempt to recreate the background in which he was brought up and to point out the main influences which nourished his mind as a child and a young man may help future biographers and literary historians.

1. '*The Sea Town*', *Kingdom of his Childhood.*

Born in 1914 in South Wales of Welsh parents, he was brought up in Swansea. An old lady remembers him at seven as the fair, curly-headed boy of a painting by Sir John Millais – 'Bubbles'. Perhaps the portrait given by the poet himself in one of his short stories is, if not as romantic, more suggestive and true than the old lady's idealised recollection: 'Four boys on a roof . . . one small, thin, indecisively active, quick to get dirty, curly . . .' He was a happy child, full of life but dreamy and imaginative, and he regretted to have to give up his explorations in Cwmdonkin Park to enter, at eleven, the Swansea Grammar School, where his father was an English master, revered by his pupils for possessing the secret power of making them love and enjoy what he taught them. The young Dylan, esteemed as a friend, admired as an excellent runner indifferent to fame, disconcerted his school-fellows by steadily remaining at the bottom of the class, though the son of the English master. He was a bad and weak pupil in every subject but English, where he was exceptionally brilliant. He revealed his literary and artistic gifts in school activities: he animated the Reading and Debating Societies, and the dramatic group was proud of his acting in the role of Oliver Cromwell in Drinkwater's play, and of Roberts in *Strife* by Galsworthy. In 1929, he became the editor of the school magazine to which he contributed generously: stories, light verse, parodies of modern poets like Osbert Sitwell, Sassoon and Yeats, an article about modern poetry, written at fifteen, and no less than twenty-six poems in six years. Most of them already reveal his emotional and imaginative nature, witness this poem written by the small boy of Form 3:

Rose-red banners across the dawn
Brown sails at sea on a misty morn,
Racing shadows across the corn,
These are the things that I love.

First dim star in the twilight hour,
Drenchings sweet of the hawthorn flower,
Wall-flower kissed by a silver shower,
And the clear blue sky above.

Wistful song as the shadows fall,
The whisper of trees and soft bird call
A glimmering moon – and over all
The tang of a wind from the sea.

or two 'Images' written in 1931, and already more original:

I

Here is the bright green sea,
And underneath a thousand fishes
Moving their scaly bodies soundlessly
Among a bright green world of weeds.

These thousand pebbles are a thousand eyes,
Each sharper than the sun;
These waves are dancers;
Upon a thousand, pointed toes
They step the sea,
Lightly, as in a pantomime.

II

My golden bird the sun
Has spread his wings and flown away
Out of the swinging cage
You call the sky,
And, like his tired shadow
White with love,
My silver bird the moon
Flies up again
On to her perch of stars.

In other literary works written while he went to school, many qualities of the future poet and story-teller can already be detected: a certain morbidity, a sprinkling sense of humour, and a liking for cascades of alliterative sounds: his 'story of a boy with homicidal tendencies who came to a sad end' is entitled 'The Terrible Tale of Tom Tipplewhite'. His childhood and his school-days made him familiar with the Welsh Nonconformist creed and rites, to which he probably owed his thorough knowledge of the Bible, from which later he was to borrow so many symbols. The Bible was certainly the only book which could be said to have widely contributed to his intellectual formation. As a schoolboy, he was more attracted by the direct visions and sensations received from the outside world than by the second-hand and dead revelations found in books. To walk in the districts of Swansea where he was brought up is revealing; interesting discoveries can be taken back. The unique situation of the school itself must have attracted the young poet of Form 3, more than his master's teaching. Built half-way on the slope of Town Hill, the school, overlooking the low part of the town, opens its windows upon Swansea Bay. The immensity of sea and sky in the blurred distance gives an impression of infinity probably perceived by the sensitive and dreamy Dylan Thomas. From everywhere in the Uplands, you can recapture the same vision above the serrated rows of chimney-pots. At the very top of the seaward hill, all the streets meet to vanish abruptly, leaving you alone with the impression of having reached one end of the world. Beyond the band of low town, too narrow to be seen, the sea again stretches, on the right hand, to the rocky end of Mumbles Pier where the light-house, a glow-worm in its head, takes the place of the castle as soon as daylight fades away. Gripped to the slope, near the Thomases' house, Cwmdonkin Park opens its gates upon a kingdom of fairy visions 'of form and colour, sunshine and shadow' which caught the attention of young Dylan Thomas. The steep path, winding on hill-side, between willow groves and rhododendron mazes, leads at the top to a green screen of trees, whose dark figures stand out against the fused shades of clouds and waves in which the park seems to plunge its root.

Are these vistas of the ever-recurring sea as a distant background responsible for the sea imagery so rich in Dylan Thomas's poetry? Are they the origin of the frequent associations of the deep with the universal womb? Perhaps Dylan Thomas's stories are full of echoes of his dreams as a child, who 'in the warm, safe island of his bed' was haunted by 'sleepy midnight Swansea flowing and rolling round outside the house'. This is confirmed by a B.B.C. broadcast entitled *Swansea Revisited* in which Dylan Thomas devoted a large section to his life in school and in Swansea, still remembered with emotion.

2. *Departure from Wales – 'The Land of my Fathers. My fathers can keep it'.*

At seventeen, Dylan Thomas left school. It was 1931, the bitterest year of the post-war distress in Wales; tin-plate factories were shut, unemployment bred poverty and moral despondency. Dylan Thomas sometimes mentions 'the cranes and the coaltips' so typical of the Welsh valleys; he never refers to his period of misery, or to the industrial activities of his home-country. It shows probably his attitude of complete detachment from any economical, social or political problems. He had nevertheless to cope with material difficulties and to find a way of living. For a time on the staff of the *Herald of Wales*, a Swansea weekly paper, he wrote critical articles about local poetry. Unsatisfied, his possibilities being constantly bridled, he thought of leaving Wales, as if, seeing Swansea with the eyes of a grown-up, he could no longer bear the new face of the town of his happy childhood. 'Young Mr Thomas was at the moment without employment, but it was understood that he would soon be leaving for London to make a career in Chelsea as a free-lance journalist; he was penniless, and hoped in a vague way to live on women'. If this Mr Thomas of one of his stories is not the poet himself, his situation must have been very similar. His intense nature, enjoying all the pleasures of life, was perhaps responsible for a few pranks which did not make him very popular (Wales was still in the thirties, the strict Nonconformist country where deacons had the right of discussing or condemning your private life).

In an address to a Scottish Society of Writers in Edinburgh, Dylan Thomas gave the reason for his exile:

'I am a Welshman who does not live in his own country, mainly because he still wants to eat and drink, be rigged and roofed, and no Welsh writer can hunt his bread and butter in Wales unless he pulls his forelock to the *Western Mail*, Bethesdas on Sunday, and enters public-houses by the back door, and reads Caradoc Evans only when alone, and by candlelight. . . .

'Regarded in England as a Welshman (and a waterer of England's milk), and in Wales as an Englishman, I am too unnational to be here at all. I should be living in a small private leper-house in Hereford or Shropshire, one foot in Wales and my vowels in England. Wearing red flannel drawers, a tall witch's hat, and a coracle tiepin, and speaking English so Englishly that I sound like a literate Airedale, who has learnt his s's and c's by correspondence course, piped and shagged and tweeded, but also with a harp, the look of all Sussex in my poached eyes, and a whippet under my waistcoat.

'And here are Scotch writers at home, their only home, and greeted by writers of England and France, and a border case like myself!'

In the end of the address, more humorous than bitter, he seemed to be just laughing at some of his countrymen, who considered his departure from Wales as a second betrayal, the first being to write in English when born a Welshman. An echo of the severe accusation at the beginning is found in *The Three Weird Sisters*, whose script was written by Dylan Thomas. This film is bitterly resented by Welsh people, as it dwells upon the weaknesses of Welsh people, describes the Welshman as having 'a lie in his teeth and a hymn on his lips'. Under this caricature, there is pitiless grudge, probably due to his young, violent and intransigent nature; like many artists he knew 'hard times' at the beginning of his career, the more so as it began in an industrial town, at a time when the economic crisis was at its climax. Wales had nothing to offer to a young poet in those difficult years.

3. *Literary Years – London and Oxford.*

His vocation was happily stronger than material handicaps. He had already written some of the poems of *Eighteen Poems* – first book published in 1934, owing to the initiative of the editors of 'Poets' Corner' in the *Sunday Referee*, when he left Wales for England. London was the only place where he could find opportunities of revealing his literary gifts, and have his books published. *Twenty-Five Poems* followed *Eighteen Poems* in 1936, after having been published in different reviews, such as *New Verse*, *John o' London's Weekly*, *Contemporary Prose and Poetry*. It was then that Miss Edith Sitwell wrote in the *Sunday Times*: 'Here alone, among the poets of the younger generation is one who could produce sonnets worthy of our great heritage.' Just before the outbreak of war in 1939, *The Map of Love* was published, consisting of poems written in the last two years and of stories, some of which were written before he was twenty. *The Map of Love*, dedicated to Caitlin, his Irish wife, celebrates two great events of the poet's life: his marriage and the birth of his first son. (Cardiff Museum exhibits a portrait of Dylan Thomas and a portrait of Caitlin by the Welsh painter Augustus John.)

The same year, *The World I Breathe* was published in America, adding new stories to stories and poems previously published in the first three books. In 1940, Dylan Thomas published his first and only book of stories, largely autobiographical, which constitute the light section of his works. It was the first book of Thomas's to be translated into French by M. F. Dufau-Labeyrie. During the war, unfit for military service, Dylan Thomas worked in London, on the staff of the B.B.C., and after the war for the Third Programme, and writing documentary film scripts for the Ministry of Information, such as *Our Country* partly published in *Wales*. In 1942 *New Poems* were published in America.

In 1946, his new book of verse *Deaths and Entrances* made him known to a wider public, and was highly praised by press opinions.

In the same year, *The Selected Writings of Dylan Thomas* were published in America; new stories, 'Quite Early One Morning', 'Memories of Christmas' and 'Conversation: About Christmas' were found in *Wales* and in *Picture Post*.

Taking advantage of the acceptable compromise offered by the B.B.C. and film firms, which allowed him to supply the needs of his family, without forcing him to leave the fields of artistic creation, he made several important broadcasts: 'A Holiday Memory' and 'The Crumbs of One Man's Year' published in the *Listener*; and in the Return Journey series, 'Swansea Revisited'. He wrote, at the same time, several film scripts, *The Three Weird Sisters* and *These Are The Men*.

The listeners of the Third Programme became acquainted with his voice: he often participated in poetry readings, illustrating talks about modern poetry. The rich intonations of his voice, his expressive recitation, brought a great illumination to the poems and stories that he read, and the conviction to the listener that Thomas's poetry, more than any other kind of poetry, must be read aloud to be really appreciated. When reading verse of other poets, he generally chose visionary and religious poems, such as Blake's 'Tiger, Tiger' or Vaughan's poems. The controversy of opinions over his reading of the part of Satan in *Paradise Lost* still reverberates. He was heard too in radio plays, in the role of Agamemnon, for instance, in *Trimalchio's Feast*, a dramatisation from the *Satyricon* of Petronius, written by Louis MacNeice, and in several Shakespeare productions. Though these productions required often his presence in London, he always refused to live in this 'nasty grey cantankerous place, full of corpses which I dislike so much'.

He lived for several years with his wife, three children and old parents in South Leigh, a small hamlet, near Witney. Being a few miles from Oxford he used to spend many merry evenings there in the company of a few friends, generally of Celtic origin; to the academic entertainments of the time-honoured University town they preferred a stroll at night in the picturesque lanes of the old city, going from pub to pub; never so happy as when their unusual garb, or crude language, scandalised their neighbours who knew how to drink beer and remain formal and dignified.

The same informality, the absence of any restraint, was the ruling law of his family life. Walking along the broken and muddy path leading to his house, isolated and lost in a large, foggy meadow, Dylan Thomas complained to me bitterly. Though in the heart of the country, he could not find any peace at home: a caravan, outside the house, was the refuge where, locked up a part of the day, he could find the solitude and peace necessary to his work.

While despising the tea drinkers and asserting manly tastes, his favourite breakfast being a kipper and a pint of beer, he had a childish and genuine face, the expression of which has been happily recaptured by the painter, Alfred Janes. He hated meeting people, especially critics, who wanted him to speak about his poetry. Indifferent to their opinion and to literary fame, he advised me to 'write whatever you like about my poems, it does not matter'. He forgot to answer questions. He interrupted himself to introduce you, through his mimicry, to Mr Kipper-whipper, who existed but in his imagination, or to scribble on a scrap of paper strange drawings or upside-down angels with devil hooves - bad or good his poems, bad or good his behaviour, it did not matter to him—then he would draw a caricature of himself: fat, slovenly, untidy, a fag-end at his lips, and a pint of beer at hand. Then, conscious that the interview must be unusual for somebody coming from a world of conventions, he concluded and repeated again and again, 'You must be disappointed, I am an awful man.' An awful man? No, but an exuberant personality, full of zest, with an insatiable appetite for life and its pleasures; and an artist, whose first gift was enjoyment, an unbridled enjoyment of the abundance and luxuriant richness of the world.

This attempt at a portrait, owing to the short time spent with the poet while I collected material for my thesis on his work, gives the impression of a jovial personality. That is only one side of him, his works revealing often the inner struggle of a soul who courageously tears the veil of conventions and habits to find and reveal the true faces of life and death, terrifying as they may be.

To counter-balance my first impression, it may be useful to read this other portrait of Dylan Thomas, written by one of his dearest Welsh friends, Vernon Watkins. The unusual method of expression of the poem, directly borrowed from Dylan Thomas and conveying apocalyptic visions, seems to suit better the strange and true personality of Dylan Thomas. (Dylan Thomas used to exchange with Vernon Watkins long letters, where he discussed his poems and asked for advice):

He has sent me this
Late and early page
Caught the emphasis
Of last night's cartonnage,
Crumpled in the post
Bringing to lamplight
Breath's abatement,
Over- and under-statement,
Mute as a mummy's pamphlet
Long cherished by a ghost.

Who for annunciation has
The white wings of the sheldrake,
Labouring water's praise,
The blind shriek of the mandrake,
Broken shells of story,
Torn earth for love's near hand
Raised from Time's estuary,
Fed by the raven's bread;
A trespasser in tombs,
He bids the grey dust fall,
Groans in the shaping limbs:
'All stars are in my shawl.'

Who feels the deathbound signs,
Mocks the Winged Horse's fake,
Telling, as with closed eyes,
Love's language to remake,
To draw from their dumb wall
The saints to a worldly brothel

That a sinner's tongue may toll
And call the place Bethel.

Trusting a creaking house,
His roof is ruinous,
So mortal. A real wind
Beats this house of sand
Two tides like ages buffet.
The superhuman, crowned

Saints must enter this drowned
Tide-race of thy mind
To guess or understand
The face of this cracked prophet,
Which from its patient pall
I slowly take,
Drop the envelope,
Compel his disturbing shape,
And write these words on a wall
Maybe for a third man's sake.

(From 'Portrait of a Friend',
published in *Ballad of the Mari Lwyd.*)

After I met Dylan Thomas at South Leigh, he returned to Wales, to the Boat House, Laugharne, still with a simpler garage-workroom retreat from a simple house, though he was more often absent as his work and fame grew together. He visited Prague, Paris, Persia, Italy, and made three triumphant tours of the U.S.A.; his *Collected Poems* have sold nearly 10,000 copies, and won him the William Foyle Poetry Prize; his filmscript *The Doctor and the Devils* was the first 'book-of-the-film' to be published before the film was made, and was acclaimed for its atmospheric power as well as its originality; his single appearance as a story-teller on television nearly shook that unhappy medium out of its prolonged trance. He had been invited to compose a libretto for Igor Stravinsky, and at the time of his death he was working on a novel *Adventures in the Skin Trade*, a play in verse *Under Milk Wood*, and a long poem 'In Country Heaven'. He seemed to be riding a surge of creative activity to new achievements and international acclamation.

We cannot estimate what he might have achieved. His latest work since *Deaths and Entrances* has shown a greater objectivity and clarity without loss of intensity, and a better control of his verbal dexterity. The dominating quest for light and truth is made with a coherence and consistency that come from a singleness of purpose. His ruthless self-analysis and pitiless searching bring him face to face with problems which, consciously or unconsciously, beset all men. Those who are aware of having to face the same struggle, who take time, 'to arrest for the space of a breath, the hands busy about the work of the earth' in order to listen to him, are moved by its quality and sincerity. He searches for truth among those obscure forces which, identical in all men, make them feel that, beyond races, philosophies and religions, they are all in the same ark. Stripping his own being of darkness, Dylan Thomas gives to the world his own problems, his own battles, and sometimes his own victories in moving stories and imperishable poetry. To sum up his work, I should quote his own remark to Henry Treece: 'I hold a beast, an angel, and a madman in me, and my enquiry is as to their working, and my problem is their subjugation and victory, down-throw and upheaval, and my effort is their self-expression.'

Daniel Jones

OUR FIRST MEETING, nearly thirty years ago, is described in *Portrait of the Artist as a Young Dog*. I forget how the fight began. Dylan was slight, with curly hair, large soft eyes and full lips; he looked almost effeminate, but he was very tough. My own appearance was much the same, and I wore spectacles as well. Each of us seemed an easy victim, but as soon as the fight started contempt changed to respect and we became friends. This meant almost daily meetings between us for the next ten years, at his house, at my house, or, during school hours, in Cwmdonkin Park. We read aloud to one another, usually our own poems, and exchanged criticism; and some part of the time was always spent in writing, either separately or in collaboration. Music was not forgotten; I played my compositions to Dylan, and we extemporised together on the piano in four-handed duets, or on strange instruments of our own devising.

Five, Cwmdonkin Drive, and Warmley, the two houses, were very different in atmosphere. At Dylan's we had a gas fire that spluttered, an asthmatic sheep that coughed in the field opposite, and always a few owls hooting from the woods. I remember one terrifying night when we stared at one another in the gathering darkness until our heads became griffin and wyvern heads.

Warmley was not so mysterious, but it was more popular for several reasons; there were, for example, the Broadcasting Station and the Cricket Pitch. The Cricket Pitch in the back garden was about twelve feet long; every fine evening we played there without subtlety, hurling or driving the ball with the utmost force at one another, while old Harding, the neighbour, leaned on the wall smoking his pipe, sometimes calling out with perfect solemnity 'Well played, sir!' and finally asking, with a certain wistfulness, 'Will you be playing again tomorrow evening?'

Through the W.B.S. system, which consisted of two loud-speakers connected to the pick-up of a radiogram, we were able to broadcast from the upstairs to the downstairs rooms. I still have some of the programmes: 'The Rev. Percy will play three piano pieces, Buzzards at Dinner, Salute to Admiral Beattie, and Badgers Beneath My Vest'; 'Rebecca Mn will give a recital on the Rebmetpes'; 'Locomotive Bowen, the one-eyed cowhand, will give a talk on the Rocking Horse and Varnishing Industry'; 'Zoilredb Pogoho will read his poem Fiffokorp'. These broadcasters became real people to us, and we collaborated in a biography of the greatest of them, Percy. Here is a description of one of the trying experiences we inflicted on Percy's old mother: 'Near the outskirts of Panama the crippled negress was bitten severely and time upon time, invariably upon the nape, by a white hat-shaped bird'.

In prose collaboration we had to consult together all the time; the alternate sentence method proved unsuccessful. In poetry collaborations, however, we always wrote alternate lines; I had the odd-numbered lines and Dylan the even-numbered, and we made it a rule that neither of us should suggest an alteration in the other's work. These poems, of which I still have about two hundred, are a different matter from the W.B.S. fooling. It is still play, but it is what I would call serious play. The poetic style of Walter Bram, as we called ourselves, is baffingly inconsistent; it is fragile, furious, laconic, massive, delicate, incantatory, cool, flinty, violent, Chinese, Greek, and shocking. One poem may begin 'You will be surprised when I remain obdurate', and the next, 'I lay under the currant trees and told the beady berries about Jesus'. Some of the poems are very, very beautiful; very. Especially those that tell of singularly gentle and godlike action by the third person plural.

They had come from the place high on the coral hills
Where the light from the white sea fills the soil with
  ascending grace.
And the sound of their power makes motion as steep
  as the sky,
And the fruits of the great ground lie like leaves from
  a vertical flower.
They had come from the place; they had come and
  had gone again
In a season of delicate rain, in a smooth ascension of
  grace.

We had word obsessions: everything at one time was 'little' or 'white'; and sometimes an adjective became irresistibly funny in almost any connection: 'innumerable bananas', 'wilful moccasin', 'a certain Mrs Prothero'. These word games, and even the most facetious of our collaborations, had a serious experimental purpose, and there is no doubt that they played an important part in Dylan's early poetic development.

His own poetry passed in ten years from simple lyricism, reminiscent of W. H. Davies or De La Mare, to the violent imagery of the poems that first appeared in Victor Neuberg's corner of the *Sunday Referee;* on the way he came more or less under the influence of early Yeats, Aldington, Sacheverell Sitwell, Lawrence, and Hopkins, in that order; but of course there were many others.

Apart from purely literary influences Dylan was at this time self-sufficient. At the school, where his father was Senior English Master, everything offered to him was rejected. It is true that he edited the school magazine and wrote nearly all of it; that he acted in the dreary Drinkwater plays with which we were afflicted; and even argued in the debating society, if a triumphant use of the illogical can be called arguing; but school subjects were treated by him with disdain.

This was consistent; at that time, and throughout his life, Dylan hated the academic. But in those early years his antipathy had less discrimination; it was directed not only against the fossils but against much that was significantly alive as well, if he happened to find for it an academic association. For this reason, perhaps, his enthusiasm was limited almost wholly to contemporary verse; poets of the school text-book were suspect, and for the time being he kept them at arm's length. Passionately absorbed in language, he had no interest in languages, preferring to take whatever might trickle through the translator's sieve. For him, the impact of literature could only be weakened, and its vitality robbed, by study; even the word 'literature' itself was suspect in its associations. The conventions of prosody came under the ban; Dylan was aware of them, but he contemptuously reserved them for humorous verse or parodies. For his serious poetry he preferred then, and afterwards, a convention of his own, the syllabic number of the line; this convention, while giving characteristic limitation to a poem, could never be formulated for poetry; its life could co-extend only with the life of one poem.

This early stand against the academic was very valuable to Dylan; he would have needed twice the time to accomplish all that he did accomplish if he had not discerned clearly and from the beginning the things that were of no use to him, or if he had not steadily ignored them. In these early years, words occupied Dylan's mind to the exclusion even of the things with which they have some connection: to him, the cushat and the ring-dove were as different as the ostrich and the humming-bird. Later, there was a change. He passed through the narrow gate of words and found a world more spacious than the world he had left, filled with the same things, but magically transformed.

Cecil Price

JUST A YEAR AGO, Dylan Thomas came to the University College of Wales to address a student society. He did not look a particularly impressive figure as he sat listening to the chairman's introductory remarks. His navy blue suit and jersey, full belly and balding crown made one think of a decayed seaman of the type found in small fishing villages. But there were features that belied this impression; his protruding eyes with their hazy sea depths, his thick lips, tiny hands and fingers. Then the man rose and, rhythmically swaying on the ball's of his feet like a small child reciting, he let loose the wanton power of his voice. It transformed him. It robbed us of critical power and made us yield to the spell. I use the cliché deliberately: for Dylan Thomas, words were full of witchery. His poetry was incantation, a charm to rob evil and good of their influences and leave us all naked things of sense. His voice was the supple instrument; it communicated the splendour, terror and simplicity of his world.

It is not generally known that Thomas was the grandson of a Welsh preacher. It seems to me an important fact, explaining what he revolted against and what he loved. In Wales the preacher is associated with the puritanical outlook, a code that Thomas mocked and feared. The preacher is also the man of eloquence, filled with the rapture of words. The tones of his voice are so carefully matched with the ideas he suggests that his audience is lifted out of itself, captured, yet at the same time feeling aesthetically the beauty of the performance. There is an untranslatable Welsh word – *hwyl* – that describes the peculiar chanting tone which marks a preacher's peroration. The tones that Dylan used in delivering his verse were often those of the *hwyl*, without the monotony of that convention. In them was a wild exultation, a singing note, a variation of effect from phrase to phrase. It was evident that he was a man who cared for words with a religious intensity. By the time he read the last poem in his selection, there was in the audience that curious crackling atmosphere that can be raised in Wales only by hymns and words.

Meetings end, tension slackens. I met him afterwards, and noticed that he was sweating heavily. We talked about our boyhood days in Swansea, chuckled over an old cinema called the 'Ups', and some schoolboy characters we had both known. His recollections of taking part as a young man in a Swansea Little Theatre production were much hazier. I said how much I had enjoyed the radio programme on Swansea that he had written for the 'Return Journey' series, and asked him how he had managed to remember the names of all the shops destroyed in the bombing. 'It was quite easy', he answered. 'I wrote to the Borough Estate Agent and he supplied me with the names.' I could think of nothing to say but, 'Why is it that no one ever credits a poet with common sense?' I asked him when we could expect him to finish 'Prologue to An Adventure', the dazzling prose passage that appeared in the first issue of *Wales*. 'It isn't the kind of thing I could really go on with', he replied. He mentioned some of the work he had in hand and his plans for the future.

Some months later I wrote to congratulate him on the first instalment of *Adventures in the Skin Trade*. He replied in a typically droll way and said he hoped to finish it before long. He would then publish it in America, like his next book of poems – as a paperback. 'To be sold in every drugstore, with a naughty cover'.

Dylan Thomas was a Swansea boy, more gifted than any, but essentially what the old men of the place would call 'a piece of Swansea china'. He himself declared, 'Never was there such a town as ours, I thought.' He described it vividly:

> 'an ugly lovely town (or so it was, and is, to me) crawling, sprawling, slummed, unplanned, jerry-villa'd and smug-suburbed by the side of a long and splendid-curving shore where truant boys and sandfield boys and old, anonymous men in the tatters and hangovers of a hundred charity suits beachcombed, idled and paddled. . . .'

It is impossible to read his poetry without finding references to this particular locality. He had a strong sense of place and an ability to evoke its peculiarities. At the same time, he was able to incorporate these known places into the invented mythological world of his own. 'The horseshoe bay' is an apt description of the view from above the town and in its context has a strange symbolic value. The beach is mentioned over and over again, in his poetry and tales. So is Cwmdonkin Park with its keeper (Smokey), its hunchback, deaf-and-dumb children, reservoir, bandstand. They are actually and symbolically part of the world of his childhood, and his literary creation.

'This sea town was my world', he wrote. 'Outside, a strange Wales, coal-pitted, mountained, river-run, full, so far as I knew, of choirs and sheep and storybook tall hats, moved about its business, which was none of mine.' Here he is making a distinction between the curious Anglo-Welsh nature of the town and the characteristics of the rest of Wales. Swansea is neither a truly Welsh industrial town like Llanelly, nor a cosmopolitan, anglicised seaport like Cardiff. The centre of the town is English in speech, in outlook it is neither Welsh nor English but something peculiar to itself. Its chief diversions are soccer, county cricket, the theatre and the 'pictures'. The town stands on a frontier, and has all the vitality of its position. A mile from its centre, the Welsh-speaking area begins, and a very different habit of mind and culture. Rugby football and choral singing are the amusements; preaching festivals (in Welsh) draw large crowds. Swansea is a bustling, lively, sociable place, delighting in quick wit and repartee.

Dylan Thomas belonged to the English-speaking part of the town, and his memorable experiences in the 'strange Wales' that was Welsh-speaking seem to have begun with his childhood holidays in Carmarthenshire, thirty-five miles or so from Swansea. This setting provides the foreground for tales like 'The Peaches' and 'A Visit to Grandpa's', and for poems like the long epigraph to *Collected Poems*, and 'After the Funeral'. It is difficult to decide how far he was affected by Welsh literature in his own creative work. Some critics have found in his verse the subtleties of *cynghanedd*, but this seems unlikely to be correct, except possibly through the influence of Manley Hopkins.

I have dwelt on the man and his background because I believe much of his work (and most of his prose) owes its inspiration to particular places and people; but it would be an error to suggest that all his work is of this kind.

Pamela Hansford Johnson

I WROTE to Dylan Thomas in September 1933, admiring a poem of his printed in the *Sunday Referee*. He replied at once, and we corresponded steadily until the spring of 1934, when he came to stay with my family. He was nineteen, I was twenty-one. He arrived very late on a dull grey evening in spring, and he was nervous, as I was. 'It's nice to meet you after all those letters. Have you seen the Gauguins?' (He told me later that he had been preparing the remark about the Gauguins all the way from Swansea, and having made it, felt that his responsibility towards a cultural atmosphere was discharged.)

He was very small and light. Under a raincoat with bulging pockets, one of which contained a quarter-bottle of brandy, another a crumpled mass of poems and stories, he wore a grey, polo-necked sweater, and a pair of very small trousers that still looked much too big on him. He had the body of a boy of fourteen. When he took off the pork-pie hat (which, he also told me later, was what he had decided poets wore) he revealed a large and remarkable head, not shaggy – for he was visiting – but heavy with hair the dull gold of threepenny bits springing in deep waves and curls from a precise middle parting. His brow was very broad, not very high: his eyes, the colour and opacity of caramels when he was solemn, the colour and transparency of sherry when he was lively, were large and fine, the lower rims rather heavily pigmented. His nose was a blob; his thick lips had a chapped appearance; a fleck of cigarette paper was stuck to the lower one. His chin was small, and the disparity between the breadth of the lower and upper parts of his face gave an impression at the same time comic and beautiful. He looked like a brilliant, audacious child, and at once my family loved and fussed over him as if he were one.

He stayed with us for a week or so on that occasion, for six weeks on the second, and for varying periods over a year or more. Gauguin wore off quickly. We walked over the Common on summer evenings to a little pub in Clapham Old Town, sometimes we took the bus to Chelsea – which seemed to us a cultural Mecca – and sat in the garden of the Six Bells, watching the little fountain drip on to its muddy stones, the men playing on the bowling green, which was still there in those days. I read his poems, and criticized them with a kind of bold reverence; he read mine, and criticized them by ridicule which was hilariously funny and also perfectly just. Sometimes we wrote doggerel poems together, in alternate lines.

At home, he liked my mother to type his stories from his dictation. Sometimes they were stories of inconceivable impropriety by anybody's standards. My mother (abandoning the keys): 'Dylan, you *cannot* say that.' Dylan, with a wave of the hand: 'Put it in, Mrs Johnson, just put it in. It's all right – I assure you, it's *perfectly* all right.'

In our quiet, middle-class neighbourhood he not infrequently caused a stir; he meant to. I remember the disquiet of my aunt, one cold and foggy autumn morning, when she came downstairs to find Dylan about to go out into the busy main road wearing a blue and violet paisley dressing-gown that had once belonged to my six-foot uncle, and his own new, black, poetic felt hat. 'Dylan! What *do* you think you're doing?' Dylan (cowed, but with a look of unutterable appeal): 'Only going for cigarettes.' My aunt: 'Dylan, you can't go out like that! Come in at once!' Dylan (raising his hat in respect and acquiescence): 'Yes, Miss Howson. If you like. There may be something in what you say.'

I lost touch with him at the beginning of the war. I only knew him as a boy. He is that to me still.

Augustus John

ALTHOUGH, as I have related elsewhere, I had made the acquaintance of Dylan Thomas in London, it was at Laugharne, a remarkable little town between Carmarthen and Tenby, that our friendship was renewed; though not without undergoing a severe test at first as I shall show.

I had at this time formed what was almost a habit of visiting Richard Hughes, the novelist, who then occupied an attractive house under the shadow of a dilapidated castle. This tall ruin, commanding the estuary with the sea beyond, stands above the Lower Town with its Flemish population of cockle-gatherers, and is the most conspicuous feature of Laugharne.

On one of my visits (no doubt with the permission of Hughes, for he certainly raised no objection) I invited Caitlin Macnamara, who was sitting for me at Fordingbridge, to come down from her home in Hampshire for a change of air and scene (Mrs Hughes herself being absent at this time although I had a portrait of her on the tapis which was due for completion later). Dicon Hughes, always hospitable, at once allotted Caitlin (*pronounced Kathleen*) a room with a bath which his new guest, unused to such luxury, took full advantage of (for nothing can keep Caitlin out of water, no matter what its temperature might be).

Provided at this time with a car, my model and I proceeded to explore the countryside. One day on setting forth as usual, I saw to my surprise Dylan Thomas, standing as if in doubt, on the side of the road. I pulled up of course and, after the necessary introductions, invited him to join us which he did with alacrity. It appeared he had been considering a call at Brown's Hotel in Laugharne, where he was well known, but now proposed another place of refreshment somewhat further inland towards which accordingly I directed the vehicle, but not before Caitlin, who usually sat at my side, had joined Dylan at the back, and, as an occasional glance informed me, both were already making the very best of the situation! A more instantaneous case of mutual 'clicking' can hardly have occurred in history! To intervene would have been madness, so accelerating somewhat, I hastened to the pub indicated, where at least I might find temporary relief. Though somewhat disturbed, I behaved with tact on this occasion. I felt I was to some extent responsible for Caitlin, and would have to devise some means of asserting my authority. Such an opportunity occurred next evening, when we rejoined Dylan at Carmarthen. As the evening wore on I had to remind Caitlin that it was now high time for our return since no doubt supper awaited us. But she showed no inclination to move, so jumping into my place at the wheel, I turned on the engine, whereupon Dylan came forward with the proposition that he should come too! I had to point out that, as a guest of Dicon Hughes, I could hardly bring home a stranger at that hour of the night. This rather specious argument was effective, for Caitlin, after a last embrace, now took her seat beside me and off I drove, leaving Dylan disconsolate on the pavement. It was well after closing-time . . .

Dylan later on became friendly with Richard Hughes, who, with his customary good nature, was sometimes able to help him out of certain difficulties, thus earning his rather meagre gratitude.

After the marriage the happy couple took a house at Laugharne. I had recommended this house. Tall, narrow and detached, it faced the Estuary and looked like a stage house with a certain air of mystery about it. It was also very damp. Dylan had a number of admirers in this part of the world who would look him up. Once when I was staying there, one of such pilgrims arrived and was provided with a bed for the night. We had all passed the evening at Brown's Hotel, which I have seen described as Dylan Thomas's favourite pub. (The fact is it is the only one in Laugharne, except for one other in the Lower Town, which is frequented by the Flemish colony of cockle-gatherers and is less distinguished than Brown's.) To return to our guest, Caitlin told me next morning, after he had left, that during the night, upon hearing strange noises coming from his room, she had entered to find the visitor stark naked on the floor and in an attitude of prayer! Leaving the suppliant to his devotions she retired on tip-toe.

At one time Dylan joined the Communist Party. He was no student of sociology but felt I suppose some fellow-feeling for the under-dog. After all, wasn't he one himself? King at least of the pub, like some other monarchs in history his relations with the *bourgeois* were precarious and mostly limited to monetary transactions. These, requiring few acknowledgments, got of course none from Dylan or his wife. On finding that, as a Communist, he would be expected to use his poetic gift for propaganda purposes, he wisely detached himself and returned to his favourite bar, a free citizen once again. Laugharne is one of the few 'unreformed boroughs' in the kingdom, and flourishes under the mild rule of a *Port-Reeve*. Here at Brown's Hotel gather a genial company of friendly leg-pullers who employ a more restricted vocabulary than Dylan's especially since he returned from perfecting his own among the dead-beats of Greenwich Village. Now that he will return no more, the tavern has lost its finest ornament and even the beer, much of its virtue.

I cannot speak of Dylan Thomas's poetry, never having been able to remember a word of it, though I did enjoy his recitations delivered in that rich sonorous voice. Some hold, and I am inclined to do so myself, that the best English in this island is to be heard in Carmarthen County, a largely Welsh-speaking area. However this may be, as a 'Pembrokeshire man' I found Dylan's English irreproachable.

The art of Dylan Thomas, intricate in form, with its wit, wisdom, tragic sense and underlying passion, seems to call for the instrument of his own wonderful Welsh voice, which, for those who have heard it, will never be quite stilled. 'Poppycock!' said one accomplished writer to me, but one of our neighbours, Lord David Cecil, was, I think, agreeably impressed by Dylan's style and personality and was, besides, by no means unappreciative of his poetic gifts. But this critic missed the secret hidden under Dylan's elaborate rhymes, nor could he have guessed the source of the inspiration which later rocked the U.S.A. from New York to San Francisco. Dylan Thomas was 'possessed', by no ordinary devil, but by the most ancient spirit of them all, (who sometimes masquerades in dark places) – the Lord of Laughter; the Elemental *Clown*. . . .

William Jay Smith

DYLAN THOMAS TOLD ME ONCE that he found it difficult to converse with actors because they had only one subject of conversation – themselves. The Welsh writer was, of course, himself an actor, inspired reader, superb mimic, irresistible comedian, soulful clown; words rolled and danced on his tongue; but more than an actor, he was a poet, and of himself he rarely spoke. When he did, it was in asides, quick, bubbly, embarrassed, as if he wanted to get on with something more important – the story to be told, the joke to be brought to the proper roaring conclusion. How much indeed there was to get on with, and how lively and real it was to those of us who listened!

Oddly enough we met at All Souls in Oxford. A. L. Rowse had invited us to lunch, and I shall never forget the first sight of Dylan and Caitlin in those august surroundings, Dylan in a bright checked suit and rakish pancake cap, Caitlin all gold and red, completely the dancer, seeming to whirl in her bright skirts even when still. They were 'country', as one of Eudora Welty's Mississippi characters might put it, and they didn't mind letting the world know that there was something more important than literature, and that was life. Let geese honk below the windows, and beer spill over the tables; life was to be lived. It was life that counted.

There was not much of the 'literary' about Dylan Thomas, but he knew his craft as only the finest craftsman can; and he was brilliant, when he chose to be, in literary asides. If he spoke of poetry, it was usually to praise the poems of a friend, or to quote some lines from Hardy. He could be devastating, too, with quick thrusts at certain contemporaries, at the bumbling, the pretentious, and the boring.

This perhaps is worth putting down. I remember that once in the midst of a dinner-party, when the conversation had turned to literary topics, he broke in. 'There's nothing so beautiful', he said, and his hand shot up, 'as a lark rising from a field. That's what we . . . we . . .' He left the sentence for us to complete.

I did not see him again after that year at Oxford but I never cease hearing of the effect he had in this country, of the sense of vitality – and nobility – he communicated wherever he went. His poetry, written from the roots of language, goes to the roots of life; and it touches us all.

In a house opposite the hospital in Greenwich Village where Dylan Thomas died a short time ago. I write these lines. I look up, beyond the neon lettering outside, toward those windows where he breathed his last; and as I do, the traffic noises subside, a familiar voice again fills the air. And the lark rises.

Ralph Wishart

I HAVE KNOWN Dylan Thomas for over twenty years and can remember the time when he used to bring to my shop review copies of thrillers for me to buy – mostly on Friday evenings – so that he could have a few extra shillings to spend over the week-end; that was when he was working for the *Evening Post*.

You can read all about his early days in Swansea in his book *Portrait of the Artist as a Young Dog*, and believe me that 'young dog' has certainly left a pedigree behind him. After he left the *Post* he went to London and I only met him on rare occasions when he had the opportunity of coming to Swansea and Gower for a breath of real fresh air. But when he returned to Wales he settled in Laugharne and then I saw much more of him – more of him in more senses than one as he had then put on a lot of weight. When he was in my shop and met many of his friends his Rabelaisian laugh used to ring around the book-shelves. He always called in at my bookshop to see me before going to cricket matches and was most anxious to know what cowboy films were on as he thoroughly enjoyed this type of entertainment, but of course on all his Swansea visits he would want to see his real pal, Dr Daniel Jones.

This year he had been in more than ever because of his B.B.C. programmes, and I should like to mention here that Aneurin Talfan Davies helped him very much to get his poetry over the air so that all his countrymen should have an opportunity of hearing his works.

Sometime ago Dylan and Danny Jones, the composer, were

n the shop (after 'stop-tap') and I showed them a copy of an early women's magazine containing many of the *Mystery of the Red Barn* type of stories. This started a friendly battle as to who should have the book and I eventually decided by the toss of a coin. On this occasion Danny won; they walked out of the shop arm-in-arm as good friends as ever, Dylan well muffled up in his duffel coat, without a hat and the wind blowing through his curly hair. He seemed to have no care in the world and he and his friend appeared like two colliers out for the day.

His presence in the shop was electric and I could never be cross with him although he would mix up my bookstock and do his best to persuade people to buy books they did not want. Despite the sophistication in his poetry I knew him as a whimsical, boyish type, a sort of Peter Pan and William rolled into one.

I remember one Saturday night, when Dylan and his wife Caitlin went shopping together, they brought the goods back to my shop and what they had bought was nobody's business – most of the articles were hanging out of the bags. When they left to catch the train to Laugharne Caitlin left the bags in my shop and there was I running madly after them, managing to reach them just as the train was leaving. This was the sort of fun I always associated with Dylan's visits and I remember too how he used to love to select copies of *Chums* and other boys' books, partly for his children and partly, I think, because he liked them himself.

But I know from those about him how hard he worked at his poetry, sometimes spending a whole day to write just a few lines. Tragically enough, only recently I tackled him about producing more work and he told me that next year he had planned poems, stories and film scripts because as he said, 'Plenty of work meant plenty of money.' Dylan and Caitlin came to the shop the afternoon before they left for London, from where Dylan was to catch a 'plane to New York, and I remember him telling me how he hoped to come back home for Christmas with more fame and more money.

It seems such a pity that a number of great Welshmen have to go abroad not only to earn money but to die; such as Dr Vaughan Thomas, who died in South Africa, and our friend Dylan who died in America. So please, if Wales should produce other great men – and of course we shall – let us see to it that we do not allow them to end their days far from home.

I shall always treasure the two copies of his books which Dylan gave me, one inscribed, 'To Ralph, the Books', and the other 'To Ralph the Books – again'.

Lawrence Durrell

MUCH WAS WRITTEN about Thomas immediately after his untimely death, but for the most part it took the form of obituary, eulogy, and criticism. Fifty years from now his readers will want to know other things, about the way he looked and talked and wrote – for these are the little things which bring a poet alive to his readers; they are perhaps worth jotting down, even though I was not a close friend of his and my memories of him are of an early period, when *Eighteen Poems* had woken the world of poetry up to the fact that a new and original poet had sprung out of Wales. Others will have better stories of his latest period. It is to be hoped that they won't be lost, or snowed under by anecdotes of his wildness and improvidence only. For he was an original in his way.

I first met him quite by chance; on a flying visit to England I had been commissioned by Henry Miller to investigate the story that Anna Wickham, the poetess, had a large private diary for publication, parts of which might be regarded as actionable if produced in England itself. I called on her to see if there was any truth in the story. She was a rather formidable person, of intimidating size and forthrightness – and I soon found out that her diary was a myth. (She afterwards hanged herself from the window-sash of her house because cigarettes went up in price – a noble protest at the English way of life). While I was talking to her, Thomas came into the room and introduced himself. He had caught the name of Henry Miller – whom he deeply admired – and wanted to know what was going forward. He was then a slim, neat young man with well-trimmed hair and a well-cut suit – anything less like the sub-lunary golliwog I was to meet years later cannot be imagined. His voice was low and musical, his smile ready. Since he wanted to know more about the Paris Group, as he called it, I was delighted that he should elect to share a long bus ride back to Notting Hill Gate with me; we talked and became good friends. He was full of eager questions about Miller, most of which I was able to answer; and in return I questioned him about his own work which he took seriously but not too seriously. He was particularly amused by our attempts to revitalise the *Booster* (Official Publication Of The American Country Club, Paris, France). By some stroke of fate this periodical, so like the *Hairdresser* in format, had come into the possession of Alfred Perles who had been instructed to turn it into a Paris version of the *New Yorker*. As Perles cordially detested the paper's owner, he decided to make it really good; and this is where we came in. The *Booster* became so good so quickly that within three numbers it had not only lost all its advertising but had provoked the President to the Club to threaten us with an action under French laws of obscenity. It became an act of wisdom to transfer the *Booster* to London where it lived on for two numbers under the incognito of *Delta*, before dying. Some of Thomas's work was first printed here. It is worth mentioning, perhaps, that today bound sets fetch up to sixty pounds second-hand!

All this gossip seemed to delight Thomas, who confessed that he found the English literary scene rather dull and he promised us contributions, which he duly sent so long as we were in Paris. I found him then very self-possessed and single-minded and with a marvellous sense of the comic. He was not, I thought, very widely read – indeed, reading bored him somewhat. He liked some novels, and mentioned Dickens and Lawrence with enthusiasm. But though he had heard of Freud and Jung, he had not at this time read either. He listened with attention to what one had to say but gave the impression of knowing exactly what interested him, and being unwilling to waste energies outside his chosen field. I imagine true poets must be like that, shielding their sensibilities against distracting intrusions from the world of ideas. I liked him awfully, too, because he believed in hard work and said that he never released a poem until he had tested every nut and bolt in its body. We drank a farewell beer at the local and promised to keep in touch, which we did for years, exchanging vigorous and jolly messages whenever I happened to be in England but too far away perhaps to reach him.

I tried, I remember, to persuade him to come back to Paris with us and then on to Corfu for a summer. I thought the Mediterranean would blind him with its colours and perhaps help him dig new veins for his verse – the image is a happy one, for his poems rattled and banged away in the darkness like convoys of coal-trucks. And you could always hear the sound of the rock-drill in the best of them. But he sheered away from France and Greece – and wrote saying he preferred to mix his colours from the greys and browns of Wales. He couldn't be budged on this.

Later that year (1937, I think) when the editorial staff of the *Booster* took incontinently to its heels and fled from the threat of persecution by the French to the more liberal atmosphere of London, I found myself piloting Miller (trembling and swearing) past the Customs at Dover. (He had been turned back once before and had developed a formidable phobia of English Customs officials). Furtively in another part of the crowd came Alfred Perles wearing dark glasses which would have deceived nobody – so like an illegal psychoanalyst did he look at the best of times. We joined forces on the train and there was much rejoicing. We had a bottle of beer and an editorial conference in which we decided to change *Booster* to *Delta* and see just how much English printers could be made to stand.

Miller had compiled a list of people he wanted to meet, at the head of which stood the name D. Thomas, followed in brackets by the words 'crazy Welsh poet'.

Anais Nin's husband, Hugo Guyler the painter, also happened

to be Hugo Guyler the banker and patron of the arts; he allowed us to make his London flat our headquarters and thoughtfully furnished it with six cases of a good Bordeaux against such entertaining as we might have to do. And here we organised a few dinner parties which would enable Henry Miller to meet writers of his own calibre. They were good evenings. For a while it was hard to locate Thomas, and then I ran him down. He was living in Hammersmith and was delighted at a chance to meet Miller. But, alas! on the evening in question he kept us waiting hours and we were on the point of giving him up for lost when the telephone rang. He said in hollow, muffled tones: 'I can't find the flat so I'm not coming'. He wasn't tipsy. He just sounded terribly nervous and ill at ease. 'Where are you now?' I said, 'because I'll get a taxi and fetch you'. That startled him. 'As a matter of fact', he said, 'I'm just too afraid to come. You'll have to excuse me.' He then told me that he was telephoning from the pub immediately opposite the house. 'Stay there', I said, and ran out across the road to meet him and lay hands on him. I hadn't seen him for some time and he had altered a good deal. He was the golliwog poet of the later portraits – (there is one of him by that marvellous photographer, Bill Brandt, which should by now be on every bottle of stout in the kingdom). He was ruffled and tousled and looked as if he had been sleeping in a haystack. He had a huge muffler round his throat. He was also extremely jumpy and touchy and said he was too frightened to move from the pub and that I should stay there and have a drink with him. This I did, and after a bit his nervous aggressiveness died down and I was able to suggest dinner. I painted a ludicrous picture of poor Henry Miller walking round and round the dinner-table cursing him until I prevailed upon him to come with me. Once we left the pub he completely changed, became absolutely himself, and took the whole thing with complete assurance and sang-froid. Within ten minutes the nervous man was teasing Miller and enjoying Hugo Guyler's good wine – and indeed offering to read us his latest poems, which he did there and then.

Miller was delighted, too, and Thomas thereupon launched into a fragment of poetic prose with his curious pulpiteer's thrasonical voice; I didn't awfully like the way he read – and only when I heard him on the radio did I realise the full power and beauty of his voice.

We talked and drank late into the night and altogether it was a splendid evening; and from then on we met fairly frequently, though he would never come direct to the house. He always rang up from the pub and forced me to have a drink with him there before he would come into the house. I don't know why.

I had several chances of discussing poetic theory with him then, and he answered questions with complete certitude, honestly and quickly. He had few preconceived views about what poetry should or shouldn't be. He wrote slowly, I found to my surprise, and with difficulty in that small square hand – I always imagined his work falling out red-hot into the mould. He also mutated adjectives and nouns until he squeezed them into the right shape to suit his theme. He went on worrying them for ages before he was satisfied. I saw one phrase which filled a whole exercise book, repeated over and over again in different ways.

We argued a good deal, too, and I remember accusing him of being more interested in sound than in meaning – which he denied. But he agreed that he played all his shots, so to speak, from up at the net; every one was a smash-hit. He liked the simile and said with approval: 'That's it. No mercy on the reader.' But he was robust and without any self-importance and rejoiced in a laugh.

I was reading a good deal in the Museum at this time, and used to spend my lunch hours drifting about the manuscript room. It is always thrilling to see a page of the original Don Juan, or something in Keats's own handwriting. I never tired of it. One day, in an unfrequented corner of the room, I saw what I took to be a page of Dylan Thomas. I was surprised to find it was a page of an Emily Brontë MS, and I was so struck with the similarity that I bought a sixpenny facsimile and posted it to Thomas. The next day he wrote: 'Strange that facsimile by E.B. I thought it was a rejected poem of mine when I opened it. Yes, it's my handwriting, and I can read every word of it.' A day or two after this I happened on a picture of the three Brontë girls (is it by Bramwell, unfinished?) and I was struck by a resemblance between Emily and Dylan Thomas. The dark, slightly popping eye, the toneless skin and dark hair. . . . I told him about it, and he was amused and delighted; and when I accused him of being a reincarnation of her he agreed at once and added: 'And what is so strange about that? She's the only woman I've ever loved!'

I remember several meetings that spring, before I went abroad again; not all are worth writing about – for some were boisterous and silly, and some unproductive of anything but good-natured noise. Thomas, under the physical and mental robustness, was quite a sensitive person and rather tended to use his boisterousness as a defence against people who might bore him and make demands on him. He did not care for conversation about writing, and was not really interested enough in ideas to give much thought to them. These things invaded the privacy he felt he needed for his work. He wanted to make himself more sensitive and less conscious. 'You know', he once said, 'when I'm in company which contains admirers or fans or fellow-writers, I begin to feel I'm under false pretences. That is why I act the clown.' And he could be a splendid clown. When he was in a rip-roaring mood he seemed to attract to him everything that was fantastic and unreal in the air around him. I went for one pub-crawl with him which was as full of comic and unreal incidents as an Irish novel. Indeed the grotesque and unreal in events and people always stepped to Thomas's elbow when he started clowning. It was as if he had touched off a secret spring of lunacy in reality itself. It was a splendid form of safety, I suppose, to move in a coloured cloud of real-life fantasies. Once I visited thirteen drinking clubs in an afternoon with him in an attempt to trace a pair of shoes which he had absently taken off in one of them – he did not remember which. The types of people we met, and the hallucinating conversations which ramified around these shoes, would have made a whole novel. In one place three old men helped him crawl under a bar to see if they were there, and one of them got stuck and couldn't be got out; in another he nearly got tattooed by an elderly Indian: in a third. . . . It was like a Joyce Cary novel. And finally, he told me, that when he got home he found the shoes standing beside his bed. He had simply forgotten to put them on. . . .

Yes, a splendid clown and a splendid poet. But under the clowning and the planned appearances of this wild and woolly public figure there was a somebody quieter, somebody very much harassed by a gift; and I like to think of him in those early days. I am sure others who knew him well will have more interesting memories of him. I hope these lines may persuade his friends to write them down before they fade.

Roy Campbell

WHEN I FIRST MET Dylan in London, he was sylph-like in appearance, with curly golden-ginger hair: but he had the same blazing eyes and the same blazing voice which remained unchanged until his death. Unlike most sylph-like poets he was very manly, athletic, and a great runner, though there was something wrong with his reflexes and he never learned to fight; which was a great pity in one so extremely aggressive and pugnacious.

I did not see Dylan again till the time of the blitz in London when I was chief air-raid warden of Post 33 in St Pancras district. I went into the Yorkshire Grey, the nearest pub to our post, when I came off duty, and there were Dylan and his beautiful wife Caitlin: but how changed he was from the sylph-like figure I had met the last time, only four or five years ago! He was quite stout now, but I recognized the voice and the eyes. What he had lost in beauty he had made up in character, wit, and knowledge. Those extraordinary bumps on his forehead had grown more rugged. He was less self-conscious and had none of that English reserve and restraint which he had affected for the first half hour when I met him first. Success had made him modest instead of having the usual opposite effect.

Dylan had failed his medical test for the army, and he and Caitlin were broke. My three pounds a week did not carry far: so one day Dylan and I decided to go on a borrowing raid. 'But you must stay outside, Roy', he said. 'We'll never raise a penny if they see you with me, except in the case of so-and-so and so-and-so.' Dylan proposed to make a vast tour (on a day when I was off duty) of all the newly-rich poets in their new offices in the Central Office of Information and the Ministry of Information. The only two of these new plutocrats to whose presence Dylan admitted me were fairly crackling with Bradburies as they rose from their seats: you could hear the new bank notes crinkling and crankling against their ribs as they moved! But we raised no cash. Dylan said it had been the same in every office where he had been without me. We stood outside the M.O.I. scratching our heads. 'What about His Grace?' I asked; 'he lives just around there.' 'You mean the Archbishop?' gasped Dylan; 'I wouldn't dare.' 'Come on, you'll see. He's not only a saint in his poems, he's a bloody saint in his life too.' We went to see Eliot and that great man helped us so lavishly that it lasted till by some curious coincidence we both got our first considerable radio jobs, almost simultaneously, and were able to pay Eliot back. (Dylan never forgot his kindness. Neither do I.)

Dylan got his first radio job through his own deserts, the beauty of his voice and its amazing strength. I got mine by chance. The British imagined that Hitler was about to march through Spain, through Gibraltar and they wanted someone from the civil defence who could speak Spanish and Portuguese to broadcast to Spain and Portugal instructions about fire fighting and air-raid precautions. After the blitz stopped I joined the Welsh Fusiliers as a private. I lost Dylan then for three years, as I ended up in the Far East. When I came back discharged from the army with wounds, as a cripple, with a thirty per cent disability pension of eighteen shillings a week, I was incapable of other work than the work I found as a Number 3 grade temporary assistant clerk on the War Damage Commission for about six months on two hundred and fifty pounds a year. During this period Dylan and Caitlin, who were by now quite well off, were extremely generous and more than made up for any help I ever gave them when I was a warden.

Later, when Desmond McCarthy had got me a fine full-time job on the B.B.C. (as the end of a long story I save for another time), I had four years with an immense salary and the chance to find work for Dylan. It was about then that the famous Third Programme was started with Barnes at the head, myself in charge of the Literature, and Commander Ian Cox, also a disabled ex-service man, in charge of the Science. Ian and Dylan and I became very thick from then on. I showed them a secret which I derived from my experience as an air-raid warden. All the pubs round the B.B.C. (which is in Marylebone) open at 11.30. In St Pancras district they open at 11.00. My district had abutted on Marylebone and I knew of a point where the boundary ran straight through the middle of a hidden public house at the very tip of a sort of narrow promontory of the St Pancras district, which juts for about half-a-mile into the Marylebone district to within only a couple of hundred yards of Broadcasting House. During the blitz I had been called to the bar and had pulled the proprietor, his wife and two barmen from under the counter. They had given me five bottles of whisky to take back to our wardens' post and I was very much *persona grata* with them. It was in this pub that Dylan and I arranged all our poetry programmes, beside pints of beer. Dylan was the best all-round reader of verse that I ever produced, though John Lawrie ran him close, and an Irishman called Hutchinson. Dylan only had one weakness – he could not read correct poets like Pope or Dryden. He was best at the 'wild and woolly' poets. I used to keep him on beer all day till he had done his night's work and then take him down to the duty room where the charming Miss Backhouse or Miss Tofield would pour us both a treble whisky as a reward for our labours. It was with Blake and Manley Hopkins that Dylan became almost Superman: but we had bad luck with Dryden. Dylan had got at the whisky first and he started behaving like a prima donna. He insisted on having an announcer instead of beginning the programme right away as we used to on the Third Programme. There were only two minutes to go and I rushed back to the studio and found Dylan snoring in front of the mike with only twenty seconds left. He was slumped back in his chair, with an almost seraphic expression of blissful peace. I shook him awake, and, to his horror and consternation, began announcing him, not in my South African accent, but trying to talk like an English announcer, with my tonsils, in an 'Oxford accent'. Dylan nearly jumped out of his skin with fright and horror: and was almost sober when he got the green light, though he did bungle the title as 'Ode on Shaint Sheshilia's Day'; but after that his voice cleared up and I began to breathe again. When he had finished reading the 'Ode' I got another fright: he began to beckon me wildly with his arms and point to the page before him. I got the engineer to switch off the mike and slipped into the studio again. Dylan had forgotten how to pronounce '*Religio Laïci*'. I told him and slipped out. He had about three shots at it, bungled it, gave it up; and then went on reading. The next day I was hauled up in front of George Barnes, but he was a good boss and had a sense of humour. I promised to keep an eye on Dylan: Dylan promised me to keep an eye on himself – and he kept his word. I used him for several readings, a wonderful performance that he gave of Cervantes's *Two Dogs*, and many other poetry readings: and his performance was always flawless from then on. The performance he gave of Davies's *Super-Tramp*, which he read as a serial, was superb.

After about four years on the B.B.C. I began to long for work. My malaria had left me and my wounds had healed. Life in the bureaucracies is rather like a marathon of shop-walkers. The job I liked best on the radio, apart from producing Dylan, was being in charge of all the travel and adventure talks, which enabled me to meet interesting people. My wife, to whom I gave half my salary, saved up enough to rent a small farm in Portugal for three months, so I begged off the rest of my contract with the B.B.C. and was graciously granted my resignation. I had to say goodbye to Dylan, but we got the farm working, and at last I am growing my own bread and wine as a tenant farmer, and writing in between times. I went on a lecture tour to America in 1953 and was hoping to meet Dylan in New York or Chicago. When I was in Seattle

I saw his face looking at me from a newspaper in a news-stall. I don't know what gave me the premonition, 'Dylan is dead'.

Dylan was not only a great poet. A great poet is sometimes a mere medium. He was a deeply religious and great-hearted man who put love and friendship before everything else. He was never out of love with his beautiful wife and muse, Caitlin, who really inspired him in the old-fashioned manner. He was so generous that he often harmed himself to help others. If ever he was wrong about anything, his conscientiousness and humility were such that he would apologise to the humblest person whom he thought he had hurt. He had no fear of opinion, as he showed by befriending me so nobly during my five years' ostracism by almost everybody, except Eliot, Wyndham Lewis, and the Sitwells.

John Lehmann

EVERY ONE OF US will have his own special memories of Dylan Thomas. The most vivid among mine are, first, our weekly meetings in a pub during 1940, when I was trying to persuade him to finish his remarkable short novel – the only one he ever wrote – *Adventures in the Skin Trade*. I published the first part ('A Fine Beginning') in *Folios of New Writing*, and was immensely enthusiastic about it; but he treated all my cajolings and homilies as a huge joke – to which I was privy – and his work on it ran down like a clockwork toy. I got to know Dylan rather well; but I never got the completed manuscript. The second memory that stands out is of a poetry reading in the latter years of the war: I was to choose the poems and Dylan was to read them. The meeting was small, but there were ardent fans of his in the front row. Dylan, who had been in the highest spirits before, was not at his most lucid when it came to the reading: I thanked my stars that the poets themselves were not there, because the pages refused to come into focus before his eyes, and he rewrote the poems on the spur of the moment, according to his fantasy, from the few words he occasionally caught sight of. Astonishing improvisations: but not what the poets meant. The fans never batted an eyelid. Then I asked him to read some of his own poems: the change was immediate and miraculous. He knew them by heart, and the poems sobered and mastered him, using him as an instrument for a performance of the highest power and beauty. I remembered that evening on the last occasion of which I saw him, when he recited the magical 'Prologue' to his *Collected Poems* on my 'New Soundings'

Programme in a B.B.C. studio. What struck me particularly then was the immense trouble he took over every detail of timing, volume, expression, and the incantatory gestures he used to work himself up to the right pitch. And yet, heard at the other end, all was divine ease and haunting melody, captivating innumerable listeners who could not have told you afterwards what the logical meaning of the poem was. How fortunate we are that so many records of his reading of his own poems exist, for, more than with any other poet of our time, the voice heightened and illuminated the power of the word.

Mario Luzi

DYLAN WENT TO FLORENCE for the first time in 1947 and by chance his visit coincided with the presence there of Spender: one sensed at once how fundamentally different the two poets were, Spender displaying a lively intellectual curiosity in personalities and art, Dylan appearing not to be in the least interested, his main preoccupation being to find a place where the wine and beer were good and a comfortable lodging. He chose the well-known Café Giubbe Rosse and a lodging in the country suburb of Mosciano, gravitating between the two.

Entering the Giubbe Rosse late of an evening, he was to be found entrenched behind a small forest of bottles, a full glass in his hand, and one wondered whether those large pale blue eyes were gazing upon something ineffable or merely into vacancy. He would begin to speak, then lapse into silence, perhaps because the listener did not understand English, perhaps because what he had to say was inexpressible in any language. He talked little, preferring gestures of comprehension or dissent, remaining isolated within his own solitude, his friendliness apparent in the offering of drink.

His wife's problem was to push him into a taxi and get him home. One evening, expected to supper with the poet Montale, he was reluctantly dragged from his bed and remained drunk all the evening. Invited on other occasions to their houses by his translator Bigongiari and Rosai, the painter, he seemed at first to enter into the conversation, a glow of fiery youth in his eyes, but almost at once fell back in his chair and slept heavily.

And yet, in spite of his drunkenness, his reluctance or inability to speak, his myth remains. These things merged into an impression of incommunicability which, strange though it may seem, roused sympathetic liking and commanded respect. Those who knew little or nothing of him clearly recognized that destiny or a fatal play of natural forces was at work within him. Moreover, he felt and repaid as best he could the sympathy which surrounded him, as for example when, at a lively gathering in the house of Parronchi, he suddenly became animated, reading aloud from Milton and Shakespeare, giving a melodious, profound and extraordinarily vigorous rendering, which left a deep impression as of a new discovery of the old texts and of the reader.

In the summer he left for Elba and years of silence were broken when he wrote a long poem 'In Country Sleep'.

(Translated from the Italian by Monica Painter)

EDITOR'S NOTE: Mario Luzi's valuable piece must be completed by an equally authentic document, the confession Dylan made to one of his English friends: 'What a sun-pissed pig I am not to dip a bristle in Chianti. A few days ago I climbed a tree, forgetting my shape and weight.' Dylan, as usual, was terrified by 'intellectuals' and complained to the same friend: 'We have got to know lots of the young intellectuals of Florence, and a damp lot they are. They visit us on Sundays. To overcome the language, I have to stand on my head, fall in the pool, crack nuts with my teeth, and Tarzan in the cypresses. I am very witty in Italian, though a little violent; and I need space. Do you know anybody in Florence nice to have a drink with?'

Theodore Roethke

It is difficult for me to write anything, stunned as I am, like many another, by the news of his death. I knew him for only three brief periods, yet I had come to think of him as a younger brother: unsentimentally, perhaps, and not protective as so many felt inclined to be – for he could fend for himself against male and female; but rather someone to be proud of, to rejoice in, to be irritated with, or even jealous of. He was so rich in what he was that each friend or acquaintance seemed to carry a particular image of him: each had his special Dylan, whom he cherished and preserved intact, or expanded into a figure greater than life: a fabulous ageing cherub, capable of all things. I think Thomas often knew exactly what each person thought him to be, and, actor that he was, would live up to expectations when it suited his mood. Often this would take the form of wry, ironical, deprecatory self-burlesque: as if he wanted to remind himself of the human condition. Like Chaplin, whom he loved, he could laugh at himself without being coy, and call up tenderness in those who rarely felt it.

The demands on his body and spirit were many; his recklessness, lovely. But even his superb energies felt the strain, I should say, on lecture tours when he was set upon by fools. Any kind of social pretentiousness disturbed him, and particularly in academia. The bourgeois he did not love. And he could, and did, act outrageously, on occasion, snarling from one side of his mouth to a gabbling faculty wife that nobody ever came to America except to get fees and drink free liquor; only to wish, wistfully, the next five minutes, to someone he respected, that he could stay in this country for a time, and maybe even teach: show the young what poetry really was. But even in black moods, his instinctive sweetness and graciousness would flash through. More than any other writer or artist I know, he really cared for and cherished his fellow-men.

I first met him in 1950, in New York. John Brinnin had written twice that Dylan Thomas wanted to meet me. I found this hard to believe, but when I came down from Yaddo in May, still groggy from my own private wars with the world, it seemed to be so.

Someone had lent me an apartment up-town; he was staying down-town on Washington Square. We sometimes alternated: one would rout out the other, different days. He had been built up to me as a great swill-down drinker, a prodigious roaring boy out of the Welsh caves. But I never knew such a one. Some bubbly or Guinness or just plain beer, maybe; and not much else. We would sit around talking about poetry; about Welsh picnics; life on the Detroit river, and in Chicago (he greatly admired *The Man with the Golden Arm*); the early Hammett; and so on. Or maybe bumble across town to an old Marx Brothers movie, or mope along, poking into book shops or looking into shop windows. One night he insisted I come along, with others, when some fellow Welshmen, in America for twenty years, entertained. And then I saw what he meant to his own people: to those hard-boiled businessmen Thomas was the first citizen of Wales, and nothing less.

Sometimes he would recite – and what that was many know; but I think off-stage he was even better, the rhythms more apparent, the poems rendered exactly for what they were. I remember he thought 'After the Funeral' creaked a bit at the beginning: that he had not worked hard enough on it.

He had a wide, detailed and active knowledge of the whole range of English literature; and a long memory. I noticed one day a big pile of poems – Edward Thomas, Hardy, Ransom, Housman, W. R. Rodgers, Davies, and others – all copied out in his careful hand. He said he never felt he knew a poem, what was in it, until he had done this. His taste was exact and specific; he was loyal to the poem, not the poet; and the list of contemporaries he valued was a good deal shorter than might generally be supposed.

He was one of the great ones, there can be no doubt of that. And he drank his own blood, ate of his own marrow, to get at some of that material. His poems need no words, least of all mine, to defend or explain them.

Alastair Reid

WHEN I WAS AT SCHOOL in Edinburgh as a boy, I bought for no reason a copy of *Eighteen Poems*, and carried it everywhere until I had pawed the cover off. For no reason, because I was not then faintly interested in poetry as poetry; I read the book with awe, in a pure literary innocence. It was an astonishment that nowhere fitted into the world as I knew it then. Walking home across the park, I would say single lines to myself over and over again. The words seemed to me as absolute and inevitable as air, and I could not conceive of them as ever having been written by anyone. Even now, through the clutter of literary know-how that accumulates round our reading, I think the poems insist on a similar innocence from anyone who wishes to read them well.

The matter of all the scattered fragments of conversation I had, here, there, and everywhere with Dylan Thomas was most of the time words themselves; or if we talked of things outside them, the words chosen took more than their customary share of attention. He often suspended talk to roll the last words, his own or anyone else's, round his head. Sometimes, in the middle of someone's sentence, he would hear a word he wanted and would save it, saying it over once or twice to make sure it was still there. He would talk to anyone about anything, listening intently to their words, because it always seemed incredible to him that there could be a word for things. I remember both his delight over subtitling himself for an advertising man, 'The Ugly Suckling', and his astonishment when we found once on a menu that the word 'live' backwards spelt 'evil'. It was the same astonishment that he would fix suddenly on a man rolling barrels in the street, or a face, or an egg.

He was, I think, very shy of the unspoken; when he met people, he would always wait, outside of them, until they had spoken for a time. Once in New York, not long before he died, he was talking about writing. 'When I experience anything,' he said, 'I experience it as a thing and a word at the same time, both equally amazing.' He told me once that writing the 'Ballad of the Long Legged Bait' had been like carrying a huge armful of words to a table he thought was upstairs, and wondering if he could reach it in time, or if it would still be there.

The relation between a poet and his poetry, like that between husbands and wives, is often very far below the surface, unexpected, confusing, perhaps impossible to find. With Dylan Thomas, it was clean and clear. When he was busy with them, existence and language were to him twin miracles. His poetry was trying always to make them simultaneously dawn, as they dawned on him. It seems to me that his poetry, whatever its literary fate, covers prior to anything the miracle of the first speaking creation, the wonder of words bringing about the wonder beyond them. And sometimes, in the middle of talk, one saw in the same way the man who praised existence because it would have been inconceivable to him not to, who wrote with a grateful amazement that such a thing as poetry was possible at all.

Richard Eberhart

THERE WAS SOMETHING IMPISH about Dylan Thomas and there should be something impish in me now to tell the truth about him. There should be such a thrust, but such a thrust would jar things and it is not time to tell the truth. Perhaps it is never time. Perhaps the truth would be Comic when we live under a predilection that it is Tragic. The fact is that we live the truth but cannot tell the truth. Poetry is involved in the truth and is the final truth, but, by paradox, it is a parcel of myth; which is to use the word not in peroration but in praise, and to use another word were probably better. Say then poetry is myth or sleight-of-hand-sleight-of-mind tricks to show iridescent qualities of the soul. Is not Thomas's poetry a continuous artifice in this sense, a series of masks each paradoxically revealing the truth, or part of the truth, and is not his conscious craftsmanship itself an ability of the self to fend off reality so that reality will not be used up, a deftness to vary the conception with every poem, with every year, with every new insight, a consuming making of reality in the form of poetry, so that the total depth of life will never be exhausted?

Thus his poems, every one a struggle, were composed at once with dynamic energy springing from some genius not to be quite described or quite named and at the same time from some sly, cool, subtle, controlled intellectual craftsmanship, so that he knew, quite well, what effects he was preparing as he prepared them. He composed harmony from the fusion of these two forces.

One should talk of the impishness, if that is a good term for it, in Dylan. I should recall a blonde girl living in our house when he first came to Cambridge for his first reading, and by what impishness he astounded her on the ride over from the South Station to Cambridge; how he astounded Matthiessen before the reading; how he delighted everybody in his actual performance; how he shocked and astounded everybody at the Advocate party afterward, and I should tell just what he said; how he astounded everybody later in the evening at Matty's, and I should tell just what he did; how he still astounded a late small group at Wilbur's; and how my wife and Charlee Wilbur had finally to deposit him in his Harvard guest house in the small hours; and just how they did it, how they had to do it.

I should then have to go on to reveal those startling truths of his progressions near by, with friends, to various places for readings.

But it is not time to tell the truth, maybe it is never time.

Everybody connected with him has his own adventures to remember.

I should have to tell how, on his second trip here, when he stayed at our house, my wife tried valiantly to get him to eat something, but only succeeded in four days with one piece of bacon; how I had to (and was delighted to) get him up in the morning by plugging his mouth with a bottle of beer, this wonderful baby.

I should have to recount how, just after dinner before I was to introduce him at the Brattle Theatre for his first reading of verse drama in America under the auspices of our Poets' Theatre, he had not yet decided what to read, and with what instantaneous deftness and command he decided, once several of us had ransacked book-cases and thrust probable books into his hands, exactly what he wanted to read and was prepared for action on the instant. Then to leap on to the stage and give a stirring, memorable reading from Webster, Marlowe, Beddoes, *Lear*, and finally his own poems.

I should have to recount many charming episodes, as that my wife, when we took him to the airport early on a cold morning to take a plane, clad in the dirty, thin one suit he had brought from Florida, gave him my naval officer's raincoat, which we never saw again. Incidentally, how at the airport, amazed as always at American gadgets, he delighted in the machinery that produced cokes, and had four before stepping on to the plane. And how, through the aid of John Brinnin a very long time later, Dylan sent the coat back from Wales, but this time it was an odd, little, tattered British affair all buttons and flaps, no bigger than he, his own coat, which I could not wear.

I should have to recount a time with Dylan and Caitlin which was to have been a half-hour at midday but which went on in talk and drink for ten hours.

One should tell the truth. One should put down all the stories before time dims their contours or presses them into some unnatural shape. In fact, the impishness I began on as a quality of his was less apparent from his second visit to these shores, and could not be made out as a permanent characteristic.

If I were more impish myself now I should relate the truth! One cannot tell the truth. It would be too harsh, too unbelievable; too rich, too deep, too wild, and too strange. The truth is more dramatic than fictions. It should be confided in this case to private papers and left to posterity. One has to defend Dylan against the total humanity of the man.

Others knew Dylan much better than I did, but I loved the man. I hope all who knew him will want to write down their impressions. He was so natural, friendly, jolly and bright (without ostentation) that personal reminiscences of him should be preserved. Already there are critical appraisals; time will accrete more of these.

One shudders at the depths of the truth. I found myself thinking, after the shock of his death, that he had been a long-term suicide and that a drive to destruction was inextricably bound up with his genius, somehow, itself; that his high and wordy nature demanded the extreme penalty for being completely itself; that he could no more escape his death than he could his genius; and that he lived and died to exalt mankind and to express something recurrent and ineffable in the spirit of man, the strength of the imagination, the exaltation of the soul.

David Daiches

I LAST SAW DYLAN THOMAS in America nearly three years ago. He had come to give a poetry reading at Cornell University, where I was then teaching. He had been given a very rugged time in New York, where he had been almost killed with kindness: round after round of heavy parties had rendered him sick and exhausted. I met the 'plane on which he was due to arrive from New York but found that he was not among the passengers who alighted. I entered the 'plane and found Dylan fast asleep in his seat. He had been feeling sick, and had promptly filled himself up with sleeping tablets which he had obtained in New York because of his inability to sleep in the steam-heated hotel bedroom. I got him home and put him to bed, and an hour or so later, with the help of black coffee (my suggestion) and cold beer (his suggestion), got him on his feet. It was a cool, bright winter's day, and we decided that a brisk walk would clear his head.

We went out in the clear, frosty air, and walked across the suspension bridge which leads across a picturesque gorge to the Cornell campus. He stood a long time leaning on the bridge, looking at the ice and snow. We talked about life in villages in Wales and Scotland and the pros and cons of being a village worthy. I then took him to the university, where a sudden queasiness overtook him and before I could stop him he had crammed a handful of sleeping pills into his mouth. We hurried home, and he was soon fast asleep. I had invited some people to dinner to meet him, but Dylan slept all through dinner, He was due to give his reading at 8.30, and I was worried. But we got him up at 8, spruced him up with cold water, and somehow got him to the hall in time. I was afraid that he would prove incapable of talking. But as soon as he got on to his feet, and saw the large audience in front of him, his somnolence fled, and he proceeded to give a most brilliant performance. 'I'm just an old ham,' he said to me as I was taking him back to my flat afterwards. 'I always respond to an audience.'

He was in good form that night. He talked wittily to the several guests we had in to meet him after his reading, and gave a fine reading of 'Poem in October' for the benefit of my wife who had been unable to come to his public reading. Then, about midnight, we drove him to Syracuse, N.Y., and put him on the night train going west. He had a sleeping berth reserved, but he had only the vaguest notion of the various places out west that he was due to visit. And he had forgotten the name of the man who was supposed to be meeting him at the station where he was to get off. He sat down on his berth, looking utterly forlorn. 'Westward into the night', he said. 'I feel frightened. I don't think I shall ever come back. Perhaps I shall die in Utah.' Then the cry of 'All aboard' went up from the platform and I left him sitting there, sleepy and lost, deliberately frightening himself with melodramatic pictures of the lonely terrors of the West.

Marjorie Adix

THE FOLLOWING IS AN ACCOUNT of a conference held by Dylan Thomas with students at the University of Utah last spring.

I met Dylan Thomas yesterday – that doesn't mean I rushed up and told him how wonderful he was; it means that I sat three feet away from him in the Union lounge while Professor Brewster Ghiselin and his following questioned him for an hour-and-a-half. Throughout it all you could feel the relationship between Dylan Thomas and Ghiselin – tremendous respect on both sides, and yet too great a distance ever to be close. Both of them shy men, really, who have hung their souls out on the line, yet kept firmly established egos: Ghiselin, the scholar-poet and host, never quite sure that his man wouldn't get up and leave through the open window; and Thomas, out of place, uneasy at being exposed on all sides, yet on his best behaviour, sticking it out.

Ghiselin led off with a brief introduction and then asked why a poet went around on a reading tour. Thomas, looking down at the table, facing no one, said softly: 'My God, that's a hard question! I'm afraid I shall have to answer it straight: it's a way of seeing the country and I haven't any money. It's a matter of ego as well.'

GHISELIN: But why is the poetry read aloud? Does it aid understanding?

THOMAS: People come to have a look at me. Here's a little fat man come to make a fool of himself, they think, and since they don't listen to what I read, it doesn't matter whether I make sense or not . . . But that isn't quite fair of me – I am enjoying myself.

GHISELIN: You read much on the B.B.C. Do you feel that poetry must be read aloud before it is complete? Does it bring you closer to the meaning?

THOMAS: Yes – perhaps it helps in the interpretation or emphasis. It brings you closer to the poet.

STUDENT: Do you listen to the sound of your own words? Is that as important to you as the rhyme and metre?

THOMAS: Oh, God, that's a hard one, too! Yes – you can struggle with rhyme and metre and style and still not have a poem. I'm sorry I'm not answering the way you would like.

STUDENT: But why do you read your own poetry?

THOMAS: For the noise it makes. And for the memory of the experience of writing it. But it has already said everything it had to say.

STUDENT: Do you say the words aloud as you write them?

THOMAS: Yes. That's why I live in a hut on a cliff.

ANOTHER STUDENT: Is it necessary for a poem to have an outcome? Robert Frost says that a poem should be resolved. It should not be too obscure to be understood. I have difficulty in understanding you, especially your early sonnets.

THOMAS: Then you should read Robert Frost. . . . But you are right: to the poet, at least, there is always an outcome. Those sonnets are only the writings of a boily boy in love with shapes and shadows on his pillow.

GHISELIN: I've wondered about the sonnets. I could never see anything very deep in them. It's good to know I need search no further.

THOMAS: Well, they would be of interest to another boily boy. Or a boily girl. (*Long pause*). Boily-girly.

Here Thomas laughed to himself and seemed lost in very amusing word combinations – while everyone sat petrified, until somebody brought him back to us:

'Is it ever fair deliberately to confuse the reader?

THOMAS: I thought someone would take me up on that. No –

it is a deliberate avowal of your own inefficiency. It is impossible to be too clear. You can state too bluntly all you know, or put down very clearly what you intend, which may be very narrow and even cruel. But we don't know about anything. Especially people, nobody knows. There are scientific terms, but – why doesn't the water fly out of the ocean when the earth whirls? Because it is a ball of magic. It is impossible to be too clear. I am trying for more clarity now. At first I thought it enough to leave an impression of sound and feeling and let the meaning seep in later, but since I've been giving these broadcasts and reading other men's poetry as well as my own, I find it better to have more meaning at first reading.

GHISELIN: But, on the other hand, isn't it possible to narrow and fix a meaning to the exclusion of richer levels of meaning?

THOMAS: Oh God, isn't an education wonderful!

GHISELIN: I shall be silent from now on.

THOMAS: No, I mean it as a compliment. You say things so well, and I'm ashamed to be flippant and go down the side-alleys. . . .

STUDENT: Do you find it necessary to study other things in order to find increasing satisfaction in your own poetry?

THOMAS: There is never any satisfaction – that's why I write another poem. Do I study other things? Yes, people. (*Long pause, the questioner nodding thoughtfully*) then: Me!

ANOTHER STUDENT: Why do you write poetry, Mr Thomas?

THOMAS: Because I have the time. Because I have to live, too; (*mumbled*) I don't know why. It is very slow work, however. Only five poems published in the last six years. It is slow, but sometimes there is just nothing better to do. Sometimes it feels very good to have a blank piece of paper in front of you, and you put down the first line. Then you look at all the paper and think, 'Now I've got to rhyme this'. And it's work! Oh God, it's awful! . . . I write some very bad poems.

STUDENT: What happens to them?

THOMAS: I keep them – too much of an egoist to throw them

away. But neither do I do as Rossetti did, who buried them with his wife and had to dig them up later. I keep them in a drawer.

STUDENT: What do you do with them?

THOMAS: Nothing. When it's written it's finished.

GHISELIN: Perhaps you don't read your old poems over because there is a chance you might become infatuated with them and continue to write the same poem over and over. Some poets do.

THOMAS: Jove! I never thought of that! I wonder what's in the drawer. (*Pantomime.*) This isn't so bad after all! Delightful! (*He was gone again.*)

STUDENT: Who decides whether your poems are good or bad?

THOMAS: I do. Nobody reads the bad ones.

STUDENT: Then you don't ask a publisher for an opinion?

THOMAS: Oh, no. If he didn't like one that I thought was good, it would be too terrible.

STUDENT: If your own poetry gives you no satisfaction, is there any which does?

THOMAS: That's easy: Shakespeare!

STUDENT: Who is the best of the moderns?

THOMAS: The nice thing about poetry is that it isn't a competitive field. There isn't any *best*; but I do like Thomas Hardy, D. H. Lawrence, W. H. Auden and—— (Here, Dr —— on my left squealed in surprise, and I missed the fourth name).

STUDENT: How do you tell whether a poem is good or not?

THOMAS: If I like it.

STUDENT: But what do you go by?

THOMAS: I like one because it is better than the others. (*Silence.*) Before I find a poem I like I have to pass over a great many that I don't like. When I find one I like, I read it. I don't know why. The big problem is to find the poem, then read it – hang by your ears from the chandeliers, or however you read poetry – and enjoy it.

GHISELIN: Perhaps we should do as you suggest and like a poem because we think it better than others, but students have to pull it apart and analyse why they like it and write it all down for a professor.

THOMAS: People who think they know T. S. Eliot find it unbelievable that he enjoys Kipling, that rowdy rhymester. That is, the people who think they know Kipling too. Some of his poetry is excellent.

(Very long pause. Dylan Thomas sips at his glass of water like a kitten bobbing its nose in a saucer. The glass is still full at the end of the session after at least a dozen embarrassed sips.)

STUDENT: Do you address your noise only to yourself?

THOMAS: Oh no. No. Yes – well, I *am* lots of people. I think I am lots of people at any rate. Of course, I know, and the birds know, I'm only a fat little fool ranting on a cliff, but it seems that I am lots of people.

YOUNG LADY: Has your style changed?

THOMAS: Style? Yes. No – I'm still after the same things if that's what you mean.

GHISELIN: Your poetry seems to open little doors in quite ordinary and common events, sometimes by only shifting an image slightly to one side to let in the new idea.

THOMAS: How nicely you say it! That is exactly what I would like my poetry to do some day.

LADY: Do you revise?

THOMAS: No, I work it out a phrase at a time. It is very slow, but when it is once finished, all the revision has been done, and I don't change it.

LADY: Then it may take several days?

THOMAS: Months. Years. It might never be finished. But I am a patient man.

GHISELIN: You always seem to put in your poetry just what you are seeing at the moment – the heron, and the birds near the estuary, for instance?

THOMAS: Yes – yes. I wanted to write about the cliff, and there was a crow flying above it, and that seemed a good place to begin, so I wrote about the crow. Yes, if I see a bird, I put it in whether it belongs or not.

GHISELIN: Do you leave it there?

THOMAS: If it is happy and at home in the poetry, I do. But really I should get a blind for my window.

STUDENT: But you do have some idea of what you are going to say?

THOMAS: Sometimes. You don't just sit and wait for the little doors to open. Twenty years ago I would have said 'inspiration'. It's hard work. But sometimes the mood is enough. Say a poet is gay and he wants to write a gay poem – about anything. It is spring, or he has a new pair of shoes, or his wife has left him. Everything is gaiety. But then, suddenly, in the middle of the poem, he might miss his wife. It would be a very sad poem. You can't always follow your original plan.

ANOTHER STUDENT: Do you pay any attention to critics – for instance?

THOMAS: Yes. Sometimes I wake up in the night and wonder about them. I don't know what they have against me. As far as — goes, it is a personal matter, I'm sure. He just can't abide me. He can't stand to read me at all. I don't know why. I pay attention to the praise too – it's easier to take, although it isn't any truer and I don't believe it any more than the other. I mean, I can't be bought with a few sentences. I don't think they will change me. I know what kind of a man I am. (*Quietly.*) Thirty-seven years with the same head. . . .

And so it went on, until Ghiselin asked Thomas to read one of his poems. He arose for the first time, gathered up his five books and stuffed them in his briefcase. I thought he was offended, but he finished stowing them away, kept one out, and turned back to us:

'I brought all these books in case I would be too frightened to answer your questions. I haven't answered them, but I wasn't frightened. Thank you for asking me'.

He smiled and sat down again, and began to talk in a soft voice about his father, who, he said, had been a militant atheist, whose atheism had nothing to do with whether there was a god or not, but was a violent and personal dislike for God. He would glare out of the window and growl: 'It's raining, blast Him!" or 'The sun is shining – Lord, what foolishness!' He went blind and was very ill before he died. He was in his eighties, and he grew soft and gentle at the last. Thomas hadn't wanted him to change. . . .

And all at once the little poet began to read, and his voice raged and surged with power and anger and a terrible desolation. He read 'Do not go gentle into that good night'. It was slow and rhythmic and deep. His eyes were bent down on the book, but he was not reading, for they would remain fixed for a long time and then wander over both pages for a moment and then freeze again. I can't express how startling the change was in him, from the shy, humble, apologetic, patiently eager man, to this tidal wave of humanity. I was uneasy at first because I felt that in either one position or the other he was only acting, but I could find no trace of insincerity ever. I suppose he knows best. He is lots of people.

Philip Burton

JUST A FEW DAYS BEFORE he flew for the last time to America, Dylan Thomas spent an evening with me, chiefly to discuss some of his future plans. A few weeks before, we had met by arrangement in Swansea. I had been anxious to hear about the final form of a work for radio which he had first outlined to me in a memorable session at the Café Royal more than six years before. That work, which we had originally discussed under the tentative title of *The Village of the Mad*, had now become *Under Milk Wood*. He had already taken part in New York in some public readings of an incomplete version of it, and it was for some further readings, now of the finished work, that he was flying to New York again. At our Swansea meeting Dylan soon dismissed *Under Milk Wood* because he was on fire about a new work. He delighted me by saying that he wanted my collaboration in it, for it was an entirely new venture for him – a stage-play. He said he would come to see me in London, on his way to America. I rather doubted whether, besieged by his many friends and in the rush of departure, he would be able to find the time, and I reconciled myself not to hear from him until he came back from America, but I was wrong. He was clearly so obsessed by his new play that out of his last hectic days in London he set aside a whole quiet evening to visit me for a talk about it. His death makes my memories of that last evening peculiarly precious and acutely poignant, for he talked with his infectious gusto of his future work.

It is significant that we discussed his newly completed radio-play, *Under Milk Wood*, a libretto for an opera, and a stage-play, the latter two unwritten but planned in media new for Dylan. Hindsight wisdom inevitably gives an added depth to some of the things that Dylan said that evening, but it is now clear to me that he felt he was coming to the end of his first lyrical impulse. He talked with affectionate warmth of a new poem he had written about his father, and he talked as though it was likely to be the last of its kind. He said: 'I've got another twenty, or perhaps twenty-five, years to live. I've got to try new things. This play is the beginning.'

Before we had been talking long about the play we found it necessary to find a working title for it. We decided on *Two Streets*. My part in the discussion was to suggest how Dylan's vision might best be realized in the physical opportunities and limitations of the stage, for the play was to have little resemblance to the normal, commercial three-act entertainment. To begin with, there was to be no interval. On this point Dylan was adamant. The possibility of members of the audience trooping to the bar in the middle of the performance of any play of his made him very heated indeed. Even the cinemas had better manners; they sold ice-cream only between films. A play must be an unbroken experience, like a film or a symphony. If it turned out that *Two Streets* was short enough to warrant including another short play 'or something' in the programme, then the bars could ply their trade between the plays; otherwise, no. *Two Streets* was to be 'a simple love-story'. It was to be set in a small industrial town in South Wales, and it would tell of the lives of two families who live unknown to each other in neighbouring streets. The play would begin with the birth of the boy in one family and the girl in the other, and it might possibly end with their first meeting, in a dance-hall. There was to be little realism in the presentation, and the families would live their separate but unconsciously interwoven lives at separate ends of the stage, until at last the boy and the girl met in the middle. The first character to form a link between the families would be the midwife attending both mothers. What a rich, Dylanesque character she would have been! I suggested that the centre of the stage throughout the play might be dominated by the voice of the valley itself, a character who would become different things at different times, a voice that the families sometimes listened to and sometimes ignored; he could be a preacher, a politician, a football-supporter, a recruiting-sergeant, a poet, a cheapjack selling the valley in the depression, a bureaucrat, a multiple-shop owner. . . . In this part I saw Dylan himself; he would have been superb. But even if he did not play it himself – and, although he revelled in acting, the nightly discipline of a successful run was not for him – such a fat star-part would have enhanced the play's chance of a profitable production. Dylan took warily, but I think kindly, to my idea of the central character, and we were both going to ponder the form and shape of the play in preparation for our next meeting. His last word about *Two Streets* was memorably characteristic. During the discussion he had enjoyed treating me as an obstructive stage-producer whom he had to badger and plead with. In the actual staging of the play his mind's eye had not seen much beyond the opening, and for this he begged with comic fervour: 'Please, please let me have two prodigiously pregnant women.'

We drifted into talk about the opera libretto he was going to write for Stravinsky. I gathered that there had been a change of plan about this. Originally it was going to be sponsored by some Boston foundation, but Stravinsky had decided that they would be better advised to complete the opera without initial sponsorship. This left Dylan with the task of having to make his own way to Hollywood to meet the composer; the readings of *Under Milk Wood* in New York were to pay his expenses. Dylan's ideas for the opera seemed to be almost as nebulous as those for *Two Streets*, except for one little incident which for him crystallised the theme. The setting of the opera was to be the world destroyed by atomic warfare. Almost all life had disappeared. The scene was to be a cave in completely barren surroundings. Miraculously two young people had survived, and they had to find life again in an almost total absence of it. The boy was older than the girl – or should it be the other way round? – and he had dim, groping recollections of the life before the destruction. The incident that made Dylan's imagination glow was when the boy tried to remember and explain to the girl what a tree was. Another character was to be an old prophet who had survived the doom he had foretold. As I listened, it suddenly struck me that Dylan was feeling towards a sort of Garden-of-Eden story. When I told him this, he was momentarily surprised and then he seized excitedly on the idea and began to embellish and develop it with brilliant spontaneity. The theme of the opera was clearly to be one that underlies much of Dylan's work – life is stronger than death.

What else remains of that last evening? His inimitable reading of passages from *Under Milk Wood*, particularly of some revisions written on scraps of paper brought to light from his cavernous pockets—'That word won't do. The Censor wouldn't pass the word she would really use, but 'Loving' is too feeble altogether and it's got too many other associations'. After much fumbling I suggested 'pleasure'. He savoured it. 'Yes, that's better. It's a word she would use, and an actor can do something with those consonants—his wickedly funny and infinitely enjoyable judgments on some mutual friends; his titbits of political gossip; but, above all, his warm humanity that robbed his quips of all cruelty.

At the end of the evening – he had been talking solidly and wonderfully for four hours – he said quite suddenly: 'I feel ill. May I lie down?' Soon he was in a very deep sleep on my bed. When it was necessary to wake him, I found it difficult to do so, but, when he left, he was bouncing with life again and full of the usual promises of a certain future: 'I'll write you from New York, and see you as soon as I get back.'

George Barker

IT WAS ON THE WORST DAY of this or any other month of the year that he died, and no one knows why. I find it very hard to write about his death, perhaps because, for the time being, the language is at a loss, as well as we. In time to come, if there is any worthwhile time to come, much will be said about him that we do not know how to say now, not only because he was a great poet, but because he was also a very great person. But, writing this as I do so soon after his death, I have to think about him in a way which those who will write of him later may not do: I mean as a living man whom one cannot believe dead, because he had no right to die at this time. Why has he died?

He has died not because there was no more life left in him, but because the world as it is has become an intolerable place for such a man, and insupportable to such a spirit. And yet I do not think that he would ever have acknowledged this intolerableness of the world in so many words, for, as I saw him, he loved everything as much as anybody ever could, But I think he did so in spite of what everything was, as well as because of what it was. And this antinomy is a killer.

The pathologist's opinion that he died 'of a brain ailment of unknown origin' simply illustrates the undisguised intervention of the powers of darkness in our affairs: for this is one of their greatest as it is their latest triumph. With this sleight-of-hand assassination such powers now openly operate among us.

Why should I try to disguise the pessimism with which his death affects me, me personally? For many years, since we were both young, our names have, intermittently, been put together, his, as it should have been, foremost, for he goes before me in poems as he does in dying. We managed once to take each other's overcoats as we left a drinking party – and I knew whose coat I had got from the dog-eared Penguin I found in the pocket with a line of unmistakable poetry written on the back:

> The lovers scorched to ashes on the green park grass.

As I see his death it would be a dishonouring of him if I were to try to write this note about him as though it would be quickly disremembered. For, although I am at a loss what to say, the poets of this time will feel at a greater loss how to be. He showed how to walk along the street with a poem as though it were a wife and not a whore for the night or a kept-man's angel. He had married the art of poetry not in a registry office or a library or a lecture room, but in a church. Heaven only knows what in the end they will say he died of – but one of the causes may have been the knowledge that he had done some of the things he set out to do. The poems as they are make up a complete and working body, a natural organism, a shape and pattern fulfilled and functioning, like a fly's eye or a stellar system, so that, retrospectively, one could believe that he had not died too soon. He only died too soon because a man like him would always die too soon. But we are not left with fragments of tremendous mementoes, like the poems of Keats – the truth is that, just as this fable evolved in front of our eyes the wings and fire that proved a whole new dragon of poetry had been born – just as soon as he had done this, he died.

But does one fly straight to the insurance office when one hears of such a death? I do not know why this particular death is, for me, more than the eclipse of a single life – perhaps because every poet is more people than he seems to be – but I do know that I feel as if a great principle were in graver danger of extinction now that he is dead. What this great principle may be, I can only sense obscurely – I do not think that he himself would have claimed an over-intelligible familiarity with it – but this principle has to do with the conservation of the spiritual privileges of all those things we do not know, and can never know.

He speaks of this most nearly in the little note prefixed to the *Collected Poems*. 'Man was born to serve, reverence and praise God', – this is the first sentence of the Spiritual Exercises of St Ignatius Loyola. 'I write for the love of man and to praise God' – this is one of the last sentences of Dylan Thomas's. And perhaps what I mean when I say that his death has darkened a great principle is that, from now on, the praise will be a lot thinner without that voice which has, at last, welshed on us.

John Davenport

HOW DELIGHTFUL IT WOULD BE if we always recognised genius when we met it, and turned blue or red, like litmus paper. It is over twenty years now since in a London pub I met a snub-nosed little being with a check cap perched on his dirty curls – an explosive mixture of Rimbaud and Verlaine. He had just published his first book – *Eighteen Poems* – and it had made a large crater in literary London. Unfortunately for me, I was in no mood to be impressed. I had just returned from Paris. I had met Paul Valéry in the Bibliothèque Nationale; Valéry Larbaud had said kind things about my Mallarmé translations; I had been bewildered and bewitched by Léon-Paul Fargue; Paul Eluard had inscribed several volumes of his verse for me; with Marcel Duchamp I had played chess and climbed over the roof of Chartres. I was not at all prepared to bow before this bomb from the provinces.

I was, shall we say, rather an ass. I not only did not recognise a genius, I did not even realise that I had met the man who was to become one of my closest friends. As a clown, I realised that he had merits. You paid for the drinks, it was not unreasonable that you should be amused. He concealed his total contempt of his idiotic patrons with the centuries-old skill of the Celt faced with the Saxon. Perhaps the contempt was not total; he had too much humour for that; but we would have been surprised at the shrewdness of the social judgments behind the mask of buffoonery. He was the ruffianly little oddity from Wales who was the protégé of Edith Sitwell, a grubby rogue who might, or might not, be a genius. His frankly romantic poetry was disturbing to a generation brought up on T. S. Eliot, whose spokesman was W. H. Auden. Spender, of course, was romantic, but he was sentimentally interested in politics. Thomas was definitely not sentimental and, except for vaguely humanitarian leanings, was not remotely interested in politics. He was a pirate who drank our drinks and borrowed our money and kissed our girls.

This Villon-like scrounger was a great poet. Augustus John's portrait of him in 1936 is a wonderfully revealing work. I went with them to the Surrealist Exhibition in London that year. Salvador Dali, stifling in a diver's suit, was far less odd a sight than Dylan guiding his venerable compatriot through the sometimes inane mazes of that freak show. Shortly after this I went to the United States for two years. While I was away Dylan married his golden wife, Caitlin Macnamara, published his book of religious sonnets – *Twenty-five Poems* – and went to live in Wales, at Laugharne, a decayed little port looking over Carmarthen Bay towards the Gower Peninsula. In the summer of 1938 I wrote to him, and shortly afterwards drove down to see him in his strange habitat – he was a sort of Roi d'Ys.

A lovely, lost place, Laugharne; a place of sea birds and shellfish – a bit of Brittany. Incidentally, although Dylan knew no French, and read few French books, even in translation, he greatly enjoyed Louis Guilloux's *Le Sang Noir*, which had come out in English. He would have understood Corbière, too, had he read him; and, of course, many other French writers, notably Rimbaud, of whom he was stupidly supposed to be a disciple. It is interesting that a writer with a virtuoso's command of English should have known no other tongue; not even Welsh. His father and mother were the children of small farmers long settled in Carmarthenshire, both Welsh-speaking; but Dylan's father was a schoolmaster by profession, a teacher of English at Swansea Grammar School. Dylan was born in Swansea, in October, 1914, and was brought up in a self-consciously suburban way not to speak Welsh; but, if he did not speak it, he 'thought Welsh'. His poetry has properly been called Bardic, and he had a pride in being Welsh as violent as the most passionate nationalist could wish, although for Welsh Nationalism as such he had no use.

But to return to Laugharne. I found him living in a tall, narrow house facing the estuary. As Augustus John said, it looked like a stage house and had an air of mystery. Past it, gigantic fisher-women, shapeless as manatees, would drag themselves out of the mud to their evening potations. Their trade was cockle-fishing. Dylan loved all shellfish; and if oysters were not available, cockles would serve, or winkles. Arriving at night, we groped our way through unlit rooms to the same grinding sound one knew from the floor of Sickert's studio, where it was due to pieces of coke which had been hurled at the stove and missed their mark. On Dylan's floors it was due to the carapaces of innumerable devoured crustacea. Eventually we ran him to earth, surrounded by books and bottles, some full, some containing candles which cast a spectral glow over the tousled bard and his ardent wife, who was nursing their first child, the boy Llewellyn. Much beer was drunk, many more shells were cast by midnight on the floor; there had been readings of Blake, readings from the stories of Caradoc Evans, a quarrel about D. H. Lawrence, innumerable bawdy stories and unrepeatable gossip before we went to our unmade beds. The next morning there was great puritanical groaning – Dylan never lost his Baptist's conscience – before the party could be got into the car for the drive across Pembrokeshire to the romantically desolate Cathedral of St David, that *cathédrale engloutie*.

It was there, on the turf above the blue Atlantic, that I heard him recite the poem for his birthday, October 1938, which he had just written and which appeared in the volume *The Map of Love* in 1939: 'Twenty-four years remind the tears of my eyes'.

This meeting in Wales was really the beginning of my friendship with him and for the last fifteen years of his life it was unbroken though occasionally illuminated by violent volcanic eruptions.

Dylan on his native heath was a different being from the extravagant buffoon I had met five years before in London; and I realized, for the first time, the intense seriousness which lay beneath that social exterior that was a mixture of Puck and Panurge, with more than a touch of Falstaff. It was essential for him to work off his puppyish sociability on extravagant trips to the despised but necessary London; but his real self was under the shadow of Sir John's Hill at Laugharne, where the stilted herons and grave cormorants fished in the estuary, and the melancholy cry of the curlew haunted the air, and the night was brushed by the white owls' wings.

This idyllic but precarious existence was shattered by the war. He had just completed the semi-autobiographical prose book *Portrait of the Artist as a Young Dog*, which immediately won him a far wider public when it was published at the beginning of 1940 than any of his previous works had done. Up till then he had been known only to that small band of people in England and America interested in contemporary verse, and even they were often baffled by his obscurities. The *Portrait* was accessible to everybody. At the time of its publication he was staying with me at my house in the Cotswolds with his wife and child, and remained for several months. We wrote a satirical novel together, writing alternate chapters. It was called *The Death of the King's Canary*, but was considered too libellous for publication, as each of the large cast of characters was an easily recognisable caricature of a well-known writer, painter, musician, or absurdity.

It was a strange period in all our lives. The house was full of friends waiting for the call-up. There were the musicians Lennox Berkeley, Arnold Cooke, Humphrey Searle and Henry Boys; the novelist Antonia White; the poets David Gascoyne and William Empson looked in from time to time. Everybody was working feverishly to get some piece of work finished before he or she was caught up in the war machine. Slowly the household disintegrated; we all moved in different directions but for the same reasons, and Dylan and Caitlin arrived in London with a few borrowed pounds in a state of profound gloom. Except for a brief sojourn at New Quay, on Cardigan Bay, London was his home for the next five years.

Dylan's weak chest had caused him to be rejected for military service, and for the first time in his life – if one discounts a year or two as a reporter on a Swansea newspaper in extreme youth – he found himself offered employment, remunerative employment, in two fields. His increasing fame as a poet attracted the attention of the B.B.C. and the success of the *Portrait* made his entry into the world of films as a scrip-writer inevitable. He was an immediate success on the air, having superb natural gifts as a reader of his own poetry and that of others. His voice was immensely rich and resonant, the voice of a nineteenth-century actor, but of a nineteenth-century actor with intelligence. His gift as an extemporiser of brilliant images made him a successful writer of documentary film commentaries, from which he graduated into the world of the commercial cinema. All this was financially desirable and socially satisfying. It was also intolerable. An excellent craftsman, he was scrupulous in all the work he undertook; but the only work which had the faintest importance in his eyes was the making of poetry.

During the war years his poetry was changing into something at once deeper and more communicable. These works are to be found in the volume called *Deaths and Entrances* (1946), which contains the famous 'A Refusal to Mourn the Death, by Fire, of a Child in London'.

I saw him whenever I was in London during these years. They lived in Chelsea, first in a tumble-down, cat-haunted studio; and then in a tumble-down, landlord-haunted basement. As his expenditure was always larger than his income, more money meant no change in the Micawberish mode of living. He was the only genuine Bohemian I have ever known. He depended for security upon his growing fame, of which he was well aware, and which he consciously exploited. It affected him personally not at all;

he remained the same delightfully detached observer. There were penalties to be paid, however. His time became increasingly eaten up by the outside world. and he began to drink to excess. He had always been a Pantagruelian drinker, pouring down beer with the exuberance of a tiny giant. With increasing age an amiable habit became a dangerous necessity. Also, his lyrical impulse was slowly drying up. He published only six poems in the last six years of his life – seven, if one counts the brilliant 'Prologue' to the *Collected Poems* (1953). It was thought an irony that a man should publish his collected poems, and die, immediately after his thirty-ninth birthday, but there would have been fewer and fewer poems; and the poems of his last years all have an elegiac quality; they are all laments for lost youth. The dazzling quality of their texture and their pure Wordsworthian radiance blinded people to the fact that his genius was flaming out.

Incidentally, it would be well to point out here that Dylan always composed with great pains and difficulty, making innumerable drafts of his poems; and that he never wrote a line except when he was raptly sober. Unlike Hart Crane, he did not compose to whisky and Sibelius. He remained always the most scrupulous artist, and his technique became increasingly sure. It is sad, but not unnatural, that these last poems, *In Country Sleep*, with their Traherne-like vision of childhood, should have been those by which he became world-famous. They had behind them – and carried with them – the immense metaphysical force of his early work, in relation to which they seem like the gleaming trail of a meteor.

During these last six years Dylan lived first in Oxfordshire and finally, to his infinite delight, once more in Laugharne, where he was provided with a magically suitable house perched on a cliff – The Boat House. A daughter, Aeronwy, and another son, Colum, had been added to the family. He was a sort of elder brother to his children, who were determinedly independent. Aeronwy, aged four, was asked if she would go for a walk with him and me on one occasion. She was firm in her refusal: 'I'm not going to the village with those two dirty boys.' This last sojourn in Laugharne was broken by many visits to London to do broadcasts; by three lecture tours – increasingly, wildly, suicidally successful – in America; by a trip to Persia (Iran) to write a documentary film about oil; and by a six-month stay in Italy for the sake of his son Llewellyn, who also had a weak chest. Dylan loathed Italy, except for Elba and its iron-workers. America – where he had become the laureate of the young – he loved; but the only European town he enjoyed was Prague, to which he once paid a flying visit. He was Gothic by instinct, and mistrusted the classical – he was entirely unresponsive to English poetry between Milton and Blake – this Dionysian, who was a follower of Hermes rather than Apollo. Nor could he stand Italian literary society. He once hid in a cupboard in his bedroom in Florence rather than meet a famous fellow-poet.

In the autumn of 1953 he made his fourth journey to America. He was on his way to California, where he was to work on a libretto for Stravinsky. While he was in New York he took part in a reading of his radio play, *Under Milk Wood*, on which he had been working intermittently for six years. It was immensely successful, as it was in England and everywhere else when it was broadcast after his death. In fact, the charm of its writing and his tragic end combined to make critics and public alike make absurd claims for it. As a radio play it is marvellously successful; it is gay, it is tender; it sparkles. But it remains a radio play, no more. For Dylan it was merely a proof that he was master of that medium; for the public it was something by a famous modern poet that everybody could understand. All substitutes for poetry were for him the means to make a livelihood – and nothing more. He was pleased with *Milk Wood* but deeply dissatisfied that he had been unable to carry out the original scheme from which it had sprung, a play which was to have been called *The Village that was Mad*. This was abandoned because he was incapable of dramatic structure.

It is the fault of his film scripts, which are more remarkable for the quality of the dialogue than anything else. It is interesting to speculate on what would have happened to the Stravinsky libretto. Dylan was fascinated by the task, but dubious as to his ability to cope with it.

And then, he died, this violent, loving man, destructive of nothing but himself. His body was brought immaculately back from New York to Laugharne, where he was buried in November, 1953. It had rained all the way down from London, but it was a high, shining autumn day, of the kind he loved, by the time of the funeral. As his coffin was carried through the lych-gate of the village church a cock began crowing redly. A suitable epitaph. I walked away from the churchyard with Louis MacNeice and the village publican. It was the publican who made the perfect comment on our dead friend. 'He was', he said, 'a very *humble* man.' The man who felt that everything was mortal and everything was sacred; the man for whom everything was miraculous; who wrote his poems 'for the love of man and in praise of God'; the man who wrote:

Not for the proud man apart
From the raging moon I write
On these spindrift pages,
Nor for the towering dead
With their nightingales and psalms,
But for the lovers, their arms
Round the griefs of the ages,
Who pay no praise or wages
Nor need my craft or art.

G. S. Fraser

I KNEW DYLAN THOMAS only very slightly, but it so happens that my second most vivid memory of him – my *most* vivid memory is of his reading some of his poems – is of his standing by the bar in a pub near Broadcasting House and making an immensely long and enormously funny saga out of an incident that, for most people, would have had no 'story in it' at all. The anecdote was about a wartime railway journey in the blackout, in a carriage crammed with large, grim, silent Canadian soldiers, and about Dylan's embarrassment in opening in front of them an untidy brown paper parcel full of sandwiches, finding that the sandwiches almost choked him under the Canadians' steady stares, and fumbling hopelessly to parcel the sandwiches up again. He made this stretch half an hour, getting funnier all the time. He held one's attention partly by mimicry (you *saw* the big, bovine Canadian eyes, the munching, choking little Dylan, the embarrassed flurry with the brown paper); partly by the old comedian's trick of making you 'wait for it'; partly by the mere deadpan accuracy of the trained reporter, who subconsciously and automatically records any experience that may at any time provide 'copy'; and partly by a gift the opposite of this accuracy, a wild, wilful, beautiful, buffoonish verbal exaggeration.

It is the highest tribute I can pay to Mr Emlyn Williams's evening with the young Dylan Thomas at the Globe Theatre to say that, from now on, this memory of Thomas telling a funny story about himself will be overlaid and confused in my mind with a picture of Mr Williams telling Thomas's sad and funny stories, mainly from *Portrait of the Artist as a Young Dog*, with a supple spontaneity, as if Mr Williams himself were making the stories up as he went along.

Mr Williams's performance is not a feat of physical impersonation. In his neat, nondescript blue suit, he doesn't look in the least *like* Thomas, who threw on any clothes that came handy in the morning and generally resembled (in the phrase of an American reporter which he relished and appropriated) 'an unmade bed'. Nor are the two voices similar, apart from having the 'cut glass' quality of the Welsh voice, controlling its lilt, and consciously speaking 'beautiful English'. Mr Williams's voice is light, high, and supple; Dylan Thomas's was low, wobbly, and rich, What Mr Williams gets into the skin of is Thomas's spirit – or more precisely of his *persona*, the mask the splendid poet hid behind, the comedian at the bar. Thomas's semi-autobiographical stories and his fragment of a farcical-fantastic novel, *Adventures in the Skin Trade*, are lightweight things. He wrote them as he might have talked them; to me, at least, they come over more effectively, as talked by Mr Williams, than on the printed page. They are (as in a sense many of Thomas's poems were also) scripts for the speaking voice. They look like the most reckless off-cuff improvisation, but are in fact as taut and timed as a good music-hall sketch.

Mr Williams has had to cut very little; from a mood, to a scene, to an incident, from a character in outline to a character in action, from one small climax of humour or pathos to the next one, the stories move on firmly, never missing a trick. Jokes that seemed on the page too flat and broad, sentiment that seemed to be 'getting at you' – as in the story of the Welsh youth haunted on his holiday by his dead brother and father – are just right for the different medium (that needs a broader brush, and a less finicky fastidiousness) of the dramatically spoken word. For Mr Williams acts these stories as well as tells them; with a single chair for prop, he becomes in turn the great, fat uncle with the gravy-stained waistcoat, the tiny aunt standing on the chair to hit the uncle on the head with a china dog. Mr Williams lost his grip on me only when he read, stagily, two poems, 'The Hand' and 'And Death Shall Have No Dominion'. One remembered Dylan Thomas's own voice reading poetry – the gong booming over the sea of treacle. One remembered the truth (the serious and impersonal poet, dead too young), so much larger and sadder than the legend perpetuated here. Yet the legend was part of the truth and was worth perpetuating, and, if Mr Williams has the success he deserves, he should diffuse the legend widely: the card, the young dog, the wide boy from Swansea with a bottle on his finger, the brilliant minor writer of excellent comic tales.

Louis MacNeice

YEATS DESCRIBED THE POET as one who knows 'that Hamlet and Lear are gay'. No poet of our time was a better example of this than Dylan Thomas. When his first work appeared it was astonishingly new and yet went back to the oldest of our roots – roots which had long been ignored, written off, or simply forgotten.. He was not just a poet among poets; he was, as has often been remarked, a bard, with the three great bardic virtues of faith, joy, and craftsmanship – and, one could add, of charity. Many of his poems are concerned with death or the darker forces, yet they all have the joy of life in them. And many of his poems are obscure but it is never the obscurity of carelessness; though I, for one, assumed it might be when I first read his early work in the 1930s. Lastly, all the poems (a rare thing in this age of doubt) are suffused both with a sense of value, a faith in something that is simultaneously physical and spiritual, and with (what is equally rare in an age of carping) a great breath of generosity, goodwill not only towards men but towards all created things.

The next few years will obviously see a spate of writing about Thomas – his vision, imagery, technique, etc. – and the writers will be beset by two distinct and opposite dangers – the danger of trying to equip him too exactly with a literary pedigree and the danger of isolating him as a sport, a Villon figure, a wild man who threw up works of genius without knowing what he was doing. The former mistake has been made for years by various academic critics, often Americans, who have dwelt at length on Thomas's relations to ancient Welsh poetry or to Rimbaud; though he has something in common with both (and though Wales in general and Swansea in particular were the most important factors in his make-up), it should be remembered that he had never read Rimbaud and could not read Welsh. As for the 'wild man' conception, immediately after Thomas's death it was exploited in its most disgusting and imbecile form by certain of our daily papers. Of course Thomas liked pints of beer (so what? he also liked watching cricket) but he did not write his poems 'with a pint in one hand'; no writer of our time approached his art in a more reverent spirit or gave it more devoted attention. One glance at a Thomas manuscript will show the almost incredible trouble he took over those elaborate arabesques that could yet emerge as fresh as any of the 'woodnotes wild' expected from the born lyric poet. In fact, he *was* a born lyric poet but it was a birthright he worked and worked to secure.

His lyrical gift, though the most important, was only one of several gifts. He had a roaring sense of comedy, as shown in many of his prose works. He had a natural sense of theatre, as was shown not only in his everyday conversation but in those readings of poetry (and his taste, by the way, was catholic) which earned him such applause both here and in the U.S. He was moreover a subtle and versatile actor, as he proved repeatedly in radio performances. *And* he 'took production'. Though his special leaning (as was natural, given his astonishing voice) was to the sonorous and emotional, he enjoyed playing character parts, especially comic or grotesque ones, such as a friendly Raven which he played for me once in a dramatised Norwegian folk-tale. He could even 'throw away' if required to. And in all these sidelines – as in all his verse and prose – there appeared the same characteristic blend of delight in what he was doing and care as to how he did it.

This does not seem to me the moment for analysing Dylan Thomas. He is assured of a place, and a unique one, in the history of English poetry. But, when such a personality dies, his friends are not much in the mood for literary criticism. What we remember is not a literary figure to be classified in the text-book but something quite unclassifiable, a wind that bloweth where it listeth, a wind with a chuckle in its voice and news from the end of the world. It is too easy to call him unconventional – which is either an understatement or a red herring. It is too easy to call him Bohemian – a word which implies affectations which were quite alien to Thomas. It is too easy even to call him anarchist – a better word but too self-conscious an attitude. Thomas was an actor – and would that more poets were – but he was not an attitudiniser. He eschewed politics but he had a sense of justice; that he once visited Prague proves nothing as to his leftness or rightness; it merely is one more proof that he thought men everywhere were human. Both in his life and his work he remained honest to the end. This, combined with his talents, made him a genius.

PART TWO

The Poet

Map of Llareggub

HUGH GORDON PORTEUS

'THE WORK OF THIS YOUNG MAN is on a huge scale,' says Miss Vurble Burble, in the purple blurb on the dustwrapper of Mr Dylan Thomas's new book, *The Map of Love*. This is indeed a large-scale map of a very small and gnomic piece of territory. 'Geography's about maps, Biography's about chaps', says the clerihew. But not for Dylan. In his autogeography he maps chaps, or he eddies in Finnegan's wake sketching the biographies of bald or hairy hills. A map is a representation of surface features. To snatch and fix the living surface is a Welsh gift. And if anyone can map a chap, in this supremely superficial manner, or hand over intact to the eye the palpitating superficies of life, it is Mr Augustus John, whose splendid portrait of Dylan serves as frontispiece to this book.

Beneath pensive temples, crowned with a crop of sunflower curls, the eyes are big Welsh lollipops, about to roll, the nose an inquisitive and substantial knob, awaiting the flowering of the lush mouth. This is to flutter the fans, perhaps? It may do a good deal towards establishing Dylan as the 'wild pet for the supercultivated' that Mr Eliot once found people apt to deem W. Blake. But this is Dylan's danger, not his destiny.

Mr John's map of Dylan is of course a *physical* map. And what everyone wants of a chap now is a *political* map. This nobody has ever been able to do, for Dylan. Yet it is felt everywhere that D.T. is one of those unavoidably significant and exasperating *incorrigibles* about whom something must be done. He found himself launched, some years ago, in his pubescence, as a sort of overdue prodigy. His demise was daily expected. He persisted, however, in drugging the constipated poetic market with salutary tisanes of an alarming purgative power. He refused to play marbles with the usual politico-literary gangs. He cocked snooks in all directions. Moreover, it was soon discovered that he was not a true naïf at all. Even in his poems, *form* was found lurking, and at the core of his most fey and incontinent outbursts the presence of an intellectual principle could be detected. And ever since, he has clung to the role of impenitent highbrow Tom o' Bedlam, obstinately and indefatigably edgaring away, in spite of everyone and everything. All this is naturally considered deeply unsuitable and provocative. So D.T. has been written about a good deal, and given a lot of nonsensical sobriquets. (He has been hailed in China as 'the happy worrier', and in America as 'the poetic athlete', even!)

Dylan's trouble is a simple one. Anyone who wishes to entrench himself in the public's fancy has first to patent a little manner. But also anyone who once becomes celebrated for a little manner will find it very difficult to escape being committed to it for life. Dylan invented an *idiom*, consisting of a few tricks of verbal and metaphorical violence, like an infectiously engaging lisp or stutter, as found in the repertoire of a successful social clown. Dylan became trapped in this mechanism, it seems, and now many besides Dylan are slaves of these easily mastered tricks. It is impossible to pick up one of the little magazines now without being affronted by the spectacle of this contagious eruption. The little manner is being mass-produced *ad nauseam*. One can have too much of a good thing. No artist worth his right hand should allow himself to get cheaply standardised and multiplied in this way. And it is not Dylan's monotonous idiom, in any case, but his psyche, that is interesting. This is less tittupy than it looks.

Like many who affect a distracted style, spouting their messages through a cast of idiot-puppets, set in a fantastic landscape, Dylan is actually remarkably well-balanced. He has a strong head and a sound critical faculty, (as readers of the *New English Weekly* have good cause to know, from his acute fiction-reviews). He has also an innocent eye – ('innocence, two flowers wagging in a sow's ear',) – and a sort of *mandragora* outlook, that enables him to see 'creation screaming in the steam of the kettle', or 'the necks of the screaming weeds', or 'the sheep's fleas staring out of their hair', just as naturally as he notes 'the sour churning of water over pebbles' or that 'the creams of the sea ran unheeded over her feet'. He is afraid of this sensitive impressionability, and so turns the gently inhabited organisms of his world into laughable toys. There is no 'poetry in the pity' nonsense. 'Pity the hare', he thought, 'for the weasel will drink her'. There the pity is in the poetry, as it is when 'her foot lay on his like a mouse'. He enters the creatures and the network of vegetable veins with ease. He can inhabit the loony, the mouse, the louse, the parson, the larch, in a series of quick-change striptease acts; it is only *words* that sometimes transfix him. Metaphor and rhetoric clot the clarity of all his verse. His prose, on the other hand, is often apt to run flat, to lose the intensity it owes to a personal vision, and to trickle into pompous-pathetic fine-writing. Then it has to be artificially juiced up with an exotic word or image. The introduction of crypto-prurient ex-presbyterian *objets trouvés* like nun's thighs, or green or bald-as-badger women, is one cheap way to keep the pace hot. Or he warms up with a new word, like the verb to brother: 'He brothered the world about him. . . . There is rain on my face, there is wind on my cheeks. He brothered the rain.' But this is just the wind on the heath's brother, in a borrowed vision. I call attention to the texture of Dylan's writing because that is, if not the most individual thing about it, all that can be discussed in a brief review with any profit. And needless to say, Dylan's writing, poetry or prose, good or bad, is among the very little *intensive* writing worth scrutiny at all today. There are 115 pages of it in his new book, which is made up of sixteen new poems (some however have appeared more than once in magazines); and seven prose-pieces. These are not sketches or stories, nor yet prose-poems, but rather lyrical fables, and they have a formal excellence that it is difficult to demonstrate. 'The Mouse and the Woman' is one of the most characteristic; and better, in my opinion, than the title-piece. It is about a madman and his woman, but also 'It is the telling of a creation. It is the story of birth'; a story in which 'real things kept changing with unreal, and, as a bird burst into song, he heard the springs rattle far back in its throat'. It is an asylum nightmare, full of symbols and arranged like a fugue, with a mouse theme that runs in and out with an hallucinated conviction.

> '. . . the mouse had waited for this consummation. Wrinkling its eyes, it crept stealthily along the tunnel, littered with scraps of half-eaten paper, behind the kitchen wall. Stealthily, on tiny, padded paws, it felt its way through darkness, its nails scraping on the wood. Stealthily, it worked its way between the walls, screamed at the blind light through the chinks, and filed through the square of tin. Moonlight drooped slowly into the space where the mouse, working its destruction, inched into light. The last barrier fell away. And on the clean stones of the kitchen floor the mouse stood still.'

Out of such humble material, dramatically dignified and poetically heightened into momentous episodes, Dylan makes his maps of love. This is masterly; but are his maps of any use? For Auden, for example:

> . . . maps can really point to places
> Where life is evil now:
> Nanking; Dachau –.

For Dylan, they lead to the Jarvis hills, the trickling water, the ninth field, the cattle's hay, to a toy and daffy Welshscape over which 'the sun turns at the edges of a thin and watery sky like a sweet in a glass of water'; or to a queer escape-country for the comfort of the overbepoliticked; or to Dylan's own land of Llareggub, seen through the looking-glass. There is room for Dylan's country, on the larger literary map, and it should have some visitors this balmy season.

Dylan Thomas: A Pioneer

FRANCIS SCARFE

I. *Points of Contact*

DYLAN THOMAS IS ONE of the most promising of the poets under thirty, but he has suffered through catching the public eye a little too early, which resulted in unfounded criticism by both his supporters and detractors. He was promising in 1934 (*Eighteen Poems:* Parton Press) and promising in 1936 (*Twenty-five Poems:* Dent). To those who have followed his production since then he is still promising, and this premature estimate of him is being made to clarify the nature of that promise.

For many people his poems are puzzles, seeming to offer at first reading no more than a forbidding cliff, impenetrable to reason, from which there jut great crags of capricious imagery. Some people (notably Miss Sitwell) read him for his sound, but though the words peal fully and roundly, the rhythms are monotonous enough to make this pall. But many a good poet is monotonous. The only satisfactory approach seems to be to plumb these images and verbal din and see what lies beyond.

The poems, especially in the 1934 and 1935 volumes, seem to have three noticeable points of contact. Discussion of the Metaphysicals, Sitwellism and Surrealism is irrelevant. The dominant points of contact seem to be James Joyce, the Bible and Freud. The personal habits of language and mythology of Dylan Thomas can readily be identified through these three sources. The first is linguistic, the second mythological, the third psycho-pathological, the key to his interpretation of his world.

II. *Language*

It is agreed that James Joyce's language in *Ulysses* is simple enough. It appears difficult only when sentences and parts of sentences do not appear logically related. *Ulysses* is the masterpiece of the unexpected: the element of surprise, so puffed by Poe and Baudelaire, and so unclassical, dominates every page. The words are not odd, they are merely at times oddly related. Later, when Joyce evolved a composite language, it appeared to some people (like myself) more satisfying and logical than the jargon of *Ulysses*, because this new language has a recognisable basis in philology. In *Ulysses* there are such elementary experiments as 'A screaming bittern's harsh high whistle shrieks. Groangrousegurgling Toft's cumbersome whirligig turns slowly the room right round-about the room.' This is simple, it reveals meaning, is emotionally apprehended. 'Steel shark stone onehandled Nelson, two trickies Frauenzimmer plumstained from pram falling bawling.' Though the words are simple, this is not easy. It is not readily apprehended either emotionally or by analysis. It lives only in its context. Such writing reveals in miniature the linguistic habits of Dylan Thomas.

His basic device (which Joyce later systematised) is the invention of words. This device is fully in accord with Dylan Thomas's own statement, 'Poetry is the rhythmic, inevitably narrative, movement from an overclothed blindness to a naked vision', and his definition of his poetic activity as '. . . the physical and mental task of constructing a formally watertight compartment of words, preferably with a main moving column' (*New Verse*, October 1934). Dylan Thomas, in writing poetry, is not expressing so much as discovering his feelings. This is as it should be, for the reading and writing of poetry at any time are largely acts of discovery. The poet conventionally offers what he knows he has found, but Thomas offers the process of discovery itself. This unfinishedness is regarded by some as an insult to the reader, but in reality it is characteristic, honest, and one of the most attractive aspects of his work.

The invention of words, then, is inevitable in the expression of the half-perceived, incoherent sensations and ideas. And as his pen hovers between a host of choices, seeking some short-cut to expression as the Surrealists do by automatism, Dylan Thomas invents such terms as 'man-iron', 'bonerailed', 'seaspindle', 'sea-struck', 'all-hollowed', 'pin-hilled', 'natron'. The presence of puns in these composites ('all-hollowed') indicates his pedantic dry humour. At other times, instead of fusing ideas together in this way, Thomas distorts their usual meanings, as in 'minstrel angle' (ministering angel?), 'triangle landscape' (here triangular + trinity, formed by the crosses of Christ and the robbers), 'ship-racked gospel', and the like. Real obscurity only starts when a false epithet is used, of which Joyce was rarely guilty. These are sometimes immensely expressive, as in 'dead nuisance' or 'iron mile', but the trick annoys when it hides rather than reveals meaning, as in 'colic season', 'cadaverous gravel', 'metal neptune'. This emotional use of epithet resembles fake Surrealism. Real Surrealism is practically reached in his fourth trick: 'man of leaves', 'tree of nettles', 'wood of weathers', 'sixth of wind', 'house of bread'. This is very charming at first, but it bores by repetition. The final trick is the inaccurate use of verbs, which abounds in these poems in such lines as:

> Through the rampart of the sky
> Shall the star-flanked seed be riddled . . .
>
> ('Poem 5')

Most of these verbal tricks are from time to time completely successful and justified, as in the ten 'religious' sonnets in the *Twenty-five Poems*, where 'gallow grave', 'mountain minute', even 'glove of prints' and 'linen spirit' are impressive and logical in their context. At his best, Thomas reminds us of the Old Testament, James Joyce and Hopkins all at once. It matters little whether he reads them: his language partakes of all three.

In his later poems (since 1936) Thomas has diluted these verbal surprises. That his poems still startle our complacency is a proof that his first appeal was not due to mere bogus verbalism. It is well that he is losing some of these habits, which lead to preciousness of the most pompous kind. Not that it is to be despised, for preciousness itself can reveal a wealth of unsuspected fact. All poetry is precious.

III. *Biblical Symbolism*

I do not agree with a critic who said that there were two types of poems in the 1936 volume, 'sense' and 'nonsense' poems. The poems scarcely differ in method, and are made sensible by the pervading presence of the Bible and sexual symbolism.

Genesis, the Garden of Eden, the Fall, Adam, original sin, the presence of Cain, Job, Jacob, Abraham, Lazarus, the legends of Christ and Mary, form the bulk of the reference-matter, and even subject-matter of the *Twenty-five Poems.* The fervency of these references is due to the fact that the Bible appears as a cruel and crazy legend, as seen through childish memories of hot-gospelling and the diabolical grimace of the Welsh Bethel. The Biblical element is further confused by a primitive metaphysics, related in the last analysis to a sexual interpretation of the universe:

> Dawn breaks behind the eyes;
> From poles of skull and toe the windy blood
> Slides like a sea;
> Nor fenced, nor staked, the gushers of the sky
> Spout to the rod
> Divining in a smile the oil of tears.
>
> ('Light breaks where no sun shines')

The philosophy is simple: the universe is sexually dynamic; bird, beast and stone share the same (sexual) life with man (an advance on the pretty pantheism of Wordsworth), but, for ever conscious of a sense of sin, Thomas conveys this as something terrible:

> The horizontal cross-bones of Abaddon,
> You by the cavern over the black stairs,
> Rung bone and blade, the verticals of Adam,
> And, manned by midnight, Jacob to the stars;
> Hairs of your head, then said the hollow agent,
> Are but the roots of nettles and of feathers
> Over these groundworks thrusting through a pavement,
> And hemlock-headed in the wood of weather.
>
> ('Poem 25': II)

Why horizontals and verticals (genitals would do)? The same arbitrary association links Abaddon, Jacob and Adam. Hollow agent (joke) is Death. Only 'cross-bones', 'cavern' and 'hemlock' produce horror. These lines form part of a sonnet relating growth from childhood to manhood. Death is present from beginning to end.

The '*horreur de la vie et l'extase de la vie*' of Baudelaire are evenly balanced in Dylan Thomas. His universe is dynamic, frighteningly active and alive:

> And now the horns of England, in the sound of shape,
> Summon your snowy horsemen, and the four-stringed hill,
> Over the sea-gut loudening, sets a rock alive;
> Hurdles and duns and railings, as the boulders heave,
> Crack like a spring in a vice, bone breaking April,
> Spill the lank folly's hunter and the hard-held hope . . .
>
> ('Poem 10')

But, in consequence, death itself appears not as a negation, but as an equally dynamic force, as old as Adam:

The wisemen tell me that the garden gods
Twined good and evil on an eastern tree;
And when the moon rose windily it was
Black as the beast and paler than the cross.

('Poem 3')

Death, not life, is the measure of time:

A worm tells summer better than the clock,
The slug's a living calendar of days.

('Poem 7')

So it is that the life-death problem in Dylan Thomas is as unresolved as the sex-sin problem. These dualisms are again related to a theological dualism, body-soul, as expressed in the first poem of the collection:

I, in my intricate image, stride on two levels,
Forged in man's minerals, the brassy orator
Laying my ghost in metal,
The scales of this twin world tread on the double,
My half ghost in armour holds hard in death's corridor,
To my man-iron sidle.

('Poem I')

This is more than lay philosophy, for it is implicit here that the triumph of the body is death of the spirit, since the 'man-iron' (flesh) and 'ghost in armour' (soul) are equally aggressive elements. It is only owing to this primitive interpretation that Thomas is able to confuse sexual and spiritual values in the ten 'religious' sonnets.

These so-called 'sonnets' (they are 14-line poems) cannot be considered separately, as together they form a unit ('Poem 25'). The technique is cumulative, impressionistic, though in one or two sonnets the subject is directly presented. Subjects, rather, for though the theme is the life-death antagonism, it is inextricably bound up with Old and New Testament mythology and sexual symbolism. It is rash to reduce such works to a formula, but for me they represent a double pattern of Biblical and sexual imagery, the recognisable characters being Satan (identified with death and sin), sex (i.e. life, represented by Adam and even Gabriel), Mary (the justification of sex through child-bearing and suffering, but none the less a worldly symbol), and Christ (victim and blood-offering rather than hero).

Sonnet II, quoted above, expresses the identification of sex with sin and nature through Biblical reference. The third sonnet is confused, and in it the Old Testament wait for the Messiah, the Paschal Lamb, the three-days' death of Christ and the Ram of the Zodiac are so related that only the author could give a satisfactory explanation, if there is one. Not that it matters, for even a few lines of that poem should show Dylan Thomas's capacity for *montage*, as he works together a sense of time, the foreshadowed conflict of life and death principles, against a scriptural and sexual background:

> First there was the lamb on knocking knees
> And three dead seasons in a climbing grave
> That Adam's wether in the flock of horns,
> Butt of the tree-tailed worm that mounted Eve,
> Horned down with skullfoot and the skull of toes
> On thunderous pavements in the garden time.

Such verse is not intellectually rich, but sensually and emotionally it is profound. The fourth sonnet is a passage of sexual mysticism, in which love and sex are identified as a prelude to the nativity (Sonnets V and VI). 'And from the windy West came two-gunned Gabriel' (V). The narrative begins moving with this first line, the gangster-disguise of Gabriel (however naïve) giving the sense of shock and incredible difficulty by the Annunciation. Again cabbalistic tricks come to the aid of the poet, who conjures us a miracle with a pack of cards and a mumbo-jumbo of literary and

Biblical allusion. Sonnet VI continues in the same vein, being a gruesome conception and nativity in one, contrived once more by a cabbalistic formula:

> He in a book of water tallow-eyed
> By lava's light split through the oyster vowels
> And burned sea-silence on a wick of words . . .

But this time the difficulties are not shirked, and all the horrors of birth (as suggested by Genesis and Milton perhaps) are conveyed in a brutally effective language:

> And love plucked out the stinging siren's eye,
> Old cock from nowheres lopped the minstrel tongue
> Till tallow I blew from the wax's tower
> The fats of midnight when the salt was singing;
> Adam, time's joker, on a witch of cardboard
> Spelt out the seven seas, an evil index,
> The bagpipe-breasted ladies in the deadweed
> Blew out the blood gauze through the wound of manwax.

The attending presence of the siren and cock (both symbolising lust and sacrifice), Adam (the sinner), and the 'ladies in the deadweed' (again sirens, Fates, Furies, acting as midwives) heightens symbolically the the horror of Christ's difficult, and indeed *unnatural*, birth. The next sonnet summarises Christ's career: not the conventional tale so much as the bringing into focus of all Biblical legend, and a new identification of man with God and the universe. Its concentrated rhetoric:

> Now stamp the Lord's Prayer on a grain of rice,
> A Bible-leaved of all the written woods
> Strip to this tree: a rocking alphabet,
> Genesis in the root, the scarecrow word,
> And one light's language in the book of trees.
> Doom on deniers at the wind-turned statement . . .

brings together the literal fanatic, doubting Thomas and the twentieth-century modernist, while before them lies a world of living fact in which spiritual and physical realities meet.

The eighth sonnet, the 'Crucifixion', is the best.

This was the crucifixion on the mountain,
Time's nerve in vinegar, the gallow grave
As tarred with blood as the bright thorns I wept;
The world's my wound, God's Mary in her grief,
Bent like three trees and bird-papped through her shift,
With pins for teardrops is the long wound's woman.
This was the sky, Jack Christ, each minstrel angle
Drove in the heaven-driven of the nails
Till the three-coloured rainbow from my nipples
From pole to pole leapt round the snail-waked world.
I by the tree of thieves, all glory's sawbones
Unsex the skeleton this mountain minute,
And by this blowclock witness of the sun
Suffer the heaven's children through my heartbeat.

[To establish a hasty glossary, it seems evident that 'Time's nerve' = Christ, i. e. most sensitive point in history; 'gallow' = shallow + gallows; line 3: 'I' = Christ (if it means Dylan Thomas the poem loses); line 5, 'three trees' = crosses; 'bird-papped' = association of dove, also undeveloped, virginal; 'pins for teardrops' – compare Picasso's imagery, the very tears wound; 'Jack Christ' – Hopkinese, Christ is Everyman; 'minstrel angle' = ministering angel, also literally minstrel angle, that is each corner of the singing sky; 'heaven-driven' – the responsibility for the 'crime' rests with God, not man; 'three-coloured rainbow' – a new covenant made by the Trinity (see Milton); 'snail-waked' – snail symbol of destruction, sloth and lust; 'sawbones' – doctor; 'mountain' – gigantic, important; 'blowclock' – literally so, or the lifeless Christ's body become a symbol.]

In a sense this poem seems to symbolise the birth of love through the death of sex. Mary suffers the true punishment of Eve – not merely the pangs of child-birth, but the death of her offspring. The full symbolism only appears towards the end of the poem, with the words 'Unsex the skeleton this mountain minute'. A similar instance of sexual frustration occurs in 'I in my intricate image', in the words:

> a cock on the dunghill
> Crying to Lazarus the morning is vanity.

The conclusion to be drawn from this fine crucifixion poem is disturbing. After presenting in all his poems a brilliant sexual interpretation of life, Dylan Thomas has here presented a sexual interpretation of death. The secret of death, and its horror, is that it is sexless. (Note: this may seem a far-fetched interpretation of a straightforward poem. The answer is that all interpreting is dangerous, and never quite in focus. The poet is rarely entirely responsible for his implications, they rest with the reader.)

These poems owe their success to their density rather than to their outlook, though the outlook is original and stimulating. One or two of them are too exclusively *montage*, but as a whole they concentrate admirably in a final synthesis the tentative self-exploration of the rest of the volume.

In Dylan Thomas's later poems this Biblical background narrows (some would say broadens) considerably. The 'Poem in October' (*The Year's Poetry*, 1935) is a variation on the theme 'In the beginning was the Word', for in it all living things and natural objects are defined in terms of letters, vowels, syllables, etc. This poem could well have appeared nauseatingly literary, were it not for the fact that the subject is sustained by a strong sense of universal analogy, the one-ness of life, and justified by the poet's presence in the poem. This is a good instance of Thomas's pseudocabbalistic mystery, an effect which is readily obtained with few properties, but for a full development of which Thomas has not the necessary background. Let us remember (as a warning to schoolgirls who regard Dylan Thomas as a magician) that Professor Saurat once affirmed that Rimbaud's 'Les Voyelles' was based on the mysteries of the Cabbala. At seventeen, Rimbaud could easily obtain a smattering (about five lines) of knowledge of those mysteries from a Larousse dictionary. . . .

Towards 1937 Thomas broke slightly away from Biblical background, only to err consciously or unconsciously towards church ritual. This may have been due to Eliot or George Barker. That it was not successful can be seen in the poem 'It is the sinners' dust-tongued Bell claps me to churches' (*The Year's Poetry*, 1937). Though there are some fine movements in the poem, in spite of the clarifying of the images the theme is less clear than in his earlier poems, and it leaves a sense of frustration. 'In Memory of Ann Jones' (*The Year's Poetry*, 1938), which is perhaps his best poem since then, is fundamentally religious, and is Biblical rather than church-going. Even the poem 'There was a Saviour' (*Horizon*, May 1940) is only a new outlet for the Messianic legend, and the typical imagery is ritualistic.

It would be ridiculous to claim Thomas for any church. It is sufficient to note to what entirely different uses T. S. Eliot and Dylan Thomas have put the Bible for purposes of poetry. Thomas is much nearer Blake, one might even say nearer Donne, but also perilously near Rimbaud's *Les Premières Communions*.

IV. *Sexual Symbolism*

'Poetry must drag further into the clear nakedness of light more even of the hidden causes than Freud could realise' (Dylan Thomas, *New Verse*, October 1934).

So wrote Dylan Thomas in his admission that he had been influenced by Freud. The influence is first of all general, understandable in a poet whose chief preoccupation is to explore childhood and adolescence. Only a reader of Freud can receive the full impact, which is enormous, of Dylan Thomas's predominantly sexual imagery. The influence of Freud would seem to go even further in view of the poet's acknowledgment that his activity as a poet is one of self-discovery rather than self-expression or even self-analysis. In their finished state the poems suggest that self-analysis could be undertaken by such a poet only by analysing what he had written. That is to say, they are not the product of analysis, but the very raw material for it. They are in the fullest sense documents: they are not intellectual or cerebral, but so spontaneous that the poet himself might well be amazed and bewildered in face of them.

The sexual symbolism in the poems seems to work largely as an assertion of sexuality, of the sexual basis of all thought and action. Secondly, the poems also contain some implied defences of this sexuality, justifications offered by the poet to society and to his own conscience. A little probing reveals not a liberated body but an obsessed mind (as in D. H. Lawrence):

> And I am dumb to tell the crooked rose
> My youth is bent by the same wintry fever.
> ('The force that through the green fuse')

Dylan Thomas's imagery is predominantly masculine, to the point of onanism and homosexuality. And although the male sexual images are bold, harsh and triumphant, there is a sense of impending tragedy and frustration.

> I see that from these boys shall men of nothing
> Stature by seedy shifting
> Or lame the air with leaping of its heats.
> I am the man your father was.
> We are the sons of flint and pitch.
> Oh see the poles are kissing as they cross.
> ('Two' in *New Verse*, June 1934)

The male is constantly expressed, naturally, in heroic images, such as the tower, turret, tree, monster, crocodile, knight in armour, ghost, sailor, Jacob's ladder, sky-scraper. But side by side with these are other equally male sex-images which carry also the idea of death and disgrace, such as the snake, the slug, the snail and the maggot:

> In old man's shank one-marrowed with my bone,
> And all the herrings smelling in the sea,
> I sit and watch the worm beneath my nail
> Wearing the quick away.
>
> (*New Verse*, August 1934)

It seems evident that Thomas's allegiance to Freud has not resulted, in his poems, in the cleansing of sexuality from the Old Testament sense of sin. Even the 'Paradise Regained' poem (as one might call the last of the sonnet-sequence) ends on a combined note of creation and destruction:

> Green as beginning, let the garden diving
> Soar, with its two bark towers, to that Day
> When the worm builds with the gold straws of venom
> My nest of mercies in the rude, red tree.

For the vision of the worm creating is only gained after the sexual immolation of the male (Christ):

> I by the tree of thieves, all glory's sawbones
> Unsex the skeleton this mountain minute,
> And by this blowcock witness of the sun
> Suffer the heaven's children through my heartbeat.

The words 'unsex the skeleton' are a good indication of Thomas's problem, the reconciling of the creative and destructive elements of sex. In view of the prevailing sense of sin, this suspicion that sex is not an end in itself, and that the ultimate objective is irremediably obscure it must be concluded that the poet's interpretation of sex is still as close to the Old Testament as to the psychology of Freud. The Bible provides the mythology by which the problem can be raised to a high and universal plane, while Freud gives the impetus to what is perhaps the most overwhelming and poignant sexual imagery in modern poetry.

V. *Shape*

'The more subjective a poem, the clearer the narrative line' (Dylan Thomas, *New Verse*, October 1934). This is eminently satisfying if considered only in reference to Dylan Thomas himself. His poems are admittedly subjective, and their structure is remarkably simple. Not only is the 'main moving column' of words present; there is in consequence a strong core of subject round which the imagery is grouped. For this reason, although many people are dismayed by the accumulation of imagery and pseudo-imagery in the poems (for he is a spendthrift poet), the poems are far from being chaotic. Thomas's fundamental simplicity is shown in two of his finest poems, 'The hand that signed the paper felled a city' and 'The force that through the green fuse drives the flower'. These two poems reveal a classical ability to develop fully a simple subject. They alone would prove him a considerable poet. (After painting his complex portrait of Gertrude Stein, Picasso needed all his genius to draw like a child.)

In many poems the overlaying of images seems to go too far. That this is not a sign of weakness, however, and that Thomas still has (or had until recently) this basis of simplicity, is shown in what appears to me his best poem, 'In Memory of Ann Jones' (1938). The poem is planned in a manner worthy of Valéry himself, and a wealth of imagery subdued to the subject. There are four phases: the burial, the feast, the character and the homage. Tied images unite these phases, all of them relating to death, her home, her character. The poem is, in the poet's words, 'a monstrous thing blindly magnified out of praise'. Here Thomas achieves a concentration which is to be found in glimpses in his earlier poems:

> I know her scrubbed and sour simple hands
> Lie with religion in their cramp, her threadbare
> Whisper in a damp word, her wits drilled hollow,
> Her fist of a face died clenched in a round pain;
> And sculptured Ann is seventy years of stone. . . .

The typical furniture of her room, which appears early in the poem ('In a room with a stuffed fox and a stale fern'), serves as a dominant tied image, reappearing brilliantly at the end to drive home the idea that her love might even bring the dead to life:

> . . . . until
> The stuffed lung of the fox twitch and cry Love
> And the strutting fern lay seeds on the black sill.

Dylan Thomas's poems are somewhat coarse-grained because of the profusion of imagery, most of it in overtones, grouped round the centre. But in the best poems, as in 'In Memory of Ann Jones', the magnifying habit scores heavily, In more recent poems there is less overlaying, and in 'There was a Saviour' there is evidence of a more refining process of selection.

VI

Technically, Dylan Thomas has achieved nothing new. His alliterative and inventive tricks are as old as poetry. His personal rhythms are not unusual when compared with those of Hopkins. He writes with equal ease in fixed and loose forms. His outstanding merit, when compared with the other young poets, is his rich vocabulary, his sensual appreciation of words, his intense persuasive idiom which reveals him as one who is reaching towards all that is most living in our language. In that respect he is an anachronism, for he has not abandoned the wealth of the past for the somewhat thin idiom of Hollywood and the Middlesex suburbs as many poets are doing.

Thomas is lacking in genuine humour, though he is humorous enough in everyday life. He displays in his writings, surely enough, the traditional Welsh easy flow of speech. But most of his jokes are either purely verbal, or sad and a little sinister. The characteristic tone of his poems is grave and depressing. There is sorrow in his wit, which is grim. This grimness is to be found also in his stories, such as 'The Burning Baby' and 'The School of Witches', where it reaches cruelty.

Dylan Thomas is fundamentally a poet of the feelings, and is not a visual poet. He does not see clearly, and consequently is a cuckoo in the nest of the *New Verse* observation poets. His main object is to feel clearly, which he has not yet achieved:

> I have been told to reason by the heart,
> But heart, like head, leads helplessly.
>
> ('Poem 19')

He seeks the world in himself, and consequently his work is entirely autobiographical.

His future depends on an enlarging of his simple vision of the sexual basis of life, and it is to be hoped that he will not abandon his essential subject. That problem itself, and his evident conflict as to its solution, should provide him with an inexhaustible and vital theme. He is potentially the most modern of the young poets now writing, because of his assimilation of Joyce, Freud and the Bible, and because so far he has rejected the influence of the generation immediately preceding his own. He, like no young poet save perhaps George Barker and Ruthven Todd, is his own poet.

Thomas is the most old-fashioned of his generation in his apparent separation of his poetry from his politics. This might yet prove valuable. Technically he has little to do save to give his verbal inventions a better grounding in reality and in philology, to concentrate even more on that 'main moving column', and to concede less to that delight in a grimace by which every poet is tempted.

Unsex the Skeleton: Notes on the Poetry of Dylan Thomas

MARSHALL W. STEARNS

DYLAN THOMAS HAS BEEN TREATED as a watched pot by his reviewers since 1934 when, at the age of twenty, he published his first book of poems. The few critics who have not indulged in hedged banalities (several American critics have limited themsleves to viewing the poet's treatment of sex with alarm) differ extravagantly in their estimates of Thomas. In 1936, Edith Sitwell stated, 'I know of no young poet of our time whose poetic gifts are on such great lines', while three years later, Herbert Read delivered the unanswerable pronouncement that Thomas's work is 'the most absolute poetry that has been written in our time'. This general opinion has been seconded by Conrad Aiken enthusiastically and by David Daiches, Peter de Vries, and Horace Gregory more guardedly.

On the other hand, H. G. Porteus compares a reading of Thomas's poetry to an 'unconducted tour of Bedlam'. A few critics have been unable to agree with themselves: Julian Symons, who once thought highly of Thomas, now refers to the poet's works as 'jokes, rhetorical intellectual fakes of the highest class', and Stephen Spender, reversing the experience of Symons, has found some merit in Thomas recently, although he once wrote that 'the truth is that Thomas's poetry is turned on like a tap; it is just poetic stuff with no beginning or end, shape, or intelligent and intelligible control'. Meanwhile Louis Untermeyer, who has just added Thomas to the fold of his *Modern British Poetry*, introduces his ward with the unexceptionable remark that 'at first glance Thomas's poems seem incomplete, if not wholly obscure, lacking correspondence with the world of ordinary experience'. In spite of this dubious recommendation, Thomas appears to be in the process of becoming a standard modern poet, slimly but regularly represented in contemporary anthologies.

In general, however, the watchers seem to have come to the conclusion that the pot may have simmered but it will never boil. The question that most reviewers are inclined to ask themselves (and answer in the negative) is whether Thomas may be considered 'promising'. I suspect that this question is no longer relevant. Thomas seems to me to be a mature poet, and although his case is extreme, it is by no means unique. In a way, he typifies the plight of the contemporary poet of indisputable ability. Perhaps the following notes, which attempt some explanation of what Thomas is trying to do and how he goes about doing it, will shed some light on the problem. I am limiting myself chiefly to the subject matter of the poetry and the method of composition. Before proceeding, however, I should like to acknowledge my debt to Thomas's friend, Henry Treece, who has generously permitted me to read the manuscript of his book on Thomas.

The importance of Thomas is two-fold: he is an original poet and a great influence upon his fellow poets. The decay of the Auden-Spender-MacNeice influence and the growth of a new romantic movement in England have been ably outlined by Daiches in *Poetry* (June 1943). The pioneer group in this alleged renaissance call themselves 'The Apocalypse' (evidence of the continuing influence of D. H. Lawrence), and they point to Dylan Thomas as their more immediate predecessor; the group is led by Henry Treece, G. S. Fraser, and J. F. Hendry, and it includes about a dozen authors. The merits of these men, which are by no means inconsiderable, are discussed by Francis Scarfe in his *Auden and After* (1942).

The Apocalyptics have announced a programme and published

two collections of their work, *The New Apocalypse* (1940) and *The White Horseman* (1941). At first, they were more or less occupied with distinguishing their own group from the Surrealists, pointing out that they, like Thomas, did not indulge in a 'perpetual flow of irrational thought'. There was a definite relationship between the two, however, for the Apocalyptics simply chose Thomas and Surrealism as logical points of departure for their own movement, leaning toward Thomas wherever the two were at odds. The Apocalyptics were more definite in their rejection of their immediate predecessors. 'The younger generation of poets', writes Fraser, 'today, tend to derive from Pound and Eliot, through Freud and the Surrealists, through, especially in the very recent past, Dylan Thomas, more or less side-tracking the influence of their immediate forerunners (Auden, Spender, MacNeice).'

This isolation of Thomas, even as an influence, points to his uniqueness; he assumes a lonely but pre-eminent role among a welter of so-called ancestors of the Apocalyptics. In 1939, Treece and Hendry, attempting to define their poetic preserve and prevent poaching, announced in an advertisement: 'Apocalyptic creation is a European movement or tendency [this apparently for the benefit of a newly formed American group] whose immediate forebears are Kafka, Epstein, Picasso, the later Yeats and Dylan Thomas.' Thomas has been similarly linked with Revelations, Shakespeare, Webster, Blake, Donne, Hopkins, and others, on comfortably equal if not superior terms.

For so young a poet, Thomas has published much. Four books have appeared in England: *Eighteen Poems* (1934), *Twenty-Five Poems* (1936), *The Map of Love* (1939), and *Portrait of the Artist as a Young Dog* (1940). A generous selection from the poet's first three books appeared in the United States under the title, *The World I Breathe* (1939), and a group of seventeen old and new poems entitled *New Poems* was published here in 1943. Little is known of Thomas's life; he is Welsh and was born in Swansea in 1914. He is now writing cinema scripts for the British Ministry of Information.

A high-pitched documentary film, *These Are the Men*, appeared recently in this country with Thomas as co-author.

I

The subject matter of Thomas's poetry has given rise to widely divergent comment. Herbert Read describes it approvingly as 'poetry of the elemental physical experience: birth, copulation, death', while Julian Symons observes: 'What is said in Mr. Thomas's poetry is that the seasons change; that we decrease in vigour as we grow older; that life has no obvious meaning: that love dies. His poems mean no more than that. They mean too little.' The fallacy in Symons' line of criticism, which paraphrases a poem and then criticises the paraphrase, is clear, but it points to the content of Thomas's verse. Further, such themes are capable of conferring timelessness and universality upon poetry.

In an early poem, Thomas considers various themes as the subject for poetry (*Eighteen Poems*, p. 16):

> And what's the rub? Death's feather on the nerve?
> Your mouth, my love, the thistle in the kiss?
> My Jack of Christ born thorny on the tree?
> The words of death are dryer than his stiff,
> My wordy wounds are printed with your hair.
> I would be tickled by the rub that is:
> Man be my metaphor.

The poet seems to be using the word, *man*, in a special sense. He rejects what he considers the static concepts of death, earthly love, and religion ('the words of death are dryer than' the corpse of Jesus), and selects *man* as the theme of his poetry, 'man living, loving, using his five senses and functioning fully', as Drew and Sweeney have said. And more. Man for Thomas is man from seed to grave, with the emphasis on the grave, and the poet constantly attempts to view the entire progression simultaneously.

The literal truth of this statement regarding the subject-matter of Thomas's poetry may be illustrated by an example of his treatment of pre-natal experience. Describing Christ's anguish of fore-knowledge in his mother's womb, Thomas writes (*Eighteen Poems*, p. ii):

Before I knocked and flesh let enter,
With liquid hands tapped on the womb,
I who was shapeless as the water
That shaped the Jordan near my home
Was brother to Mnetha's daughter
And sister to the fathering worm.

I who was deaf to spring and summer,
Who knew not sun nor moon by name,
Felt thud beneath my flesh's armour,
As yet was in a molten form,
The leaden stars, the rainy hammer
Swung by my father from his dome . . .

As yet ungotten, I did suffer;
The rack of dreams my lily bones
Did twist into a living cipher,
And flesh was snipped to cross the lines
Of gallow crosses on the liver
And brambles in the wringing brains.

My throat knew thirst before the structure
Of skin and vein around the well
Where words and water make a mixture
Unfailing till the blood runs foul;
My heart knew love, my belly hunger;
I smelt the maggot in my stool . . .

You who bow down at cross and altar,
Remember me and pity Him
Who took my flesh and bone for armour
And doublecrossed my mother's womb.

Although Christ-in-embryo is speaking, and the stress is upon his immediate surroundings, he foresees the course of his life from birth to crucifixion. This mixture of physiology and Christian myth is typical of Thomas, although the final quest of worshippers to pity God (who used Jesus as armour and 'doublecrossed' Mary in the sense that she gave birth to an immortal rather than mortal man) is more typical of his early work. In general, the variation of pre-natal experience plays a shrill counterpoint to the poet's theme that man is born to die.

Thomas treats the subjects of birth and growth in a similar manner (*Eighteen Poems*, pp. 23–24);

All world was one, one windy nothing,
My world was christened in a stream of milk . . .
The body prospered, teeth in the marrowed gums,
The growing bones, the rumour of manseed
Within the hallowed gland, blood blessed the heart . . .
The plum my mother plucked matured slowly,
The boy she dropped from darkness at her side
Into the sided lap of light grew strong,
Was muscled, matted, wise to the crying thigh . . .
And from the first declension of the flesh
I learned man's tongue . . .
The root of tongues ends in a spentout cancer,
That but a name, where maggots have their X . . .

Here again, the poet's view of his chosen subject, man, is predicated upon and takes its direction from the grave; he feels that death alone connects man with reality.

The major theme of man in Thomas's poetry is variously accompanied by the minor themes of religion and sex, which are sometimes fused at a high temperature. Although the poet subscribes to no formal religion, his verse reveals the constant influence of a strong religious background in which the evangelical preaching of the Welsh Bethel plays a large part. He writes poems based upon church ritual (*Map of Love*, pp. 9–10); by the use of the pathetic fallacy, he twists the traditional symbolism of communion into far different channels, saying that man destroys himself by utilising the grape and the oat to make wine and bread (*Twenty-Five Poems*, p. 7). Biblical allusions crowd his poetry and it is evident that his emotions are deeply involved in religious matters, although his references to this subject are likely to be characterised more by rebellion than conformity.

The poet's attitude toward sex is central and closely connected with the allied themes of religion and man. The reason why Thomas feels that it should play an important part in his poetry in indicated by his answer to the question, 'Have you been influenced by Freud and how do you regard him?' (*New Verse*, October, 1934):

> Yes. Whatever is hidden should be made naked. To be stripped of darkness is to be clean, to strip of darkness is to make clean. Poetry, recording the stripping of the individual darkness, must, inevitably, cast light upon what has been hidden for too long, and, by so doing, make clean the naked exposure. Freud cast light on a little of the darkness he had exposed. Benefiting by the sight of the light and the knowledge of the hidden nakedness, poetry must drag further into the clean nakedness of light more even of the hidden causes than Freud could realise.

At the same time, Thomas defined poetry as 'the rhythmic . . . movement from an overclothed blindness to a naked vision', and added, 'My poetry is, or should be, useful to me for one reason:

it is the record of my individual struggle from darkness towards some measure of light.' This view of the act of writing as a kind of catharsis is not new but it is evident in much of Thomas's poetry; it springs apparently from a strong personal need rather than any thorough understanding of Freud.

It is clear that the poet was ridden by all the witches of a lonely adolescence, and only his undeniable talent keeps some of his poetry from being simply psychopathic. Death and disgrace conflict with the sexual impulse (*Eighteen Poems*, p. 17):

> This world is half the devil's and my own,
> Daft with the drug that's smoking in a girl
> And curling round the bud that forks her eye.
> An old man's shank one-marrowed with my bone,
> And all the herrings smelling in the sea,
> I sit and watch the worm beneath my nail
> Wearing the quick away.

The sexual implications of these lines (which include an obvious pun) are numerous and exact. More characteristically, sex and religion often interpenetrate. The fusion of the two reaches perhaps its highest pitch in one of Thomas's most difficult poems, the sonnet on the crucifixion (*Twenty-Five Poems*, p. 46):

> This was the crucifixion on the mountain,
> Time's nerve in vinegar, the gallow grave
> As tarred with blood as the bright thorns I wept;
> The world's my wound, God's Mary in her grief,
> Bent like three trees and bird-papped in her shift,
> With pins for teardrops is the long wound's woman.
> This was the sky, Jack Christ, each minstrel angle
> Drove in the heaven-driven of the nails
> Till the three-coloured rainbow from my nipples
> From pole to pole leapt round the snail-waked world.

I by the tree of thieves, all glory's sawbones
Unsex the skeleton this mountain minute,
And by this blowclock witness of the sun
Suffer the heaven's children through my heartbeat.

Although this poem is the climax in a series of ten loosely-connected sonnets, it may be treated independently without loss of meaning.

The lines may best be explained, I think, as the poet's attempt to describe the crucifixion as interpreted by Mary, the mother of God, the mother of Jesus, and the source of all creation. The key to the poem is the fundamental contrast between the earthly and the heavenly Mary. Assuming that the statement, 'I wept', in the third line, is made by Mary, the preceding lines are her description of the setting. Christ is likened to the nerve of Time, qualified by the phrase 'in vinegar', which emphasises the bitterness of the occasion as well as recalling the vinegar given to Christ on the cross. The 'gallow grave' is a typical alliterative antithesis in which the words, in addition to the connotation of criminality of 'gallow', contrast the state of being above and below the ground, death and resurrection. The phrase 'as tarred [i.e. dark and clotted] with blood as the bright thorns', may refer back to Christ or more probably the grave, bringing to mind the realistic portrayal of a tortured Saviour in the painting of Grünewald.

The fourth line emphasises the central role of Mary. 'God's' may be taken either as a possessive or a contraction; Mary belongs to God, or better, Mary is God and her grief is God's grief. And this wound of the world, the crucifixion of her son, is her wound. The next two lines describe Mary still more objectively. She is bent as the three trees or crosses on Calvary, which suggest the trinity. The words, 'birdpapped through her shift', are not as effective. They may mean that Mary is bird-breasted or soft-breasted (pigeon-breasted?), or better, perhaps, that she has small, pointed breasts shaped like the beaks of birds. Since the crucifixion ends her earthly role, she need no longer be a symbol of fecundity.

The image of tears hurting like pins is reminiscent of Picasso, and the description of Mary as the woman of the long wound is a variation of an earlier phrase, perhaps with sexual overtones (the period after *woman* is omitted in the American edition).

Lines seven to ten commence with a repetition of the first line and consist of a more detailed description of the crucifixion. Mary's reference to Jesus as 'Jack Christ' (a phrase found in Gerard Manley Hopkins) suggests Christ's relation to common humanity. This concept, and the similarly earthly detail of the nails, is contrasted to the sky, symbol of eternity, while the pun 'minstrel angle' (ministering angel?) carries the literal meaning of the angle at which the nails are driven or, more emphatically, the singing corners of the heavens. The nails are 'heaven-driven' in the sense that the crucifixion was predestined by God. The 'three-coloured rainbow' that springs from her nipples symbolises the trinity of which Mary is the mother in a strict sense. The image is one of erotic ecstasy, suggesting the stigmata and bordering upon the masochistic. Christianity leapt 'from pole to pole' around a world 'snail-waked', or slowly waking to its significance.

The last four lines contain the crux of Thomas's interpretation of the crucifixion. Mary, 'all glory's sawbones', or the doctor or salvation of the world, stands by 'the tree of thieves' or the cross upon which thieves are crucified. The phrase, 'this mountain minute', refers to the tremendous significance of the moment, but the preceding words, 'unsex the skeleton', are not as clear. Two interpretations suggest themselves. As the symbol of mortality, 'skeleton' may refer to the body of Christ which is unsexed at his death while he becomes sexless and immortal; Mary, witnessing this, relinquishes maternal claims to her earthly son. More probably, 'I . . . unsex the skeleton' may mean that Mary renounces her earthly function as mother of 'Jack Christ' and takes on her eternal role as mother of God. This is the basic antithesis.

The last two lines refer apparently to the eclipse which occurred during the crucifixion, destroying all sense of time. Mary calls it to witness that 'through her heartbeat' or by means of her son, she suffers or makes possible the 'children of heaven' or her heavenly childbirth. In brief, the sonnet is an assertion of Mary's all-important part in the holy mystery. At the most crucial moment of all time, when man becomes god and mortality immortality, she plays the one essential role, and through her, sex rises to asexual and eternal glory.

'None of the younger poets of today', say Drew and Sweeney, 'is closer to physical life in the biological sense and to spiritual life in the religious sense.' It should be added that no poet combines the two as closely, for although the dualism of life-death, body-soul, and sex-sin are not reconciled in Thomas's poetry, these elements often merge. It would be incorrect to conclude that the content of the poet's work is limited to variations on the themes of man, sex, and religion. Such a conclusion would be an arbitrary over-simplification of the most important subjects in his poetry, but although he has a considerable range of subject-matter, it is with these themes that he has achieved his best work.

II

An understanding of the poet's method of composition is essential to an appreciation of his poetry. Various critics have selected a more or less similar characteristic in Thomas's verse which may be explained by his method of composition, Thus, Symons complains of the poet's method of 'statement . . . repeated with variations', while Andrews Wanning speaks favourably of Thomas's 'intensive description', and 'unity generated by metaphor'. From a different point of view, Scarfe notes that the poet 'is not expressing so much as discovering his feelings'; and Spender remarks that it is poetry 'of being rather than thinking and knowing'. Glyn Jones isolates the most notable result of Thomas's method of composition when he writes that the poet's best faculty is his 'unexpectedness of verbal patterns'. The characteristic which these critics tend to describe is the poet's conscious goal.

Thomas has written some highly penetrating comments on his own poetry to his friend Henry Treece. In answer to the criticism that his poems are diffuse, the poet replies:

> . . . a poem by myself needs a host of images, because its centre is a host of images. I make one image – though 'make' is not the word, I let, perhaps, an image be 'made' emotionally in me and then apply to it what intellectual and critical forces I possess – , let it breed another, let that image contradict the first, make, of the third image bred out of the other two together, a fourth contradictory image, and let them all, within my imposed formal limits, conflict. Each image holds within it the seed of its own destruction, and my dialectical method, as I understand it, is a constant building up and breaking down of the images that come out of the central seed, which is itself destructive and constructive at the same time.
>
> What I want to try to explain – and it's necessarily vague to me – is that the life in any poem of mine cannot move concentrically round a central image; the life must come out of the centre; an image must be born and die in another; and any sequence of my images must be a sequence of creations, recreations, destructions, contradictions. . . . My object is, as you say, conventionally 'to get things straight'. Out of the inevitable conflict of images – inevitable, because of the creative, recreative, destructive and contradictory nature of the motivating centre, the womb of war – I try to make that momentary peace which is a poem. . . . A poem of mine is, or should be, a watertight section of a stream that is flowing all ways, all warring images within it should be reconciled for that small stop of time.

Perhaps the most revealing clue in this self-analysis is Thomas's declaration that he applies a 'dialectical method' to the handling of the imagery in his poetry. Apparently, the poet is aware of the fact that the process of thesis, antithesis, and synthesis (in terms of images) is seldom completed in his verse, but nevertheless that is his aim. Hence, realising the difficulty of achieving any final synthesis, Thomas is inclined to emphasise the conflict of thesis and antithesis in practice, implying that an ascending scale of synthesis is reached only to become a never-ending basis for further conflict.

In his handling of imagery, then, Thomas is consciously attempting an interesting experiment, although his use of the Hegelian dialectic is limited and without any ideological basis. It may be simply a rationalisation of a personal manner of expression. For the poet is anti-philosophical in a literal sense: he subscribes to no one school of thought, he has read and been influenced by few great books of the preceding ages, and he leans, one supposes, toward the opinion that little is valid above and beyond the level of spontaneous emotion. It may be added that if Thomas's use of dialectic has any appeal to the professional Marxists, it has yet to be noted; for example, Samuel Sillen quotes six lines of Thomas (at second-hand) in the *New Masses* (14 September 1943) as an example of the poverty of modern poetry.

In the light of the poet's stated aims regarding the use of imagery, it may be of value to attempt an interpretation of an early but important poem which has been anthologised by Michael Roberts (*The Faber Book of Modern Verse*) and Louis Untermeyer (*Modern British Poetry*), commented upon favourably by several critics, and never analysed. Although Thomas may have written better poetry, it is doubtful whether he has written a more characteristic poem:

> Light breaks where no sun shines;
> Where no sea runs, the waters of the heart
> Push in their tides;

And, broken ghosts with glow-worms in their heads,
The things of light
File through the flesh where no flesh decks the bones.

A candle in the thighs
Warms youth and seed and burns the seeds of age;
Where no seed stirs,
The fruit of man unwrinkles in the stars,
Bright as a fig;
Where no wax is, the candle shows its hairs.

Dawn breaks behind the eyes;
From poles of skull and toe the windy blood
Slides like a sea;
Nor fenced, nor staked, the gushers of the sky
Spout to the rod
Divining in a smile the oil of tears.

Night in the sockets rounds,
Like some pitch moon, the limit of the globes;
Day lights the bone;
Where no cold is, the skinning gales unpin
The winter's robes;
The film of spring is hanging from the lids.

Light breaks on secret lots,
On tips of thought where thoughts smell in the rain;
When logics die,
The secret of the soil grows through the eye,
And blood jumps in the sun;
Above the waste allotments the dawn halts.

This poem is in regular stanza form, with a steady rhythm and occasional rhyme. Of the various levels of meaning it communicates, I take it that the basic level is a description of the state of existence; the theme is the process of living.

In the first stanza, the clue to the moment of existence which the poet is describing occurs in the 'warring images' of the last line. Since no flesh yet decks the bones, Thomas is probably referring, as he does elsewhere, to the period during or immediately after conception. Thus, the 'light' of prescience 'breaks' within the embryo, as the blood pushes through its veins like the tides of the ocean. The phrase, 'broken ghosts with glow-worms in their heads' seems to be in apposition to 'the things of light', and to describe these intimations of consciousness or foreknowledge as they present themselves to the child in the womb. The contrast between the concrete and abstract nouns is great, although its success is precarious, and the reader is perhaps reminded of the poet's request to take his poems literally, seeking for no more detailed meaning. More generally, the particular word-order, 'where no sun shines', is established by three repetitions in the first stanza, to be repeated with diminishing frequency in the following stanzas. Its use is both formal and functional since it ties the poem together and permits a sharper conflict of images.

In the second stanza, the sexual symbolism of the 'candle in the thighs' is clear, and that it 'warms youth and seed' makes sense. It also 'burns the seeds of age' in the sense of 'burn up', or even 'frustrate'. In the old or passionless, 'where no seed stirs', the poet says that 'the fruit of man unwrinkles in the stars'; that is, sublimation takes place and man's energies or thoughts turn heavenward or away from reality, perhaps toward religion. The word, 'unwrinkles', is capable of an ironic sexual interpretation, as well as the following phrase, 'bright as a fig'; a fig may be shiny when ripe and young, or wrinkled when dry and old. The last line varies the metaphor: 'where no wax is', where there is no flesh or vitality, 'the candle shows its hairs', the dead wick or the fleshless bone remains. This stanza contrasts the states of being young or old, virile or impotent.

In the third stanza, the statement that 'dawn breaks behind the eyes' may refer to the arrival of consciousness, presumably in the infant. The circulation of the blood in the body is referred to again and compared to the poles, tides, and wind of the earth. This image is clear, but the last three lines present a jumble of imagery. Any interpretation must hinge upon the meaning of 'gushers of the sky'. The connotations of rain, tears, and even oil-wells are reinforced in the following lines, although they are undeveloped. Further, the conceivable image of a gusher spouting to a divining rod lends itself to a sexual interpretation, while the word 'divining' may refer forward or backward and its use suggests a pun. The syntax is fluid and the reader is inclined to equate 'gushers of the sky' simply with the processes of nature and conclude that Thomas is saying that life goes on mingled with joy and sadness.

The fourth stanza, with its contrast of night and day, winter and spring, may best be interpreted in the light of the poet's belief that the soul should be stripped of darkness. The ball-in-socket image states the relationship; inside the socket is likened to the pitch-black moon of the unknown and the unconscious, the outside to the illumined bone of truth or self-knowledge. The last three lines, as is the case generally throughout the poem, are a variation of the preceding idea. 'Where no cold is', or where the warmth of knowledge exists, the 'skinning gales' or the process of living ('skinning' because they flay or lay bare) loosen the 'winter's robe' or release the cold impulses of the unconscious. Again, a sexual interpretation of 'skinning gales' is possible. The 'film of spring', or the prelude to self-knowledge, then becomes visible, existing just beyond the eyelids. The contrasts in this stanza lend themselves to multiple interpretations, and the poet is in danger of losing any precise meaning in a welter of connotations.

The last stanza is perhaps the most elusive. The process of self-exploration is described in terms of the visible or conscious tips of buried thoughts which 'smell in the rain'. This last phrase is striking in its context but ambiguous. It may mean that the rain of self-analysis nurtures suppressed thoughts as they break through the soil of the unconscious, a meaning developed in the following lines, or more plausibly, that these beginnings of conscious realisation are evident in the rain or process of existence. The next three lines, beginning with 'when logics die', are a little out of key, for they appear to be an endorsement of the intuitive existence; dispense with logic and the eye learns the 'secret of the soil', while life becomes full or the 'blood jumps in the sun'. The last line, however, is effective. In sudden contrast, Thomas reminds us that above the 'waste allotments' of life, death is hovering. 'Dawn', a word analogous to the words of light with which the poem is teeming, comes to an end. Day may follow, but it, too, will halt. We are born to die.

A few qualifications should be added to this analysis. The interpretation is arbitrary and literal on a minimal level of meaning. Although I have taken my cues from the poet's own statements wherever possible, I am aware that I do scant justice to the wealth of implication in the poem. Again, it is an early poem and by no means illustrates the whole range of the poet. In this poem, certain of Thomas's stylistic habits, such as Biblical allusions and the use of compound words, are not represented. More central characteristics, such as the choice of subject-matter, the method of composition, and the devices of technique are well displayed. I suppose that few interested readers will deny the poem some success. That it is characterised by synthesis rather than progression need startle no one who is familiar with T. S. Eliot's *Waste Land*.

The poem is a good example of Thomas's dialectical method in practice. It is full of warring images which occasionally result in direct contradictions, such as 'things of light' filing through flesh where there is no flesh. Unfortunately, the 'warring images' are sometimes at war with themselves; the 'momentary peace which is a poem' does not eventuate, and the over-worked reader sometimes finds himself undergoing the discouraging experience of appearing to discover an adequate or even thrilling meaning of a phrase (on what was doubtless intended to be a lower level of connotation), only to realise upon careful re-examination that the phrase is more complex than he first thought and rather defies interpretation. A truce dictated by exhaustion rather than by Thomas results.

Yet the effect is frequently electric, and it may be observed that the most obscure phrases in the poem, such as 'broken ghosts' and 'gushers of the sky', owe little of their difficulty to the dialectical method. Thomas's obscurity seems to arise in part from his fluid syntax, although his diction and language are seldom as simple as they appear in this poem. Perhaps Henry Treece has come close to the core of the problem when he says that the poet's obscurity is 'produced by the inability or lack of desire to conceive himself as being one unit of reality . . . he is unwilling or does not wish to orient himself, to exist as one personality'. Such an explanation is given support by the poet's all-embracing concept of his chosen subject, man, as well as his previously discussed treatment of the nativity from the point of view of Christ and the crucifixion from the point of view of Mary. Further support may be found in Thomas's dialectic. Although it may be of doubtful value to speculate upon the question of how the poet arrived at his dialectic method of handling imagery, one may be permitted to wonder whether or not it mirrors an inner confusion. If it does, and I see little reason to doubt it, the poet has chosen a functional manner of expressing his experiences in the world of today.

Thomas typifies the problem of the poet in our time who has something original to say and an original manner of saying it. Writing ill-paid poetry in a complex age of prose, where the emphasis is upon originality, he has often sacrificed clarity in order to forge a highly individual idiom. This idiom is new and therefore difficult and, largely for these reasons, unpopular. But it is also, I feel, valid. The poet may write better poetry, but I do not think that he will develop into a more easily-classified type of poet, nor do I believe that there is any reason to expect a gradual journey into lucidity. Thomas's influence upon his fellow poets is demonstrably great and it may well become greater. His historical importance is assured, but whether or not his poetry will live rests upon whether or not the general reader is willing to make the effort to understand the poet. There is a small group today who are willing to do so. In the history of poetry, the number of people who found any poet worth the effort of comprehension was never great, and Dylan Thomas will have to be satisfied with less.

In Defence of Dylan Thomas

ROBERT HORAN

Sir:

IN YOUR WINTER '44 ISSUE,[1] Arthur Mizener speaks of

> '. . . the widespread adoption among the younger poets (I mean those who have developed since Auden) of the decorative baroque style; Barker, Thomas, Rodgers, Shapiro, Lowell – the real interest of poets like these is, not in the subject in the ordinary sense, but in the verbalised details of the subject; and the characteristic product of this kind of interest is a poem in which a very simple structure of meaning supports a vast and intricate elaboration of highly coloured details.'

Critical estimation should establish the wide differences rather than the surface similarities (rhythm, landscape, vocabulary) among these writers. The separation of subject and detail, in Thomas particularly, is not justified. It requires that we assume that the actual subject is not proposed, illuminated and exactly defined from line to line or image to image throughout the whole poem, but that it is a special and separate 'motive' of the poem, in terms of which any particular verse is a modifier and expressive agent. (There is, certainly, a margin of difference between intention and execution, but this is another distinction.) The subject *is* the detail, it exists through the complex of relations between rhythm, texture and association developed in each and all of its 'ornaments'. The extraordinarily acute analysis by Francis Scarfe of one of the

1. *The Kenyon Review.*

sonnets of Thomas (in *Horizon*) reveals that whatever philosophic equivalent or literal subject matter may be separated from Thomas's work by no means indicates 'a very simple structure of meaning'. If we recognise the complexity of Thomas's ornamentation as an expression of the necessities of his subject matter, rather than as indulgent verbalising, it is possible to find there a distinct subtlety of judgment. But this requires the exploration and evaluation of the whole poem, not as a single set or series of ideas ramified by so many turns of imagery and reflection, but as a unity of parts whose permanent separation risks serious misunderstanding.

I should like to defend or explicate the opinion that Thomas is not merely the most promising of the younger poets, but that his work has an energy, an impact, a structural and an emotional strength that is rare in any period and almost unique in our own; that his violence is not to be dismissed as histrionic, his embellishment a baroque elaboration of trivial material, his manner perversely private nor profligate, nor his method the instrument of sentimentality (if we understand sentimentality as an excess of feeling and manner in relation to the fundamental perception). I shall be contending that his imagination is remarkable to the degree that it transforms, actively, rather than describes, passively, the objects of his attention.

It is undeniable that his perspective has been, on occasion, one of self-pity and abuse, a severe but relished melancholy; that his symbolism has been recurrent, romantic and sometimes pushed beyond the formal limit of his control. But these are redeemable and increasingly redeemed features of his work.

Is the insistence of his style, embedding the content of any given poem in layer upon layer of imagery and texture, to condemn him to a relative obscurity in the gilt disguise of a 'baroque'? It may be admitted that Thomas is a difficult poet, guilty of some uses of language private beyond style, but also difficult in the sense that he requires of his readers something of the creative sensibility that is requisite to the work of James Joyce. We have heard, and are again hearing, that Joyce is 'not interested in the subject in the ordinary sense, but in the verbalised details of the subject'. Perhaps there is an unintentional clue in the word 'ordinary'.

There is a kind of subject matter currently passing for profound and personal content among both younger and older poets. Auden, for instance, has evolved a cryptic, Noël-Coward shorthand, cautiously glamorous, flattered by his own sensitivity like a public-school prodigy. Saturated with self-consciousness, more and more poems appear from the tomb of Henry James or the bier of Freud. These are gratuitous identifications with tradition, distinctly 'literary subject matters', apathetic and indulgent, conditioned by an attitude toward experience that begins to sound professional, as if it were lived through in order to be written about. Thomas has escaped this contagion, this small and anxious form of exploitation, even if at the cost of publication in the *Atlantic Monthly*.

Thomas's subject matter does expose incongruities and uncertainties in the shape of guilt, laceration, expiation. It is an effort to free memory from the strictures of paternity, from religion and from death; to establish the unique individual, not merely as the victim, but as the agent, of choice; not alone *created by history*, but *creative in history*.

> The ball I threw while playing in the park
> Has not yet reached the ground.

Because his imagination is essentially heretical, he is moved to examine the nature of his choice: the pagan, the magical, the abandoned. On occasion, as in the early short stories in *The World I Breathe*, it is the image of the devil that is invoked to supplant so wicked and exacting a Saviour. Thomas's sense of the limitation of time, its circuitous pattern that returns us to the shores of childhood and rescues the least hour drowned in our memory, his preoccupation with the forms and faces of death, are shipwrecked everywhere in his poems.

In the final direction of the elementary town
I advance for as long as forever is.

This double fear and fascination toward death cuts short or obliterates any feeling of peace or stasis in his poems, as if they were to be confronted with a last judgment on the following page. In this desperate intention to render instantaneous his whole emotional world, Thomas may be frequent in failure, but he is unique in accomplishment. The violent delivery indicates desire driving itself toward necessity, desire to free himself from the infantile kingdom where freedom is synonymous with sin and from the world of social sentimentality, immoral in Joyce's sense of refusal to accept 'the enormous responsibility for a thing done'.

It is true that poets of Thomas's generation have become embarrassed by the inertia or the violence of their material. Inasmuch as the spontaneous work of such writers tends to withstand the formal control and organisation which is necessary to realize it fully, they turn, instinctively and with apparent apology, to a frame, a 'classical' control of energy. These poets serve a kind of metrical penance for their emotional sins and excesses, as if it legalised their intentions and restored them to the sanctity of tradition. They hold on to an orthodox form and a combustible content. A cage in one hand and a wild beast in the other. But, although these are simultaneous upon the page, they rarely enclose each other. More often, the poem is constricted in its prison, without pulse or breath, emasculated by a technical rigidity that is fatal in its perfection. This stringent and foreign discipline is not a sophistication of form, but is a compromise with meaning, arising from the failure to define and identify the exact emotion and experience that constitute a poem. It is the result of radiant but inexact feeling. Thomas has been caught in this territory on several occasions, but he has learned to sacrifice less frequently the explosive imagery of his poetry to a monastic shape. In the beautiful series of ten sonnets he has created a rhythmic singularity, resetting the value, weight, speed, and texture of language to his own purposes, stamping the irregular, elided phrases with a fluidity that is entirely personal. His constant development of the scheme of internal rhyme, near-rhyme, assonance, falling, and feminine endings, have given Thomas's most formal poems fresh and fine definition. His use of rhythm that is marked and angular is observable as early as the *Eighteen Poems*, side by side with that less halted and more lyrical breath, apparent in 'The force that through the green fuse drives the flower', 'When once the twilight knocks no longer', or the poem beginning

> I see the boys of summer in their ruin
> Lay the gold tithings barren,
> Setting no store by harvest, freeze the soils . . .

Already, in these earliest poems, there was a disturbing sense of enchantment, as of a reality rushed between watery curtains, a single figure appearing with a hundred faces, that led the unwary to refer to Thomas as a mystic. Historically, in point of influence, he may seem to be so; actually, the concrete, natural weather of his observation is a real world bewitched. His refusal to ascribe infinity to the fading and the finite, to describe the temporal, failing flesh as guardian of the impaled, permanent spirit, is anti-mystical. He uses the properties of mystery and mysticism as legend and as a texture rather than as a belief; the value as ritual and reference does not presuppose a belief in sorcery. The sexual energy of his writing, the provoking and self-torturing guillotine of judgment, do not signify a deep concern with metaphysics. They underline, however, Thomas's extreme attachment to his world of Wales, a country as filled with memory as its valleys are with stones.

The poems thrown hardest against the walls of our sensibility stick the best; those that are latticed with contrition web one in, but the reader should not feel forced to escape from an insidious net.

Thomas's best poems liberate the imagination but not the conscience. He is hostile to aesthetic catharsis, susceptible to fantasy and allegory. It is a renaissance of voluptuousness that gives to his work its sensual, deceptively unintellectual surface. What suffer from diffusion are the edges of his meaning. The concentrated areas are made of brick, and no water of Celtic words can self-consciously wash them away.

An insecurity in Thomas's approach to his earliest material, and the tendency to compensate for this insecurity, which is properly the recognition of his true subject matter, led him to overestimate the power of association as an instrument of unifying meaning in poetry, to rely too heavily on cumulative rhythm and the devices of litany. A kind of interior cohesion in this work was deflected in a heavy body of incident and illustration. This attempt to surround a subject from continuously shifting levels of time, space and emotion sets up problems of perspective and chronology that cloud as often as they amplify the vision. This fault diminishes where a stable, physical point of observation has been established, permitting abundance rather than fragmentation.

The data of sensation, the result of a remarkable sensitivity to the shape, texture, and intensity of the landscape surrounding emotion, constitute, for a poet like Thomas, that astonishing weight of image and symbol that, in a poem, directly imply its meaning. We are presented not merely with the abstraction of circumstance, conflict, and judgment, but the rooms, worlds, faces, their physical atmosphere and unassailable reality.

This is powerfully illustrated in several poems from the recent collection of *New Poems*, particularly the opening 'Poem', 'Death and Entrances', 'The Hunchback in the Park', and the long 'Ballad'. The result is one of having shared an emotional territory inexplicably wide, as if, within a few lines, one ranged back and forth in memory.

> With every cry since light
> Flashed first across his thunderclapping eyes.

I do not find this to be 'difficult' poetry, or if it present difficulties it is because of its extreme precision, to which we are in reality unaccustomed, rather than because it is inexact or halting.

Thomas has not been placed in relation to any but superficial tradition's, although he bears a burden and manner shared by several of his immediate antecedents, and some more distant. Certainly he finds fathers in Donne and Blake and Hopkins, not in technical indebtedness only, but in a similar conflict between the forms of conviction and desire, expressed in the religious imagery of Donne and Hopkins, and the helpless, mystical terminology of Blake. Although Thomas is not committed to a specific orthodoxy, he is susceptible to the rigorous claims that personal religion or historical myth makes upon emotion. His rhetoric reveals a reflection of Elizabethan richness and drama, of Shakespearian tempo and detail.

There is, too, I believe, a tradition in modern poetry which Thomas shares, most intensely expressed in the work of poets like Hart Crane, Garcia Lorca, and, with a difference, T. S. Eliot. This tradition is established, not by similarities of style nor equality of conviction, nor by any comparable success of execution. Crane and Garcia Lorca are often desperate and frantic in pursuit of their subject matter, as Eliot is frequently complacent, exclusive, and pedantic. What is common to them and almost peculiar to them is the range of their feeling, and an honesty that refuses to be constricted (with the exception of Eliot's insecure exile in Anglo-Catholicism) by system. They are neither benevolent toward experience nor hostile to it; they are not essentially cynical. They may be driven by desperation, but the centre, the meaning, of that predicament is present, and is the substance and syllable of their work. The language is sensitive, the emotion is perilous, the conclusion is suspended, in that a greater rigidity of techniques and meanings would frustrate and sterilise the extent of feeling.

In Eliot, of course, there is the continual appearance of prose statements that level his intellectual perspicacity and increase the confusion surrounding his work. But this confusion is itself a manifest conflict in the poems, as in the recent '*Four Quartets*' which illuminate the tragedy of his choice, indicating his failure to be convinced fully of a system that is powerless to grant him freedom and faith simultaneously. Although his method is more exact, his manner more mature, than that of Crane or of Garcia Lorca, they maintain, at the cost of fever and melancholy, a wider view, a deeper sympathy and a more vivid reaction to experience. Thomas shares the preoccupation, the necessity to embrace the opposite poles of feeling, to extend experience and sympathy to the horizon limit. His manner has been increasingly, not toward simplicity, which may act as a deception of a different nature, but toward concentration, which is the subtler and more meaningful choice.

It has been assumed that the progress of a poet such as Thomas, as with such a poet as Hart Crane, should be, more or less automatically, toward simplification. But I should like to deny this methodology as being inconsistent with the nature of the work involved and essentially an evasion of the complexity of poetic composition. I believe that the nature of Crane's insight was complex and rich, not simply in the sense that his values were confused, though that may be easily demonstrated, but because his sympathies and his perceptions were wider than his ability at any given moment to organise them, or deduce from them more positive statements of relation. He was aware, even if intuitively, of the variety and implicit contradiction of ideas in his material, just as he palpably was aware of it in his private living. We assume that this was the operation of tragedy, that he was struck from the lists of the clearly great because of the manifold failures of his personality.

It is not the necessity of including the whole world that makes intellectual peace impossible, but the attempt to include oneself. Either one gives up the conviction personally and rides along with its logical values elsewhere, or one recognises, consciously or unconsciously, the pitfall, and delivers the dilemma in the nature of a tragedy. This is not failure in Eliot any more than in Crane. The failure in Crane was to seize upon objects of the modern and the abstracted world as a symbolisation of his tragedy, and to accredit them as semi-religious and historical myths. And, paradoxically, the tragedy is revealed in consciousness, not in unconsciousness. To the degree that we fail to see the implications of our relationship with nature and society, we can sustain hope. The more conscious one becomes of the pluralistic nature of this relationship, of its destructive as well as its constructive side, the more insistent is the tragedy. It is the tragedy of Hamlet as well as of the entire house of Atreus; it is a central motive in Dostoyevsky and Proust. It is implicit in Thomas, in Eliot, Crane, and Garcia Lorca.

In Thomas, particularly, the violence of his feeling, the variety of his expression and the disillusion that accompanies understanding, are wider than the nature of his convictions about them. It is in an effort to bring the diverse and almost uncontrollable poles of his observation and sympathy into the same poem, or into the same system of consciousness and value, that he strikes the fundamental problem of composition and experience. His poetry shows this awareness increasingly, with greater technical assurance, certainly, but primarily with finer precision of feeling and more developed insight. It is in this sense that I feel his grasp of reality is more shocking, and correspondingly more sensitised, than those around him, who are trapped in the affluence of style, and whose main consideration is to appear only temporarily baffled by the destruction of their society. Since it is a problem of every modern artist, it could hardly have been escaped by any but the peripheral and unconscious craftsmen of our time, of whom there are many prominent. It is not the solution of this problem that is imminent in Thomas, any more than it is imminent in our society, but the recognition of it, and his unique poetic approach to its discovery. If it will not give him greater hope for his future world, it shall at least give us greater hope for his future poetry.

The Poetry of Dylan Thomas

D. S. SAVAGE

DYLAN THOMAS'S STATUS as a poet is now firmly established; informed opinion both in England and in America is unanimous in its agreement that his work is not only valid and important in its own right, but that, by inference, it provides a positive touchstone for current poetic practice and appreciation. We are fortunate indeed, in these days of deterioration, to possess such a touchstone. Dylan Thomas is a primary agent in keeping poetry alive among us, and through poetry, a proper sense of life, of values. Whatever may be said of Thomas's limitations must rest upon recognition of his superb qualities – a powerful and compelling imaginative vision held in delicate equipoise, matched by a subtle intelligence, wit and verbal sensitiveness and informed by passionate feeling. The recent publication, in London, of Thomas's fourth volume of verse, *Deaths and Entrances*, provides the occasion for the following brief survey of his development up to the present.

To the question, what *sort* of a poet is Dylan Thomas, one can best reply that he is first of all *a maker*, that his poems must be apprehended as verbal structures before any attempt is made to torture a series of statements out of them. What Thomas – what any poet – says is precisely what is contained in the exact number and arrangement of words by which he says it. A clear understanding of this obvious truth will prevent a lot of idle talk about 'obscurity'. Having made this clear, it is possible to pass on to a further definition. Thomas is a poet to whom the overworked epithet 'metaphysical' may without unfitness be applied. He is a poet preoccupied, not primarily with human experience as it is commonly apprehended, but with aspects of that experience lifted out of their apparent context and seen in extra-mundane relationship to their absolute, vertical, determining conditions. Central to his work, therefore, is a proto-philosophical, impassioned *questioning* of the ultimates – origins and ends – of existence. The vision which results is not philosophical in the abstract sense, but concrete, imaginative, poetic. The poet is cerebrating, certainly, but in a primordial, mythologising fashion, dealing, not impersonally with secondary counters of thought, but imaginatively with the primary data of his own particularised existence, in which he is emotionally involved. Therefore the deep seriousness of Thomas's central vision is accompanied by a corresponding intensity of emotion, expressed in the grand, sometimes majestic, movement of his powerful and subtle rhythms.

In his poems we have no re-creation (as, *par excellence*, in the early Eliot) of a specific, localised social environment; no projection of separate human figures or dwelling upon particular experiences for their own sake. And this can only be for the reason that the vertical character of Thomas's vision tends to disrelate the components of immediate experiences in their field of local, temporal connectedness, where they are held together in a lateral sequence, in order to draw them into the instantaneous pattern of the poet's perception. His theme is thus that of the human condition itself; not, as I have said, the condition of man in his personal relationships or natural or social environment, nor even, as some have thought, his merely racial and biological origins and ends, but the essential or fundamental 'existential' human state, which is also the cosmic state, the condition of being, itself. Taking his stand within concrete, particular existence, Thomas places birth and death at the poles of his vision. His viewpoint is at once individual and universal – 'I' is also, and without transition, 'man', and man is microcosmic. The individual birth, therefore, abuts immediately upon the cosmic genesis; death, upon cosmic catastrophe. Seen thus absolutely, however, birth and death are instantaneous; time is, equally, timeless; so that human life is mortal and immortal, flesh has its ghostly counterpart; though the relationship of each to each is enigmatic. In fact, all Thomas's best poems are erected from the double vision which is the source of his understanding: their coherence and firm structure result from the 'androgynous' mating, the counter-poising in equilibrium, of contraries. Add to all these briefly enumerated factors aquasi-mystical, cabbalistic perception of the world itself as of a metaphorical nature, intimately related to the articulation of language, and you have a fairly complete picture of Thomas's mind and method of composition. This brief exposition is conveniently illustrated by a short and simple poem from his third book (references throughout are to English publication):

> Twenty-four years remind the tears of my eyes.
> (Bury the dead for fear that they walk to the grave in labour.)
> In the groin of the natural doorway I crouched like a tailor
> Sewing a shroud for a journey
> By the light of the meat-eating sun.
> Dressed to die, the sensual strut begun,
> With my red veins full of money,
> In the final direction of the elementary town
> I advance for as long as forever is.

(*The Map of Love*, 1939)

In what sense Thomas may legitimately be termed a religious poet is a question which has been too little considered. For Thomas makes central, and not merely peripheral, use of images and terminology drawn from Christian mythology, history and doctrine. And, of course, his perspectives are themselves those of religious insight. But he is a religious poet writing out of the indeterminate, sub-spiritual situation of a Hamlet. Accompanying

Thomas's imaginative activity – the very activity of course which makes him so indubitably a poet – there is, one cannot fail to remark, a moral or spiritual passivity. In his poems there is no subjective activity beyond the agonised, suffering or exultant, but always passive, acceptance of that which is given by the inexorable nature of existence; the poet is the victim of his experience. In this he is to be sharply distinguished from such poets of religious devotion as Herbert, Vaughan, Traherne, whom superficially he somewhat resembles. Their verse is packed with psychological subtleties, arising from their awareness of choice, of struggle and of meaning in personal life, whereas Thomas's poems are quite lacking in psychological interest. Thomas gains something poetically, perhaps, by his very inclusiveness, his undifferentiating, intoxicated embracing of life and death and the Yeats-like celebration of blind sexual vitality.

The knottiest problem for such a poet as Thomas is that of development. An intense imaginative activity accompanied by a psychological and moral passivity is bound eventually to result in a curbing of the growth to maturity and in consequent artistic repetitiveness and stultification. In this connection we may note the marked shift in emphasis from the earlier poems to the later. In the first, speculation and statement predominate:

> In the beginning was the three-pointed star,
> One smile of light across the empty face;
> One bough of bone across the rooting air,
> The substance forked that marrowed the first sun;
> And, burning ciphers on the round of space,
> Heaven and hell mixed as they spun.

(*Eighteen Poems*, 1934)

Later there appears a more pronounced note of bewilderment and questioning:

Why east wind chills and south wind cools
Shall not be known till windwell dries
And west's no longer drowned
In winds that bring the fruit and rind
Of many a hundred falls;
Why silk is soft and the stone wounds
The child shall question all his days,
Why night-time rain and the breast's blood
Both quench his thirst he'll have a black reply.

(*Twenty-five Poems*, 1936)

And this is succeeded, in the latest phase, by a positive, exulting note of acceptance and praise:

In
The spin
Of the sun
In the spuming
Cyclone of his wing
For I lost was who am
Crying at the man drenched throne
In the first fury of his stream
And the lightnings of adoration
Back to black silence melt and mourn
For I was lost who have come
To dumbfounding haven
And the finding one
And the high noon
Of his wound
Blinds my
Cry.

(*Deaths and Entrances*, 1946)

This rapt and exalted note, in the latest volume, as it occurs in the celebration of birth, sexuality and death, predominates in the best and most sustained poems – 'Vision and Prayer', 'Ballad of the Long-Legged Bait', 'Ceremony After a Fire Raid', 'Holy Spring' and 'A Refusal to Mourn the Death, by Fire, of a Child in London'. It expresses, certainly, a development – but a development which takes the form of an accession of *intensity;* that is, it is an introversion and not an expansion. Simultaneously, in the same volume, however, there are unmistakable signs of an effort, prompted no doubt by the poet's recognition of the danger of repetitiveness, toward the lateral extension of scope. The poems are now for the first time entitled instead of numbered, and attached to specific, recognisable occasions. It is significant, then, that the best poems are still precisely those which directly celebrate birth and death: particular, localised births and deaths, indeed, but seen still in unavoidable relation to the absolute perspectives. Yet not all the poems in this latest collection achieve the same high level. 'Poem in October', 'A Winter's Tale' and 'Fern Hill' are three of the poems which, as I have said, mark a new venturing toward the comprehension of specific lateral fields of experience. And in these poems, while the scope is indeed superficially extended, the result, removed from immediate relation to the birth-death polarity, is an unexpected diffusion and prolixity. One is led, furthermore, to wonder to what extent the too simple celebration of childhood, predominantly descriptive and correspondingly devoid of imaginative-metaphysical insight, in the last poem is permissibly to be termed retrogressive; as indicating, that is, a deliberate avoidance of the complexities (which exist on the active level of moral choice and psychological discrimination) of adult, mature experience.

Faced with a poet of Dylan Thomas's ability, a fitting humility is called for in the critic. Thomas is still developing, and doubtless will do so in accordance with a true poet's fidelity to his own vision. Yet I cannot refrain from recording my strong feeling that authentic development for such a poet as Thomas lies not in a simple, lateral widening of scope, nor of course in a simple intensification of passionate feeling, but in something much more arduous, much more difficult, but also, ultimately, much more rewarding – in a spiritual, moral and intellectual movement toward the clarification and (perhaps, even,) systematisation of the primary imaginative-poetical vision, involving struggle, discrimination, choice. This might well involve a bitter period of non-productivity, but if that were endured and overcome, we might yet find that we had in our midst a poet worthy to be classed with Dante, Shakespeare or Milton, and not merely with Hölderlin, Rimbaud or Hart Crane.

Comment on Dylan Thomas

EDITH SITWELL

'Sir George Beaumont' said Coleridge, in *Anima Poetae*, 'found great advantage in learning to draw through gauze spectacles.'

I do not know if Coleridge was intending a gibe. But in any case, no better portrait could be given of a dilettante. The amateur almost invariable softens and blurs.

A great deal of the verse that is published today is hopelessly amateurish and the authors seem to have *tried* to learn to see (they rarely succeed in doing so), through gauze spectacles.

It is very natural that people so occupied, people who spend their lives in 'measuring the irregularities' of Michael Angelo and Socrates by village scales' – in short, *les apôtres du petit bonheur*, should be scared by – should distrust – Dylan Thomas.

In my *A Poet's Notebook* I have a quotation about the painter who paints a tree becoming a tree.

This condensation of essence, this power of 'becoming the Tree', is one of the powers that makes Mr Thomas the great poet he is. His poems appear, at first sight, strange. But if you heard a tree speak to you in its own language, its own voice, would not that, too, appear strange to you?

In the essay 'Nature' (Tiefurt Journal 1782) Goethe wrote: 'She [Nature] has thought and she broods unceasingly, not as a man but as Nature. . . . She has neither language nor speech, but she creates tongues and hearts through which she speaks and feels . . . It was not I who spoke of her. Nay, it was she who spoke it all, true and false. Hers is the blame for all things, hers the credit.'

Mr Thomas, also, is a poet through whom Nature speaks.

The *apôtres du petit bonheur* regard the mind as a little machine confined in a box, which will tell the time to the minute, and which will tick at certain reactions.

Mr Thomas's mind is not a clock. It does not tell the fleeting minute.

In William James's *Principles of Psychology*, he quotes Condillac as saying 'The first time we see light, we *are* it rather than *see* it'. It is this becoming that the poet needs.

Sometimes, as with certain other great poets, a phrase, with him, will mean two things, both equally true. When Shakespeare wrote:

'Men have died and worms have eaten them, but not for love' did he not mean 'men have died, but not for love', and 'worms have eaten them, but not for love'? I think so.

In each poem by Mr Thomas, there is an infinite power of germination.

Take the beautiful 'Fourth Poem' from *The Map of Love*. This, like many another poem by a great poet, is all things to all men. It is not the poet's possession only, it is also ours. The poem moves on two levels, that of the day, and that of eternity.

The two lovers lie, in a silence of love, between the image of Life – the wandering ever-changing sea – and the image of Death, 'the strata of the shore' (the lives, perhaps, that have gone before) – 'the red rock' – and Time, that is identified with the sand:

> the grains as they hurry
> Hiding the golden mountains and mansions
> Of the grave, gay, seaside land.

These lovely lines have, I think, two significances – the grave one, of the actual mountains and mansions made golden to the young people by the light of the sun and of their love, and soon to be overwhelmed by the sands of Time – and the gay one, that of the mountains and castles made by the children at the edges of the sea, and soon to be covered over by the other sands blown by the wind.

Over the young people, 'the heavenly music over the sand' sighs to them of those yellow grains and of the wandering faithless sea – but Time is no longer terrible to them in their silence of love.

The poem is of the greatest beauty, both visually and orally.

The phrase 'the lunar silences' holds the actual light of the sea in it. The sound is like that of the heavenly music over the sand, like the sea-airs. Sometimes it changes like the wind, moves with the beauty of waves. It is of an unsurpassable technical achievement.

In that great poem 'A Refusal to Mourn the Death, by Fire, of a Child in London', with its dark and magnificent, proud movement, we see Death in its reality, as a return to the beginning of all things – as only a robing, a sacred investiture, in those who have been our friends since the beginning of time –

> the grains beyond age, the dark veins of her mother

– (Earth, her mother). Bird, beast and flower have their part in the making of mankind, and in its root. The water drop is holy, the ear of corn a place of prayer. The all-humbling Darkness itself is a begetting force. Even grief, even tears, are a begetting . . . though here this life must not come into being – (as a rival, perhaps, to the dead child). The stations of the breath are the stations of the Cross.

I do not know any short poem of our time which has more greatness.

A Comment

HENRY GIBSON

A REFUSAL TO MOURN

IT IS ALWAYS to the point to ask *why*? to the complex of thought and feeling which a respected poet offers a reader. In this poem the question may in the first place be addressed to the first sentence (lines 1 to 13). Somewhat breathlessly a semblance of sense is preserved. Mr Thomas is telling us that he refuses to mourn the death of a child. He refuses with a great deal of vigour –

> Never until . . .
> . . . all humbling darkness
> Tells with silence the last light breaking . . .

will he 'sow (his) salt seed' over the child's death. This 'last light breaking' is important, not only because it puts a limit to Mr Thomas's refusal to mourn (why, one asks, does he revoke at the last breaking? rather than at a blue moon?) but because it opens a great vista of not altogether relevant imagery to the poet's considerable rhythmical sense.

My point is that the 'last light breaking' theme is more appropriate to the deep emotional disturbance that Mr Thomas feels rather than to any situation or experience which he may consider himself to communicate. It allows him two stanzas of impressive and evocative prophetic cavorting; it provides a licence for all the eternity imagery a romantic poet might care to indulge. Mr Thomas leaves no emotive counter unturned. Every word is richly suggestive and though one can only describe the atmosphere evoked as *poetic*, one would hardly be inclined to regard the word in this case as definitive of poetry.

Just as, when stripped, the first half of the poem reveals a remarkable poverty of sense for so rich an emotionalism, so does the second half, when rendered down, leave only the most usual Georgian 'one-with-nature' sentiment. Now the Georgians had many faults, but at least they could pride themselves upon their ability to be simple with becoming simplicity. Mr Thomas puns and mixes with the most advanced company since the Surrealist exhibition, he takes liberties with language which only the genius of a Manley Hopkins could justify, he flashes and gestures, yet what he has to say has been said already and many times by men he would never wish to emulate.

One may question Mr Thomas's striking images (what does the Thames 'ride' in this context? what are 'the long friends', worms or weeds? should 'stations of the breath' in connection with 'down' suggest the Underground? why isn't the water bead a synagogue and the corn a Zion?) but such questions would simply make the point that Mr Thomas's imagery is neither precise nor deliberate. He writes under the influence of a purely personal (though quite public) inspiration, and the confused emotional statement may stand for the usual 'sensitive' reaction to 'significant' experiences in both Mr Thomas and the contemporary public for romantic writing. The concluding line of the poem with its smart consciousness of ambiguity winds up a typical peroration on death with a popular suggestion of resurrection, thus clinching the religious argument of the poem.

MAP OF LOVE, POEM 4.

This is presumably a love poem, so perhaps one is only intended to sense the excited and over-heated state of the author. At all events, though this much communicates to me, I am unable to understand anything else about the poem. In which case I can only try to indicate how the confusion of the poem is generated.

'We lying' introduces the main preoccupation of the volume from which the poem comes. 'Sea sand' has obviously suggested 'yellow' to the author. Again Mr Thomas puns with 'grave'; his 'red' rivers contrast nicely with his sand although the colour otherwise seems arbitrarily selected. 'Mock who deride who follow' is, to me, a switchback of meaning. What the 'Hollow alcove of words' is apposite to, no mere analysis can reveal. The lines:

> A calling for colour calls with the wind
> That's grave and gay as grave and sea

seems neither to define the *wind* nor clinch the argument concerning the force of 'grave' which appears to be a key image here. The first sentence of the poem appears quite lost; not in the way that a sentence which has a purpose might become lost, but in such a way as to suggest that the delights of an emotional maze mean more to the poet than the patient and disciplined pursuit of any direction.

'The lunar silences should cure our ills of the water with a one-coloured calm'; that 'should' appears to be a very personal hope. What does the sentence mean? Certainly its meaning could never be considered precise. Lines fifteen and nineteen convert the sand imagery into a 'gold' sequence. 'Grains', 'golden', 'sovereign', 'yellow' combine to suggest forcibly an imagery which bears no clearly defined relationship to the poem's central argument (that of 'lying', I presume). As so often with Mr Thomas's poems the display of virtuosity is a nine-days' wonder, and the craftsmanhip is merely concerned to revolve on its own axis.

The concluding 'thought' of the poem is pompously 'profound'. There are many popular songs which also conclude that 'wishes' breed not. However, the last line of the poem provides an interesting example of how Mr Thomas's collapsed imagery works and (perhaps) originates. Here the 'breaking' of the weather suggest to the quick romantic association the breaking of the 'heart', which in its turn introduces 'blood'. All this will be immediately recognisable as emotive cliché. It is Mr Thomas's peculiar talent of knowingness which prompts him to inject the quite irrelevant 'hill', thus giving an 'unusual' and 'thought-provoking' twist to what is both trite and thoughtlessly dull.

How Much Me Now Your Acrobatics Amaze

GEOFFREY GRIGSON

Whoever has the power of creating, has likewise the inferior power of keeping his creation in order.

W. S. LANDOR

SUPPOSE ONE WERE COMPELLED to decide between 'reason' and 'romance': it is, surely, no more the reason of 1700 that one would choose than the romance of 1800 one would easily reject. 'Romance' is too simple a pejorative. In the eighteenth century one could be 'romantic' under reason, and in the nineteenth century one could be rational under romance. The 'romance' we are drifting back to in England is a romance without reason: it is altogether self-indulgent and liquescent. An Inky Cap mushroom grows up white and firm and then flops down into a mess of ink – which is our new romance, something once alive which avoids no longer the decay into death. It is so much easier to flop, so much easier to give up the metabolism of life and literature, in a time which is contemptuous of law, and when there is no body of opinion at all clear about what is true and untrue, possible and impossible, probable and improbable. And so now a poet (Mr George Barker) can fill nine-tenths of a book with such lines as:

O dolphins of my delight I fed with crumbs
Gambading through bright hoops of days,
How much me now your acrobatics amaze
Leaping my one-time ecstasies from Doldrums . . .

and another (Mr Stephen Spender) declare:

> And there was many another name
> Dividing the sun's light like a prism
> With the rainbow colours of an 'ism'

– not only without critical eyebrow-raising, but with the evocation of the highest praise. If, in the most public way possible, in some periodical of the widest circulation and the highest repute, one were to examine such poetry, turn it inside out, expatiate with the greatest clarity and skill on the nature of poetry and its function in life, prove the awkwardnes, limpness, and absurdity of these crumb-fed dolphins, nothing would happen, no one would notice. Objection, reason, proof – all would be swamped and swallowed in the universal mess.

Thinking of some of Gerard Hopkins's strictures on Browning, I have collected a number of pieces from another book of recent poems, full of lions and amber and dust and dew:

1. . . . bird-blood leaps within our veins
   And is changed to emeralds like the sap in the grass.
2. And you are the sound of the growth of spring in the heart's deep core.
3. And I would that each hair on my head was an angel
   O my red Adam.
4. O heed him not, my dew with golden feet
   Flying from me.
5. But the sap in these dry veins sang like a bird:
   'I was the sea that knew the siren song
   And my veins heard
   A planet singing in the Dorian mode . . .'
6. Another old man said:
   'I was a great gold-sinewed King, I had a lion's mane
   Like the raging sun . . .'

7. Were those the veins that heard the Siren's song?
8. So changed is she by Time's appalling night
That even her bone can no more stand upright.
9. . . . but the long wounds torn by Time in the golden cheek
Seem the horizons of the endless cold.
10. . . . and the first soundless wrinkles fall like snow
On many a golden cheek
11. The kiss that holds . . . the rose that weeps in the blood.
12. But now only the red clover
lies over the breath of the lion and the mouth of the lover.

All these – it is Hopkins's phrase – are frigidities, all of them untruths to nature, the emerald blood jumping in the veins, the angelic coiffure, dew with feet, veins with ears, sinews made of gold, cheek wounds like landscapes, wrinkles falling like snow, the rose weeping in the veins, the earth and plants on top of the dead lion's breath – all frigidities except 2 and 8 (heart's deep core – heart's deep heart), which are specimens of the undiluted art of sinking. The poetry they come from is chimerical. The chimera has a lion's head, a goat's body, and a serpent's tail. The lion's head is a lion no longer real (as the lions of Dryden were real:

And still for him the Lioness stalks
And hunts her lover through the lonely walks).

The goat's body (and hair) is the absence of form; the serpent's tail the lines elongating into nothingness. Gerard Hopkins found it monstrous (his word once more, and I am speaking of the chimerical) – monstrous in Browning's 'Instans Tyrannus', that the sky was written of as a shield protecting the just man from the tyrant – 'The vault of heaven is a vault, hollow, concave towards us, convex upwards; it therefore could only defend man on earth against enemies above it; an angry Olympus for instance'. He held that Browning had 'all the gifts but the one needful and the pearls without the string; rather, one should say raw nuggets and rough diamonds'. His turning of concave into convex was a 'frigidity', an 'untruth to nature'. It came of 'frigid fancy with no imagination'; and frigid fancy describes the gilded stringless writing from which I have panned these dozen samples, writing of an order lower than that of Browning, and more full of untruths to nature.

Two signs of our drift into 'romance' are the writing of such poetry, and the reception of it. The reception of these poems has been marked with the epithets of greatness in a hallelujah of reviews. If the poet (who is Miss Sitwell) adds to the reassembly, to the reiteration of the great truisms of life and time and youth and age and decay and death, to the repetition of adjectives (golden, etc.) no longer valid for our sense of wonder, she has added nothing from nature. In fact, it is the ubiquitous confidence of the day that anything, any first impression, can be crammed into formless verse without the self-discipline and self-criticism which are the sources of form; the sources of that composition in which, Henry James declared, exists the 'principle of health and safety'. And that, exactly, is where our new 'romance', in all its guises, is decadent and different to, shall one say, the romance of Coleridge. It is dragging the past for verbiage, for words out of their setting, nature not at all, and the self for disorderly nonsense. Coleridge was a scientifically-minded poet, curious about self, the past, and the given nature around him. If the glitter and the excellence of a phenomenon in nature appealed to him, he did not crawl like a spaniel to its charm or mystery. He had seen, for example, the Glory, described in the *Memoirs of the Literary and Philosophical Society of Manchester*, in 1790, by a Fellow of the Royal Society. The Glory is the rainbow which surrounds the shadow of your head upon mist when the mist is in the right place below you, and the sun in the right place behind you. But instead of using the Glory as an ornament (as I have explained in writing of the Aeolian Harp), Coleridge used it in 'Dejection', and again in 'Constancy to an Ideal Object', to express his deepest exploration into the relation of man to nature:

> . . . would we aught behold of higher worth,
> Than that inanimate cold world, allow'd
> To the poor, loveless, ever-anxious crowd,
> Ah! from the soul itself must issue forth
> A light, a glory, a fair luminous cloud
> Enveloping the earth –
> And from the soul itself must there be sent
> A sweet and potent voice of its own birth.

Nature to Coleridge and Wordsworth, as romantics, may have been very different to nature as uniformity and common-sense for Dryden and for Pope. For an image, Dryden and Pope might never have used a phenomenon such as the Glory, so much outside the general experience of mankind. Yet even if Coleridge was a poet of the age of spontaneity and of expression of the individual self, his intellect never abdicated; he was born in the eighteenth century, he lived within the influence of its controls. Even if he drugged himself with opium, he only published 'Kubla Khan', it is at least worth recalling now, at someone else's request, 'and, as far as the Author's own opinions are concerned, rather as a psychological curiosity, than on the ground of any supposed *poetic* merits'. 'Psychological curiosity': this is perhaps the point for reminding oneself of Mr Dylan Thomas, who has become one of the 'greater' poets of our grey time, and before whom (so much have things changed since Sir John Squire greeted *The Waste Land* with 'a grunt would serve equally well') even the conventional critics have begun abasing themselves. Mr Eliot's poems have their seldom-mentioned shortcomings, as of some half-man who has escaped with a few guarded fragments of humanity, or divinity, from what Mr Edward Dahlberg has called 'the most clinkered land in the world for the artist to live in'; but one would not name

Mr Eliot's poems 'psychological curiosities'. Mr Eliot's poems live tightly above the waist – rather higher than that, above the heart; Mr Thomas's live, sprawl loosely, below the waist. Mr Eliot is a reasoning creature. The self in Mr Thomas's poem seems inhuman and glandular. Or rather like water and mud and fumes mixed in a volcanic mud-hole, in a young land. Those who admire his poems, one concludes, are fascinated because there is something primal and universal in the underground fury by which they are generated; but not to worry the metaphor too far, one would prefer a man's poetry to break out of the common fury at least like a geyser, at least with the force and cleanness of form, at least with the meaning of a pillar; and not with the meaningless hot sprawl of mud.

Mr Thomas is a poet, Miss Edith Sitwell has remarked, whose work is 'on a huge scale both in theme and structurally'. She must imply, not just that his poems are about birth, death and love, in his newest book, but that Mr Thomas says something about his theme, says something on a *huge* scale, and by 'huge' again Miss Sitwell must imply a scale of meditation equal to Wordsworth's in *The Prelude*. Blake's upon the contrary states of the human soul, Shakespeare's in *The Tempest*, or Goethe's in *Faust*. One cannot demolish Mr Thomas's poems by demolishing Miss Sitwell's critical discernment; but one can say that even Mr Thomas's most recent book, *Deaths and Entrances*, shows, not a theme, not meditation, but simply obsession; – obsession with birth, death, and love, and obsession mainly in a muddle of images with only the frailest ineptitude of structure. Rhyme schemes begin and break. Rhythms start off and falter into incoherent prose. Image repeats image in a tautology of meaning. If a poet rhymes, he must twist his rhymes to the exigencies of impulse, or illumination; not, as Mr Thomas very often does, twist, and so falsify, his illumination to the exigencies of rhyme. And when he determines to keep his purpose, being too unskilful in words, he nearly-rhymes. Near rhymes have their virtue, but only if they come as deliberately as true rhyme, and have, against each other, the proper weight, accent, and length; but Mr Thomas's ineptitude licenses him to write:

> Lie still, sleep becalmed, suffer with the *wound*
> In the throat, burning and turning. All night *afloat*
> On the silent sea we have heard the *sound*
> That came from the wound wrapped in the salt *sheet.*

Afloat-sheet is Mr Thomas's skill. Here, too, is Mr Thomas faltering into prose (though perhaps one should characterise his poems as attempts to falter out of prose): Some movement begins:

> Friend by enemy I call you out.
>
> You with a bad coin in your socket,
> You my friend there with a winning air

– then smash:

> Who palmed the lie on me when you looked
> Brassily at my shyest secret.

To display most kinds of Mr Thomas's formal awkwardness, it would be most fair to read through a short poem, since in three stanzas the difficulties of form are easier to resolve (and in this poem, 'On a Wedding Anniversary', see again the rhythm smashed in the third line):

> The sky is torn across
> This ragged anniversary of two
> Who moved for three years in tune
> Down the long walks of their vows

Now their love lies a loss
And Love and his patients roar on a chain;
From every true or crater
Carrying cloud, Death strikes their house.

Too late in the wrong rain
They come together whom their love parted:
The windows pour into their heart
And the doors burn in their brain.

Clouds with craters are like veins with ears; more ridiculous, in fact, than Nat Lee's night-raven with huge wicker wings, and strange eyes: 'In each black Eye there rolls a Pound of Jet'. Syntactically Mr Thomas makes wonders of awkwardness; not, one feels, from theory, but because his words are nearly automatic, his words come up bubbling in an automatic muddle.

Never until the mankind making
Bird beast and flower
Fathering and all humbling darkness
Tells with silence the last light breaking
And the still hour
Is come of the sea tumbling in harness

– construable – just, but made none the more active or effective by the confusion (or by *darkness*: *harness*).

No more, no less construable is:

There was a saviour
In the churches of his tears
There was calm to be done in his safe unrest
Children kept from the sun

On to the ground when a man has died
To hear the golden note turn in a groove,
Silence, silence to do, when earth grew loud
In the jails and studies of his keyless smiles.

– a stanza upon which Mr Thomas's explorers and admirers should meditate, for reasons which I shall give later. And like a child learning to talk, or a journalist, Mr Thomas deals in the striking, but rootless image, and in the cliché turned – *one below a time, all the sun long, happy as the heart was long – a bad coin in your socket:* word-tumbling without either gravity of point, or point of fun (as when Lewis Carroll writes 'Either you or your head must be off, and that in about half no time').

Mr Thomas does indeed work, as a child works, towards form and coherence. From the shape of one poem he must have been *looking* at George Herbert. But otherwise his poetry as near as may be is the poetry of a child, volcanic, and unreasoning, who has seldom read, and little cared for, the poets of his own language, and allowed them little power over his own manipulation – or rather automatism:

How soon the servant sun
(Sir morrow mark)
Can time unriddle, and the cupboard store
(Fog has a bone
He'll trumpet into meat)
Unshelve that all my gristles have a gown
And the naked egg stand strange . . .

The power which these poems appear to exercise over readers does not reside in sense, demonstrably; it does not reside in music, it does not reside in an ordered, musical non-sense. The unit, one realises in Mr Thomas's poetry, is neither poem, nor stanza, it is phrase or line, which by accident suggests the next phrase, or the next line, the solipsist image which suggests the next solipsism; power resides in the novel suggestion, in these massed solipsisms, of the strange, the magical, the profound; and in fact their strangeness is little else than the strangeness of Mr Thomas, their profundity little beyond the Indian-ink deepnesses of an individual, their magic little else than what appears to be a black magic. (Here perhaps I should interpolate that the second, just-construable piece which I quoted from Mr Thomas, is one made by myself of disconnected lines from three stanzas of one poem. But between, then and now, I hope any idolater will have taken his time to admire it, and to meditate upon it; for it reads, I am convinced, as authentically as most of Mr Thomas's stanzas.)

Mr Thomas, as I say, cannot help what bubbles into him and bubbles out; but to invest these black magical bubblings, as critics feel them to be, with greatness – in spite of here and there a fancy, even a 'sublime' fancy (though often it is 'the sublime dashed in pieces by cutting too close with the fiery four-in-hand round the corner of nonsense'), here and there even a poem – to do that deserves many descriptions, of which I will mention only one, that it seems a little out of date. The 'new romanticism', of which Mr Dylan Thomas's poetry is the exemplar, became articulate and 'new' some twenty years ago in the hey-day of *Transition;* and as Mr Wyndham Lewis made plain in attacking *Transition* in *The Diabolical Principle*, it was not new even then. Muddled up with politics, the 'new romanticism' of *Transition* was based considerably upon Lautréamont, whose diabolism, minus the politics (and minus a clear sense of the devil, and minus the will to be devilish) soaked into Mr Dylan Thomas in his Welsh childhood. 'That this bric-à-brac', wrote Mr Lewis of Lautréamont, 'should be seriously presented as the exemplar of the best or newest seems impossible. That it should be . . . published to catch *l'homme moyen sensuel*, on account of its blood-dripping fangs associated with the milk-white bodies of virgins, is as natural and harmless as that *Fanny Hill* should never be quite out of print, or that the *History of a Flea* or even the 'bourgeois' pornography of Paul de Kock's *Ten Pairs of Drawers* should remain scandalous best-sellers. But there, you would suppose, the joke would end – once the gull's money was safely transferred from his bank to that of the sagacious . . . literary publisher . . . But that is not the case'. Mr Thomas once defined his notion of poetry: 'Whatever is hidden should be made naked. To be stripped of darkness is to be clean, to strip of darkness is to make clean. Poetry, recording the stripping of individual darkness must, inevitably, cast light upon what has been hidden for too long, and by so doing make clean the naked exposure'. 'Whatever is hidden . . .' It suggests the disinfection of psychological ordure – as if, in Ananda Coomaraswamy's words, 'as if the artist had nothing better to do than make an exhibition of himself to his neighbour'. And what self-adulation, what absence of humility, what insolence (even if Mr Thomas is not altogether to be blamed for it), to believe in the importance to others of the 'stripping of one's own dirty, individual darkness, which must be made clean'. Art, yes, as the peeling off of the ten pairs of drawers!

Yesterday's heresy has become with the middlemen, and *les hommes moyen sensuels*, today's provincial orthodoxy. The poetry of the unpeeled drawers is now acceptable. But we should take care. What I believe should be our concern in all this war and post-war drift back into a decayed romance is not, first of all, to use 'romance' pejoratively because of any such examples, not to throw away everything that genuine 'romance', everything that poets and artists, everything that psychologists from Coleridge to Freud, everything that anthropologists have curiously revealed about the source and nature of the arts. Dryden's poetry, and Poussin's painting (even if one does not need to underwrite all the views of Dryden's age or Poussin's age about nature and reason), are always there, as models of control. It is ironic to think that we can once more read Boileau with profit; that Boileau at whom Keats had to make a long nose:

A Poem, where we all perfections find,
Is not the work of a Fantastick mind:
There must be Care, and Time, and Skill, and Pains;
Not the first heat of unexperienc'd Brains.
Yet sometimes Artless Poets, when the rage
Of a warm Fancy does their minds ingage,
Puff'd with vain pride, presume they understand,
And boldly take the Trumpet in their hand;
Their Fustian Muse each accident confounds;
Nor can she fly, but rise by leaps and bounds,
Till their small stock of learning quickly spent
Their poem dyes for want of nourishment.
With impudence the Laurel they invade
Resolv'd to like the Monsters they have made.

But still, as I say, we do not want to throw away the discoveries of the last hundred and fifty years, or the last forty years, we do not want to waste them because so many writers and artists, and so many critics, now are debasing themselves to a new exclusive set of dogmas derived from the very things discovered. Art – being an artist – is subject to entropy; or is a perpetual walking across a tight-rope, with death and disaster either side and below. And the Enlightenment of Dryden and Pope tailed off, too, by making reason's light a dogma when nothing was left to enlighten.

No one has added up and analysed the whole romantic slide with more skill and more power than W. H. Auden, in an essay, *Criticism in a Mass Society*, which was little noticed in the England of neo-romance. To the critic, he wrote, 'Slogans like Art for Arts' sake, or Art for Politics' sake, will be equally objectionable'. The critic 'will flatter neither the masses by assuring them that what is popular must be good, nor the highbrows by assuring them that what is *avant garde* must be superior. Further, he will conceive of art, like life, as being a self-discipline rather than a self-expression . . . he will distrust the formless, the expansive, the unfinished, and the casual'.

But in combating the slide into romance, into idiot romance, we have to be careful not to encourage the white and dry which sterilize the creative impulse. Even that danger does not mean that we should be afraid to recover our wits and our honesty, and speak out now and then, afraid because we may seem to be betraying a cause to the old enemy, and assuring Sir John Squire, or whoever carries his mantle in these later years, that he was right.

Postscript: As I read this in proof, I discover that Mr Thomas has also published a recipe for the writing of his poems: 'I let an image be made from my subconscious, and from that first image I let' – this is peculiar – 'its opposite emerge. These two images then war with each other, producing a third; the poem becoming a water-tight column of images.' Wyndham Lewis once defined art as 'a constant stronghold of the purest human *consciousness*'. This definition of Mr Thomas's is making art the constant stronghold of certainly not the purest (since purity implies sifting and discernment) human, or sub-human, subconsciousness.

Dylan Thomas

E. GLYN LEWIS

THE PURPOSE OF THIS ANALYSIS of the poetry of Dylan Thomas is twofold: in the first place in view of recent attacks[1] it appears necessary to make the point that this writer is articulate, that he does say something which can be recognised in terms of our contemporary idiom, and conforms to the tradition of the English language. In the second place the study attempts to describe what the poet says and to analyse in a very elementary and unambitious fashion the main characteristics of his imagination. These two aims are indeed complementary aspects of the one purpose with which we commence the study of any writer – the attempt at a sympathetic understanding. An inability to understand his attitude will invalidate any attempt we make to appraise this poetry especially, for Dylan Thomas is undoubtedly a religious poet, and without understanding, even in the narrowest sense, we can as much hope to do justice to his poetry as we can to the later poetry of T. S. Eliot – less, because the religious element in Eliot's verse is part of the dominant tradition of the West, so that partial failure to communicate may be compensated by a living context in the mind of the reader that can supply the deficiency. The poetry of Thomas, however, belongs to a disregarded and repressed but equally ancient tradition.

Before we discuss the poetry itself it may be well to consider his position in the development of contemporary European literature. He himself has disclaimed any affinity with the surrealist

1. Particularly Mr Grigson in *Polemic*, and his recent book, *Harp of Aeolus*.

group, but while we may accept his affirmation we can well ignore its implications, for that group is only an extreme manifestation of what is the climate of European writing, and few writers have effectively avoided its influence. It is a pervasive mood, an attitude and a point of view rather than a dogma, and its influence has penetrated the cinema, photography, architecture and wit, as well as painting and literature. Its main characteristic is its refusal to accept the conventional logical forms of the past, to insist upon a more penetrating and incisive glance at existence; and so 'it speaks with the vocabulary of the great vital constants, sexual instinct, feeling of death, physical notion of the enigma of space'. According to these writers, 'reason only knows what it has succeeded in learning', and in our dependence upon the validity of rational constructions we have during the past two or three centuries accumulated a superstructure of rational argument each step of which removes us farther from the primal and necessary truth of intuitive understanding. We have come so far from the first revelation that the hollowness and insignificance of our structure, no matter how coherent it may be, have become apparent in all fields of action and contemplation – literature, politics and religion. What our contemporaries have found necessary, therefore, is a transvaluation of values:

> We still live under the reign of logic . . . But the methods of logic are applied nowadays only to the resolution of the problems of secondary interest . . . Needless to say that even experience has had its limits assigned to it. It revolves in a cage from which it becomes more and more difficult to release it. Even experience is dependent upon immediate utility and common sense is its keeper. Under colour of civilisation, under pretext of progress, all that rightly or wrongly may be regarded as fantasy or superstition is banished from the mind, all uncustomary searching after truth has been proscribed . . . The imagination is perhaps on the point of reclaiming its

> rights. If the depths of our minds harbour strange forces capable of increasing those of the surface . . . then it is all in our interest to canalise them first in order to submit them later, if necessary, to the control of reason.[1]

Jacques Maritain, himself one of the most cogent and persuasive apologists for the opposite tradition, proclaims the necessity for this departure: he speaks of 'an art delivered from the ribbons and skeletons of the language factory adapted to the most superficial needs of the human being, an art that passes beyond success and the well made, beyond the measures of man and that jumps out of the shadow into the sun . . . It is certainly permissible to think that in the use of signs and forms, and in the universe of poetry, man has before him no fewer secrets to discover than in the world of the sciences and of the knowledge of nature'[2]. That is the aim of this new generation of poets – to jump out of the shadow of customary and habitual perception into the vivid and vitalising sun of novel and unusual experience; and in order to do this they are anxious to move, for the moment, in strange regions of the mind. Mr Grigson obviously would not agree with their aims: for him 'fidelity to what we can see of objects is the beginning of sanity . . . The world of objects is our constant discipline . . . Look for objects: the use of ideas (as against being used by ideas) depends upon this fidelity to objects, and objects include language, but not poetry'. He disregards, however, what Wordsworth and Coleridge and most of the great masters of literature who have written critically upon the matter have emphasised, that objects are indifferent material, their significance depending upon the light in which they are seen and the angle. It may be the light of stars Blake saw hurtling their arrows to illumine a primeval forest of ignorance with a lovely truth; it may be that strange light that never yet shone on sea or land, or it may be a very English moon-

1. André Breton, *First Manifesto*, 1924.
2. Jacques Maritain, *Art and Poetry*.

light that sits so sweet upon a bank of violets: it is the object and its occasion that matter, and should the occasion demand that lovers or poets should be translated to unwonted valleys or unfrequented and rare heights why should we complain when they return with such dazzling reports. 'All indeed is fiction and the creation of the fancy; but how otherwise can the past be invoked, or even the moment live before our eyes. It is only through truth transcendentalised that the average or approximate can come out. Such are the purposes of exaggeration; for these are in effect the fine plumes of poetry. They make a clearer lens, and magnify the detail.'[1]

For such writers, and Dylan Thomas is one of them, poetry is not so much a means of expression, an object in the sense referred to by Mr Grigson, as an activity of the spirit. In some major poets the verse offers analysis of discovery: so it is in Dryden and in Pope. The poetry is a magnificent construction erected sometimes it is true on very insignificant foundations; it is a series of variations revealing in turn different aspects of an original impulse, and the whole series is a coherent, logically related, self-subsistent and delightfully complete analysis of the theme. Other poets, however, do not offer us this analysis: frequently they present us with something less consummate and complete, frequently marked by paradox and sometimes by real inconsistency. But it is the process of discovery itself, so that the excitement of our reading derives as much from the quest as from the ultimate vision. This vision may be of profound significance, as it is in Wordsworth or Shakespeare, Milton or Keats: it may be less universal, and draw upon a more restricted field of experience, as we find in Herbert, Donne or Vaughan; but in any case it is such a truth as weighs upon the heart of humanity, and the verse vibrates in spite of its possible comparative weakness in formal excellence with a quality of magnanimity and greatness. The poetry of Dylan Thomas, however immature and however liable to freakishness and silly eccentricity,

1. Mr Sacheverell Sitwell.

belongs to the kind of Keats, obviously not in degree of achievement nor at present in security of vision, but certainly in its character of imagination. And that quality is the power to create a vision of life in terms of the lives of men and women of dramatic authenticity.

I have already said that this vision is religious, and that Dylan Thomas is a religious poet. I do not suggest that he is a devotional poet in the sense that Donne's poetry is devotional; nor that it is mystical, in the way that Crashaw's poetry flames with a visionary ardour; nor that it is metaphysical, in the manner of Eliot's great 'Quartets'. Thomas's is 'a religious sense of profane existence'; it is imbued with an intense, sometimes a precociously and hysterically intense, feeling of the unity of all forms of existence, without at the same time a realisation that the unity of existence has its reason in the nature of God and in the person of Christ, as we find in devotional, mystical, or metaphysical Christian poetry. One characteristic of the attitude of Dylan Thomas is its amoral acceptance of all experience; it has no law, no theology, a characteristic that serves excellently the need of a young man, providing richness, justifying all experience, and ensuring that 'the circle is not drawn premature'. In our poet, however, this attitude is not quite so simple nor unalloyed with Christian metaphysics. In his poem 'This side of the truth', we find from line 13 onwards that all experience is claimed to be of equal value:

> Good and bad, two ways
> Of moving about your death.

But at the end of this poem the amoral, comprehensive and unjudging attitude is called 'love' without, clearly, the implications of the Christian use of the term.

I have mentioned this poem for two reasons. In the first place it serves to indicate the poet's concern with fundamental problems of existence; and in the second place it reveals his difficulty in avoiding an amalgamation of two traditions – his devotional heritage, and the non-Christian occult philosophy to which he shows marked inclinations. At the same time the dichotomy within this poem may be an indication of possibilities in his development. In the past those writers who, like Thomas, have been drawn by a desire for absorption into the cosmic unity, who have been lured by the idea of a universal harmony, have followed diverse paths. For D. H. Lawrence the lure assumes the form of erotic love, and sometimes an exaggerated worship of family and race. For Kipling the nation may be said to symbolise the unity of the universe and to enshrine its wisdom, as the soil, the taste and smell of the country-side does for André Chamson, Barea, Silone and other regional writers. Or it may become the lure of the collective social as it does in the imagination of H. G. Wells. In whatever form this lure of the cosmos appears it denotes a 'periodic thirst to return to primitive life, to cosmic life, to find not only communion but fusion with cosmic life . . . A pagan cosmo-centricity sets itself up in the place of Christian anthropocenticity'[1].

If this lure of the cosmos affects a writer to any great degree it is probable that its expression will not be confined to any one of the forms we have mentioned, but may range over the whole field, as it does in Lawrence, for example. At the same time the emphasis may shift during the maturing of the poet's mind and with the clarification of his vision and attitude. This, I believe, has happened in the poetry of Dylan Thomas: his early poetry is manifestly and predominantly an expression of the erotic sensual lure, very much as it is in Lawrence, without the formulation of a metaphysic to explain that attitude as there is in the latter. I do not think we need quote examples of this emphasis, it is a pervading concern and an obtrusive element in his first book *Eighteen Poems*. But in the same volume we find, less emphatic perhaps but equally significant, the poet's animistic attitude, his susceptibility to the

1. Berdyaev, *Freedom and Slavery*, p. 97.

lure of the earth, the sense of the unity of man with the vast processes of nature, and the identity of all forms of life. It is revealed most emphatically, I fancy, in his poem 'The force that through the green fuse drives the flower'. The poem is not given over entirely to an expression of this attitude: the last seven lines, for example, show a typically adolescent fixation upon death, metamorphosed by Rilke into an apparently abiding metaphysic, but remaining in Thomas's early and later poetry as an abhorrent actuality. However, the animistic identity of nature and man is the poem's chief concern. The creative powers of nature and its destructive processes are identical in the great vegetative world and in man. In that sense there is an identification of these two aspects of the cosmos:

The force that through the green fuse drives the flower
Drives my green age; that blasts the roots of trees is my
  destroyer
And I am dumb to tell the crooked rose
My youth is bent by the same wintry fever.

The force that drives the water through the rocks
Drives my red blood; that dries the mouthing streams
Turns mine to wax.
And I am dumb to mouth unto my veins
How at the mountain spring the same mouth sucks . . .

This theme of 'One-ness' is not confined in its expression to the identity of man and nature within the cosmic processes; it reveals itself, too, in the assertion of one underlying principle of existence. In his poem 'In the beginning was the three pointed star' he is specifically concerned with this primordial, original principle, and each stanza is a metaphoric discovery of some new aspect. In the first stanza it is a 'three pointed star', which the poet makes clear is a sexual image. In the second stanza it is a 'pale signature', a metaphor that carries however some of the implications of the first. The poem is self-explanatory and needs no detailed explication to illustrate the point that for Thomas the one original factor in life is sex; and in this matter he shows his affinities with occult philosophies. But the poet is not content with the assertion of this factor; he goes much further. The metaphysical or mystical religious poet within the dominant Western tradition denies the reality of time:

Here is a place of disaffection
Time before and time after
In a dim light: neither daylight
Investing form with lucid stillness
Turning shadow into transient beauty
With slow rotation suggesting permanence
Nor darkness to purify the soul
Emptying the sensual with deprivation
Cleansing affection from the temporal
Neither plenitude nor vacancy. Only a flicker
Over the strained time ridden faces
Distracted from distraction by distraction
Filled with fancies and empty of meaning
Tumid apathy with no concentration
Men and bits of paper, whirled by a cold wind
That blows before and after time,
Wind in and out of unwholesome lungs
Time before and time after.[1]

Thomas too denies the significance of time, but this denial takes the form of identifying the two extremes of past and future rather than the obliteration of the whole sequence. This is expressed in several poems, but most simply, I imagine, in the poem 'I see the

1. T. S. Eliot.

boys of summer in their ruin'. In the first section he is concerned with creation, with bringing to birth and with fertility. In the second the reverse is dealt with, and man's decline, his inevitable decay, are stressed. The short final section is a synthesis of these dialectically opposed aspects; and here the identity we have referred to is made – summer and rain, the maggot and the womb, flint and soft pitch:

O see the poles are kissing as they cross.

In accepting the reality of the time sequence, Thomas differs from the traditional Western attitude; but by identifying the extremes he denies any substance to the concept. He and the Christian poets have still more in common in their willingness to enshroud the experience of time with the idea of death and the most objectionable associations. Two poems may serve to illustrate this. The first is 'Death is all metaphors', in which the process of time is identified with death. The child engendered, born, growing, maturing is merely manifesting the inevitability of death, 'for death is all metaphors', and may discover itself to us in the most varying ways. At the end he writes:

Hairs of your head then said the hollow agent
Are but the roots of nettles and of feathers
Over these groundworks thrusting through a pavement
And hemlock-headed in the wood of weathers.

The second poem commences 'It is the sinners' dust-tongued bell claps me to churches', and here time is identified with the sexual act which, holy in itself, is translated by consciousness of time into an abhorrent experience:

I mean by time the cast and curfew rascal of our
marriage,
At nightbreak born in the fat side, from an animal bed
In a holy room in a wave;

And all love's sinners in a sweet cloth kneel to a hyleg
 image,
Nutmeg, civet and sea parsley serve the plagued groom
 and bride
Who have brought forth the urchin grief.

Related to this adolescent emphasis on the need for absorption within some usually unspecified and vague 'One' is the theme of pre-natal existence. This is a commonplace of certain types of mystical thinkers, from Plato onwards: it receives remarkable expression in our literature through Vaughan, Traherne, and Wordsworth:

O how I long to travel back
And tread again that ancient track!
That I might once more reach the plain
Where first I left my glorious train,
From whence the enlightened spirit sees
That shady city of palm trees;
But (ah!) my soul with too much stay
Is drunk and staggers in the way.
Some men a forward motion love,
But I by backward steps would move,
And when this dust falls to the urn
In that state I came return.

It is, I think, a pantheistic vestige in the body of Western Christian literature, and as such it exemplifies in a particularly interesting fashion the 'lure of the cosmos' to which we have referred. From a psychological rather than theological standpoint it is a symptom of infantile regression, an unconscious desire to revert to the state of existence within the womb, a more or less undifferentiated existence in which individuality is eroded by the vast wave of the 'one spirit's plastic stress'. This infantile fixation runs through the works of our mystical poets and in a different, undoctrinal manner it characterises the early work of Dylan Thomas too. It reveals itself in the forms we have already mentioned, in the obsessive concern with and delight in sea imagery, reaching its apogee in the 'Ballad of the Long Legged Bait', and also with this concern with pre-natal existence. He differs from the Christian mystic in not formulating or adopting a metaphysic or theology to explain or to disguise this concern. But as in the works of Vaughan and particularly Traherne, it serves to create the ecstatic vision of childhood as something irradiated with a more than natural brilliance. Traherne writes:

> The corn was orient and immortal wheat which never should be reaped nor was ever sown. I thought it had stood from everlasting to everlasting. The dust and stones of the streets were as precious as gold: the gates were at first the end of the world. The green trees when I saw them first through the gates transported and ravished me, their sweetness and unusual beauty made my heart to leap and almost mad with ecstasy, they were such strange and wonderful things. The men! O how venerable and reverend creatures did the aged seem! Immortal cherubims! And young men glittering and sparkling Angels and maids strange seraphic pieces of life and beauty. Boys and girls tumbling in the street and playing were moving jewels. I knew not that they were born or should die; but all things abided eternally as they were in their proper places. Eternity was manifest in the light of the day, and something infinite behind everything appeared.

Expressed in a more contemporary idiom, without the framework of a theology and a conventional terminology, Dylan Thomas recaptures the same visionary splendour and the same rapturous illumination, and expresses it no less beautifully:

There could I marvel
My birthday
Away but the weather turned around.

It turned away from the blithe country
And down the other air and the blue altered sky
Streamed again a wonder of summer
With apples
Pears and red currants
And I saw in the turning so clearly a child's
Forgotten mornings when he walked with his mother
Through the parables
Of sun light.
And the legend of the green chapels.

But more beautifully still it finds expression in his lovely 'Fern Hill':

All the sun long it was running, it was lovely, the hay
Fields as high as the house, the tunes from the chimney, it was air
And playing, lovely and watery
And fire green as grass.
And nightly under the simple stars
As I rode to sleep the owls were bearing the farm away,
All the moon long I heard, blessed among stables, the nightjars
Flying with the ricks, and the horses
Flashing into the dark.

And then to awake, and the farm, like a wanderer white
With the dew, come back, the cock on his shoulder; it was all
Shining, it was Adam and maiden,

The sky gathered again
And the sun grew round that very day.
So it must have been after the birth of the simple light
In the first, spinning place the spellbound horses walking warm
Out of the whinnying green stable
On to the fields of praise.

The religious consciousness of Dylan Thomas is expressed not only in the desire for absorption into a cosmic whole which Shelley too experienced the desire for:

That Light whose smile kindles the Universe,
That Beauty in which all things work and move,
That Benediction which the eclipsing Curse
Of birth can quench not, that sustaining Love
Which through the web of being blindly wove
By man and beast and earth and air and sea.

This religious imagination is revealed in Thomas's concern with what for want of a better term we may call questions of human destiny – problems of will and freedom, the reason and purpose of the creation. Occasionally he feels the inevitability of forces beyond the power of man, and his verse is imbued with a sense of tragic contemplation. This is expressed in the poem commencing 'We lying by sea sand', where the pathetic impotence of man in the face of vaster forces is brought out in the last few lines:

Bond by a sovereign strip we lie,
Watch yellow, wish for wind to blow away
The strata of the shore and drown red rock;
But wishes breed not, neither
Can we fend off rock arrival,
Lie watching yellow until the golden weather
Breaks O my heart's blood, like a heart and hill.

But his book *Twenty-Five Poems* is characterised by an uncertainty about how he should approach the many decisions a young man has to make. It is not hesitancy: there is no reluctance to assume responsibility for a decision nor any unwillingness to make articulate the problem as it impinges upon his conscience. It is rather a sensibility of all the implications of a decision in any direction, and a hypersensitivity to the need to make a right decision. In his poem 'Ears in the turret hear', the poet is debating the desirability of moving away from the solipsistic attitude, feeling his way to a decision whether to remain isolated in his subjectivism or to open windows and doors upon the objective social world. Either decision carries with it terrifying possibilities, and this is expressed most powerfully in the following verses where after stating the dilemma in the first and second stanzas the poet repeats his questions with a burning urgency:

Ears in the turret hear
The wind pass like a fire
Eyes in this island see
Ships anchor off the bay.
Shall I run to the ships
With the wind in my hair,
Or stay till the day I die
And welcome no sailor?
Ships, hold you poison or grapes?

Hands grumble on the door,
Ships anchor off the bay,
Rain beats the sand and slates,
Shall I let in the stranger,
Shall I welcome the sailor,
Or stay till the day I die?

In the poem 'Should lanterns shine' the same problem is posited, this time not in terms of choice between a solipsistic subjectivism or a social communion, but rather of the opposition between intuition and reason, whether to depend for knowledge upon the infallible quick glance of the seer or to build painstakingly by careful accumulation of objectively verifiable experience, a problem that forms one of the main strands of medieval metaphysical discussion. The first stanza seems to suggest a criticism of the intuitive private judgment, for it is argued that such judgments when brought up for pragmatic or social confirmation become worthless and delusive:

> The features in their private dark
> Are formed of flesh, but let the false day come
> And from her lips the faded pigments fall
> And mummy cloths expose an ancient breast.

In the second stanza he is more explicit:

> I have been told to reason by the heart
> But heart like head leads helplessly.

And finally his decision remains unpronounced, it hangs suspended between two worlds:

> The ball I threw while playing in the park
> Has not yet reached the ground.

In the next poem, 'I have longed to move away', the problem assumes yet another form, this time the conflict between the rational form of life that has created conventions for the civilised ordering of existence, and on the other hand the eruptive Dionysiac flame that illumines life with a fierce novelty. The convention, necessary though it is to a civilised community, is nevertheless an artificial and ultimately stultifying experience. To that extent it is a lie, a betrayal of the impulse that first engendered it. The poet is longing:

to move away
From the hissing of the spent lie
And the old terror's continual cry.

But he recognises that these conventions are only the partial petrification of once vital and lovely impulses, and that the truth they distort they also preserve by virtue of that very formality which is synonymous with the petrification. They may still possess power and significance:

I have longed to move away but am afraid
Some life yet unspent might explode
Out of the old lie burning on the ground
And crackling into the air, leave me half blind.

Finally, without being necessarily part of the religious character of his imagination, but certainly very closely related to it, is the poet's hyper-sensitive reaction to society, his fear and anxiety in the face of the everyday world of ordinary men and women. In the hands of some poets this attitude may result in bitter satire, for the writer transfers his own subconscious guilt to the objective world, and finds in society those failings and defects that really motivate, subconsciously, his own wishes and inchoate desires. This is the case with that type of satirist we may call 'metaphysical', as opposed to the 'humanist' or Horatian satirist: it includes such writers as Juvenal, Hall, Donne, Swift and James Joyce. They are able to preserve an apparent integrity because they have, by virtue of their gifts as writers, been able to identify their own censored and repressed urges with the social world of which they disapprove. In Dylan Thomas this identification has not occurred, nor to my mind will it occur, for he is essentially a mythopœic poet, a visionary whose standards and values are evolved organically from his experience rather than one who brings to bear upon his experience of the world a set of clearly formulated and fixed principles of an *a priori* nature. But because the identification of repressed impulse with objective world in the form of satire has not been a feature of his poetry we are left in some poems with a sense of division, fear and anxiety. This is true of several poems, but it appears in none more explicitly than 'O make me a mask and a wall to shut from your spies'. If we compare this poem with some of those included in *Deaths and Entrances* we may see how his 'unjudging love' has helped to save him from a barren satire, and has developed into a mature and imaginative sympathy for persons in spite of what may appear to be their defects and weaknesses. He is concerned with the loving creative understanding of men and women, rather than with a judgment of their motives:

> I shall not murder
> The mankind of her going with a grave truth
> Nor blaspheme down the stations of her breath
> With any further
> Elegy of innocence and youth.

What we have said of the religious character of his poetry goes to reveal too the inherently subjective and autobiographical nature of his verse. For this there are several reasons independent of the character of the poet. The first of these is the kind of civilisation we now share. In an age of traditional conformity the young poet would have at hand a set of conventional themes that he would certainly modify but that would nevertheless ensure continuity with his predecessors, and provide for adequate communication with his reader. In the past such themes were indicated by ancient mythology, the Bible story or the legends of British heroes. In a revolutionary period such as ours not only are values questioned, but conventions are discredited; so that the poet is thrown back upon his own inventiveness for the embellishment of his theme, and more important, for the creation of any theme at all. In the second place 'Nature', which might have compensated for the loss of such conventional and accepted subjects, no longer presents, as it did at the end of the eighteenth century, an intelligible and coherent body of objects or experience: it is now conceived as dynamic, fluid, amorphous. In the same way the nature of man is differently interpreted now from of old – it is the resultant of conflicting forces, a shifting mass, for further understanding of which we are sent not to a clear set of precise principles but more and more deeply into the recesses of our own natures.

The Poetry of Dylan Thomas[1]

DAVID AIVAZ

THE QUICKEST, if a questionable, way to suggest the reputation that Dylan Thomas has already made: now thirty-six years of age, he has long been an 'influence'. The manifestos of Henry Treece and J. F. Hendry, the leaders of the 'Apocalyptic' or 'Neo-Romantic' group of young British poets, place him in first-rate company: 'Apocalyptic creation is a European movement or tendency whose immediate forebears are Kafka, Epstein, Picasso, the later Yeats and Dylan Thomas'[2]. These manifestos contain much dark talk about 'organic wholeness' and 'ideal anarchy'. The Apocalyptic programme is a denial of programme, and best defined negatively as a reaction from the social comment of the thirties. It is not hard to understand the appeal that Thomas has for the movement. His poetry is, in a sense to be investigated, organic. His images are of the natural world. He betrays no sign of social or economic bias. And his imagery and syntax, if not his metric, often seem 'anarchic' enough:

> A grief ago.
> She who was who I hold, the fats and flower,
> Or, water-lammed, from the scythe-sided thorn,
> Hell wind and sea,
> A stem cementing, wrestled up the tower,
> Rose maid and male. . . .

1. Reprinted from *The Hudson Review*, Vol. VIII, No. 3. Autumn 1950.

2. Quoted from an 'advertisement' of Treece and Hendry by Marshall Stearns in the *Sewanee Review*, Summer 1944.

He has been discussed as a Surrealist. Geoffrey Grigson, his most distinguished detractor, complains that 'his words come up bubbling in an automatic muddle . . . his poetry as near as may be is the poetry of a child, volcanic, and unreasoning'; while Miss Edith Sitwell, reading by ear, champions his cause thus: 'This condensation of essence, this power of 'becoming the Tree', is one of the powers that makes Mr Thomas the great poet he is. His poems appear, at first sight, strange. But if you heard a tree speak to you in its own language, its own voice, would not that, too, appear strange to you?' It would; but this, in itself, is to say little of Thomas's poems. It seems to me that Julian Symons falls into an opposite error[1]. He abstracts a conceptual 'meaning' from the imagery of the poems, and finds it, therefore the poems, wanting: 'What is said in Mr Thomas's poetry is that the seasons change; that we decrease in vigour as we grow older; that life has no apparent meaning; that love dies. His poems mean no more than that. They mean too little'.

Thomas has tried to explain his method of writing in a letter, quoted by several critics, to Mr Treece:

> . . . a poem by myself needs a host of images, because its centre is a host of images. I make one image, – though 'make' is not the word, I let, perhaps, an image be 'made' emotionally in me and then apply to it what intellectual and critical forces I possess – , let it breed another, let that image contradict the first, make, of the third image bred out of the other two together, a fourth contradictory image, and let them all, within my imposed formal limits, conflict. Each image holds within it the seed of its own destruction, and my dialectical method, as I understand it, is a constant building up and breaking down of the images that come out of the

1. In an interesting and careful – despite this passage – article, early criticised by John Berryman, Stearns quotes, and has appropriate doubts about, the passage too.

> central seed, which is itself destructive and constructive at the same time . . . Out of the inevitable conflict of images – inevitable, because of the creative, recreative, destructive, and contradictory nature of the motivating centre, the womb of war – I try to make that momentary peace which is a poem. . . .

I want to consider some implications of a 'dialectic' of composition later. One point seems clear: Thomas's divided allegiance to the words 'let' and 'make' does not permit one to base on this statement generalisations about the degree of reasonableness in his poetry. Evidence must come from the poems.

The following lines are typical of Thomas's early style: shifting rhythms, full rhetoric, strained syntax, and seemingly Surrealist imagery:

> Deliver me, my masters, head and heart,
> Heart of Cadaver's candle waxes thin,
> When blood, spade-handed, and the logic time
> Drive children up like bruises to the thumb,
> From maid and head,
>
> For, Sunday faced, with dusters in my glove,
> Chaste and the chaser, man with the cockshut eye,
> I, that time's jacket or the coat of ice
> May fail to fasten with a virgin O
> In the straight grave . . .

The images, when closely read, give no evidence of automatic writing. The obscurity is in the areas shaded by a conjunction of images, in the weighting of one symbol with more than one idea or quality. This kind of obscurity appears to be inherent in Thomas's dialectical method, 'inevitable' because of 'the contradictory nature of the motivating centre'. The obscurity should, I think, be challenged on grounds of method, or not at all.

The stanzas are about death and ways to transcend it. The ways under consideration are, very roughly, sexual, aesthetic, religious. The question of their efficacy is left open by the 'may' of the second stanza, the question of their relative efficacy by the interlocking imagery. 'Head' is both male sexual symbol, as elsewhere in Thomas's poems, and the mind. The first unites with 'heart' and 'maid' in sexual consummation. The second is contrasted with 'heart' and 'maid' in their sexual role, or (taking the 'heart' of sentiment, the closer definition of 'maid', the pun on 'maidenhead', and looking ahead to 'virgin o') as sensibility dissociated from mind and generation, as passion dissociated from action. 'Heart' and 'candle' in the second line repeat 'heart-head'. The words 'waxes thin' reinforce the two senses of 'head', for 'waxes' can be read 'increases' or 'candle-wax burns down': do the mind and the flesh thrive only at each other's expense? Blood is 'spade-handed' because the heart is spade-shaped and because spades dig graves; it is the naked hand of death that Sabbath-day religiosity tries to keep from sight ('glove'), to brush aside (but will the 'duster' avail against this dust?). I have trouble with 'bruises to the thumb'. A 'thumb' as, among the other things, the green thumb of the grower's art, as a palpitation of the heart: too many possible readings weaken the image for me. The children of nature ('maid') and art ('head') arise from death (time, the dead heart). The fusion of passion and action, 'chaste and the chaser', (the word-play is effective because the 'chased' *are* 'chaste', passion is the saint's way) is an attribute of divinity, the 'perfect circle' in John Donne[1] and others, and here the 'virgin o'. The eye of 'cockshut eye' is both female sexual symbol and the mind's eye, recalling the dual function of 'head'. 'Cockshut' suggests 'cocksure', in the tone of line six. The clothing of process (dust) and of art (ice, the artifice

1. The reader will become aware that most of my allusions are to currently fashionable names: Donne, Marvell, Eliot, Yeats, Rilke, Freud, Kenneth Burke. It can't be helped. Thomas seems to me to be very much of his literary time, and these are the writers he most often calls to mind.

of eternity) contrast with 'glove' of line six, but will even they serve? Finally, 'jacket' looks ahead to the pun on 'straight', death will restrain and calm (in the last stanzas of the poem we are reminded that 'everything ends. . . .').

It may be objected that, in lines demanding so extensive a paraphrase and analysis, connotations have been spread too thin for coherence; that, whatever the poet's intention, a Surrealist poetry has in fact emerged. This is perhaps true of a few of Thomas's early poems; it is not, I think, true here. The rambling of the prose only commends the tautness of these stanzas. However difficult and diffuse an image may be, we have been taught to consider it to be exact too, if its difficulty and diffuseness do not exceed that of the resemblance it embodies. The image *is* the resemblance, and non-metaphoric language cannot separate them; yet one notes how often, on the second or third reading, the verbal complexity of these 'warring' images becomes a complexity of real relationships of emotions and ideas. Even where an image is cumulative in its effect ('virgin o' containing 'maid' and 'chaste' and adding to these), or where a single image has a multiple association ('spade-handed blood'), its quality is usually 'exact' in this sense. Paraphrase only approximates it.

In Thomas's early poems especially, it is not only the weight of each image, but also the way in which the images are brought together, that give an appearance of automatism. The generative principle of the image, breeding the next, is almost always an extension of descriptive or symbolic content; the generative method, however, is very often an unashamed and inexhaustible word-play. The transition from image to image is by means of the pun, the double meaning, the coined word, the composite word, the noun-verb, the pronoun with a double antecedent. And there is a larger machinery, verbal and syntactical: clauses that read both forward and backward; uneven images that are smoothed by incantatory rhythms, rhymes, word patterns, verse forms, by the use of commas in place of full-stop punctuation; cant, slang terms and formal, general abstract wording juxtaposed in image after image, so that the agitation of each becomes the repose of the group.

Thomas employs such devices often. The surface of many of his poems is, at first sight, hopelessly crowded and confused. It is undeniably a surface of motion, yet the movement seems induced by verbal ingenuities alone. A closer reading reveals the imagery to be substantial, its movement conceptually controlled. One becomes aware how small a part the subconscious plays in this image-letting. The lines I quoted above offer the interesting possibility of an image (perhaps, since it would have reached at least three lines, the originating one) that survived the ravages of revision only as a vestige. It was an image from card-playing jargon, if it existed, and it left behind its spade-handed blood; its Sunday-poker face; the winning card up its sleeve, transformed to 'dusters in my glove', perhaps the children driven up. The conjecture becomes less fanciful when Thomas's use of card-playing imagery elsewhere is considered, imagery expressive, as here, of a fraudulent attempt at salvation ('from Jesu's sleeve trumped up the king of spots . . . the fake gentleman in suit of spades', and the like).

It surprises me that the problem of residual imagery arises so seldom in this poetry, whose method is, as we have seen, cumulative, and grounded in 'inevitable conflict'. Where such images seem to have existed, they relate only generically to the images that replace them; there are few intrusions of meaning. Another difficulty is more often encountered. This residue is not of an image that has been worked out of a poem, but of an image that shares some secondary quality with a similar image elsewhere. The shared quality disturbs the set of the imagery in both poems. The obscurity that results is different from the obscurity of Thomas's weighted images because it is not purposive, and because it is extrinsic, although not to the poetry, yet to the individual poem. Consider these lines from three poems:

Child of the short spark in a shapeless country
Soon sets alight a long stick from the cradle;
The horizontal cross-bones of Abaddon,
You by the cavern over the black stairs,
Rung bone and blade, the verticals of Adam,
And, manned by midnight, Jacob to the stars . . .

Be by your one ghost pierced, his pointed ferrule,
Brass and the bodiless image, on a stick of folly
Star-set at Jacob's angle . . .

Master the night nor serve the snowman's brain
That shapes each bushy item of the air
Into a polestar pointed on an icicle.

The images are (relentlessly, as perhaps too often in Thomas's poems) sexual, mostly 'Freudian', similar in wording (the ladder-stick-icicle to a star) and subject (consummation). I think that this is to say almost all that can be said of the first passage, almost nothing of the other two. The Old Testament imagery, in the first, is expressive of the sexual theme; the Freudian imagery is not expressive of a religious theme. The consummation is sexual; the child is 'manned' by it. This sexual residue is left behind in the stick, the star of the second passage, But here the imagery is not primarily expressive of a sexual theme. The poem in which these lines appear is a vision of general and individual process. This consummation is of vision (at this point in the poem, of vision as illusion: 'stick of folly'). In the third, the image is not Biblical, only secondarily sexual, although its terms are Freudian. The visionary is denied who sees the crystal in the melting flake. While this is similar to the theme of the second passage, the Biblical residue from the second serves only to blur the snowflake image. The residue is left, regardless of the order in which one encounters the passages. The accumulation is greatest from the third to the first, for here a simple theme is complicated by the fuller uses to which the same imagery has been put in the other poems.

This is partly responsible for the difficulty that Robert Lowell has stated: 'Icons and natural objects are often hard to tell apart'. The harder, the more poems that are read. For the reader of one poem only, the problem of the extrinsic does not enter and the difficulty does not exist. The images in the poems are descriptive or symbolic; the two kinds are seldom found together. The resemblance in the descriptive image may be of natural objects to others:

> I lordly had the trees and leaves
> Trail with daisies and barley
> Down the rivers of the windfall light.

or of objects to emotions and ideas:

> I know her scrubbed and sour humble hands
> Lie with religion in their cramp, her threadbare
> Whisper in a damp word, her wits drilled hollow,
> Her fist of a face died clenched on a round pain.

As John Sweeney and others have pointed out, Thomas's symbols are counters from Freud, myth, magic, and the English Metaphysicals. The referents are stable and familiar. There is, too, a larger symbolism, most often expressive of rational paradox, in extended figures and conceits:

> I, in my intricate image, stride on two levels,
> Forged in man's minerals, the brassy orator
> Laying my ghost in metal,
> The scales of this twin world tread on the double,
> My half ghost in armour hold hard in death's corridor
> To my man-iron sidle.

Because the ideas of this poem are paradoxical, the imagery is intricate. In a descriptive poem, such as 'Fern Hill', the images are descriptive throughout. The sexual symbols in the lines beginning 'Deliver me, my masters', pervade the lines of that poem. There is little confusion of icons with natural objects, then, in the individual poem. The difficulty is one of residue, in images that are employed descriptively in some poems and symbolically in others. For example, the image of the Jacob's ladder, in two passages I quoted above, 'stands for' the sexual referent in one, but is descriptive – Jacob's vision resembles the vision of the poet, both grand, both illusory – in the second passage. And I shall later note a descriptive image in 'Poem in October' that is obscured for me by the symbolic residue from similar images in other poems.

But Mr Lowell's comment is meaningful in another sense, and may in fact be interpreted as a tribute to the internal consistency of Thomas's world. That world is organic, the same process activates all its parts:

> The force that through the green fuse drives the flower
> Drives my green age; that blasts the roots of trees
> Is my destroyer.
> And I am dumb to tell the crooked rose
> My youth is bent by the same wintry fever.

In so far as they are subject to one force, the flower, the tree, and the poet are not only 'in themselves', but also signs of each other and of the rest of the natural world. They are, in this special sense, both natural objects and icons; images in which they occur are descriptive and symbolic images. As the flower represents the poet, so it represents the process that moves them both; and conversely, all ranks of being are implicit in Thomas's descriptions of the process:

> Here in this spring, stars float along the void;
> Here in this ornamental winter
> Down pelts the naked weather;
> This summer buries a spring bird.
> Symbols are selected from the years'
> Slow rounding of four seasons' coasts.

It is within the scope of this 'ideal synecdoche' (the phrase is Kenneth Burke's) that all Thomas's images move. Because of it, they often seem to be expressive not of resemblance, but of micro-macrocosmic identifications. The elusiveness of the word 'like' in the following lines is, I think, the elusiveness of the distinction:

> Dawn breaks behind the eyes;
> From poles of skull and toe the windy blood
> Slides like a sea. . . .
> Night in the sockets rounds,
> Like some pitch moon, the limit of the globes;
> Day lights the bone.

But even where the images are slightest – as in the pure visual description of 'Fern Hill' – they carry the symbolic weight of what I have chosen, somewhat arbitrarily, to label 'process'. This is the basic theme of all Thomas's poems.

The 'meaning' of process, abstracted from the poems, appears to be as simple as is, for Mr Symons, the 'meaning' of the poems. Process is unity in nature; its direction is the cyclical return; the force that drives it is the generative energy in natural things. Like the 'motivating centre' of a Thomas poem, it is 'destructive and constructive at the same time'; so that not only do life and death imply each other:

> A darkness in the weather of the eye
> Is half its light . . .
> The seed that makes a forest of the loin
> Forks half its fruit, and half drops down . . .

but they are, in Thomas's mind, in essence the same. As in Donne, 'that which we call life is but a week of deaths'. The flesh as a shroud is a frequent image, and frequent are such lines as

> Bury the dead for fear that they walk to the grave in labour.

In a poem which describes the progress of the sperm and the growth of the embryo, the birth of the child is their death:

> I dreamed my genesis in sweat of death, fallen
> Twice in the feeding sea, grown
> Stale of Adam's brine until vision
> Of new man strength, I seek the sun.

In other poems, the sun is both 'meat-eating', of death, and the 'arising prodigal Sun the father', of life, of rebirth by generation[1]. The worm destroys and creates: it 'wear(s) the quick away' in one poem, and 'builds . . . my nest of mercies' in another. For Donne, again, 'the womb and the grave are but one point, they make but one station'; and in a poem by Thomas, a woman speaks to her unborn child:

> . . . No return
> Through the waves of the fat streets nor the skeleton's
> thin ways.
> The grave and my calm body are shut to your coming
> as stone,
> And the endless beginning of prodigies suffers open.

With the breakdown of the conception of 'life' and 'death' as two states, all the contrasts that are implicit in the (ever overworked, ever serviceable) words 'flux' and 'absolute' necessarily break down too. Thus the German poet Rainer Maria Rilke is able to pass without transition from the statement of one idea to the statement of the other, when he writes:

> Affirmation of life and affirmation of death reveal themselves as one . . . The true form of life extends through both regions, the blood of the mightiest circulation pulses through both:

1. John Sweeney quotes these lines.

> there is neither a here nor a beyond, but only the great unity . . .[1]

And thus for Thomas the 'beyond' is 'here', the 'absolute' is located in the 'flux':

> . . . I am dumb to tell a weather's wind
> How time has ticked a heaven round the stars.
>
> The masses of the infant-bearing sea
> Erupt, fountain, and enter to utter forever
> Glory glory glory
> The sundering ultimate kingdom of genesis' thunder.

Water and sky often meet in images and symbols of absolute-in-flux. Thomas works variations into the pattern. Birds wing their way through a congeries of marine imagery:

> The shipyards . . . hide a navy of doves.
> Always good luck, praised the finned in the feather bird.
> Then she bird . . . sails the goose plucked sea.

Elsewhere, the sky spouts gushers, the sea flies, anchors ride like gulls, birds of burden are heavy with the drowned, and 'over the glazed lakes skate the shapes of fishes flying'. A characteristic bird is the shearwater, which skims the sea in flight, a characteristic phenomenon the waterspout, a whirlwind of spray and mist.

Thomas pays this process the reverence that is an absolute's due by expressing it often in the traditional images of devotion and quest. The sacrament is almost always a wordly partaking. In four images from three poems, time is a grail, gospel, saint, and priest; other images bring together the heavens and heaven, tear and church, snow and parish grave and font, dust and saviour. In the Biblical imagery itself, Christ is 'Jack Christ', 'Jack of Christ';

1. In a letter cited in the 'Commentary' to *Duino Elegies*.

his passion is Everyman's. There is a frequent identification of Christ with Adam, and, generally of Christian imagery with the imagery of process.

A usual function of Biblical imagery is neglected. In these poems Satan never tempts, Adam never falls, stern gods never lay down laws; redemption is generation, the Judgment is the day of death, of re-immersion in process. Morality is a theme for only two poems of Thomas's that I have read. In one these, there is the offhand allusion:

> The wisemen tell me that the garden gods
> Twined good and evil on an eastern tree. .

and its dismissal:

> We in our Eden knew the secret guardian
> In sacred waters that no frost could harden,
> And in the mighty mornings of the earth . . .

The other poem is as bare of imagery and as close to public statement as a poem by Thomas can be. Despite the elegiac tone and tread, I suspect that he is here defining a position in order to have done with it:

> Good and bad, two ways
> Of moving about your death . . .
> Blow away like breath
> Go crying through you and me
> And the souls of all men
> Into the innocent
> Dark, and the guilty dark, and good
> Death, and bad death . . .
> And all your deeds and words,
> Each truth, each lie,
> Die in unjudging love.

Still, he has not wholly committed himself. The title of the poem is 'This Side of the Truth'; and to write of 'the innocent dark, and the guilty dark', the 'good death, and bad death', is, the beat on 'dark' and 'death' notwithstanding, in some way to distinguish them. There is some evidence in Thomas's later poems that his world is developing. The development (I shall consider it later) may be for him the other side of the truth of process and intrinsically moral: the greater its extent, the 'better'. It remains true, however, that the chief theme of Biblical imagery is one of celebration, and not of choice.

The affirmation of process, yes. But there are other images, expressive of process, which have a sharply contrasting tone. Time, the pursued, becomes the pursuer in images that recall Andrew Marvell's 'winged chariot':

> When, like a running grave, time tracks you down . . .

> Time, in a folly's rider, like a county man
> Over the vault of ridings with his hound at heel,
> Drives forth my men, my children, from the hanging
> south.

In three early images, life is a sore, time or death an acid that will burn it out. And, as Marshall Stearns points out, the sexual imagery of Thomas's early poems is sometimes an imagery of almost 'psychopathic' revulsion.

The moon, its reflected light, its sea-flux influence, symbolises the seeming, but illusory, transcendence of death by the artist, the Christian, the lover. The 'carved bird', undying artifact, recurs often in these images; and, in one of the few direct echoes in Thomas's poetry, the Byzantium of William Butler Yeats is recalled and rejected:

> Moonfall and sailing emperor, pale as their tide-print
> Hear by death's accident the clocked and dashed-down
> spire
> Strike the sea hour through bellmetal.

The theme of art as illusion, faith as illusion, finds its most concise expression in the short poem 'The spire cranes':

> . . . Its statue is an aviary.
> From the stone nest it does not let the feathery
> Carved birds blunt their striking throats on the salt
>   gravel . . .

The aviary, contrived and confining, is the 'artifice of eternity' as it appears to Thomas. The comment in 'feathery/Carved' is clear. The poem ends:

> Those craning birds are choice for you, songs that
>   jump back
> To the built voice, or fly with winter to the bells,
> But do not travel down dumb wind like prodigals.

The poet implies that the choice is none, since both art and faith ('nightingale and psalm' in another poem, the 'voice' and 'bells' here) are illusory when they deny process.

It is the 'vision' – again, the label is mine, although Thomas uses the word often – of process that transforms the early imagery of denial ('carved bird', moon, dark, disease, and the sexual images) to the later imagery of affirmation (sun, Son, the Biblical and devotional images):

> These once-blind eyes have breathed a wind of visions . . .
> And, mild as pardon from a cloud of pride,
> The terrible world my brother bares his skin.

It sees the absolute-in-flux, and not an absolute of illusion; process, and not the individual life or death. As in the lines from 'Vision and Prayer',

> . . . I am lost in the blinding
> One. The sun roars at the prayer's end,

the 'I' is lost in the 'One'. The function of vision is to point the Way:

> . . . Seasons must be challenged or they totter
> Into a chiming quarter
> Where, punctual as death, we ring the stars . . .
>
> Murmur of spring nor crush the cockerel's eggs,
> Nor hammer back a season in the figs,
> But graft these four-fruited ridings on your country . . .

The forms of life or death in season, as the season demands; but the theme is not, I think, properly subjected to Mr Symons's rebuke. A revelation, it is expressed in images of revelation. The coming of vision is likened to the breaking of day. Hymen and caul, shell and chrysalis (and, once removed, the 'film of eye', the 'cataracted eye') are also broken in images of consummation and conception, or of birth. In more recent poems, the daybreak images remain, but the related sexual cluster has been replaced by similar images involving 'locks'. (John Berryman has remarked the prevalence of this imagery.) The locks are of an illusory art or faith:

> There was a saviour
> Rarer than radium
> Commoner than water, crueller than truth . . .
> Prisoners of wishes locked their eyes
> In the jails and studies of his keyless smiles.

Because 'keys' are either unavailable or ineffectual, the locks are broken by vision or by death, for process is reaffirmed by both:

> When the morning was waking over the war
> He put on his clothes and stepped out and he died,
> The locks yawned loose and a blast blew them wide . . .
> And the craters of his eyes grew springshoots and fire
> When all the keys shot from the locks and rang.

But to celebrate in vision is not, of course, to reconcile in fact. The problem of reconciliation – of the individual with the general process – is a major theme in Thomas's poems. More than any other, the theme sets his poetry apart from the poetry of the neo-Romantics, whose Gothic landscapes cannot sustain an imagery of paradox. In a brilliant conceit, he distinguishes the two movements:

Let the wax disc babble
Shames and the damp dishonours, the relic scraping.
These are your years' recorders. The circular world
stands still.

The recording and the turn-table that supports it move together, but there is another movement: the needle moves across the recording and plays it, the babble of the individual life ('all your deeds and words, each truth, each lie') is played out and begun again, while process turns back upon itself perpetually. Donne, in one of his sermons, employs a similar figure, to express the difference of life on earth from life in heaven:

> This life is a circle, made with a compass, that passes from point to point; that life is a circle stamped with a print, an endless, and perfect circle, as soon as it begins.

Thomas's 'circular world' is Donne's 'perfect circle' analogised to time and space.

This, then, is the mystic's plight; he cannot escape an individual history by a vision of continuity:

'Who could snap off the shapeless print
From your tomorrow-treading shade
With oracle for eye? . . .
Who could hack out your unsucked heart,
O green and unborn and undead?'
I saw time murder me.

Thomas makes use of a richly varied imagery to express the idea that what is seen by vision as duration is, in terms of the individual life, only the sum of intervals. In 'Then was my neophyte', the image is of a motion picture film, run off in reels. In 'Light breaks where no sun shines', men's lives are 'waste allotments'. In 'Especially when the October wind', the 'busy heart . . . sheds the syllabic blood'. 'Busy' here suggests the 'red veins full of money' elsewhere, blood to be portioned out in payment for measures of life. In another poem, the flesh is a:

> pinned-around-the-spirit
> Cut-to-measure . . .
> Suit for a serial sum
> On the first of each hardship . . .

This (merely clever, I think, rather than genuinely witty) poem begins, significantly, 'once *below* a time'.

Two recent poems have the death of a child as their subject. In 'A Refusal to Mourn', continuity is affirmed, but with the loss of compassion for the individual death:

> I shall not murder
> The mankind of her going with a grave truth . . .
> After the first death, there is no other.

In 'Ceremony After a Fire Raid', the tension is more finely adjusted:

> Forgive
> Us forgive
> Us your death that myselves the believers
> May hold it in a great flood
> Till the blood shall spurt,
> And the dust shall sing like a bird
> As the grains blow, as your death grows, through our
> heart.

Another aspect of the problem is that of the mystic, who celebrates the whole of life in vision, but lives in the realm of choice; of the artist, as observer and as participant:

> My man of leaves and the bronze root, mortal,
>   unmortal,
> I, in my fusion of rose and male motion . . .
>
> How shall my animal . . .
> Who should be furious,
> Drunk as a vineyard snail, flailed like an octopus,
> Roaring, crawling, quarrel
> With the outside weathers,
> The natural circle of the discovered skies
> Drawn down to its weird eyes?

The snail is a frequent image: it feeds on one vine of the vineyard; its horns are the horns of the one-many dilemma. A descriptive image in 'Poem in October' has a non-descriptive implication for the reader who recalls Thomas's use of similar imagery elsewhere:

> Pale rain over the dwindling harbour
> And over the sea wet church the size of a snail
> With its horns through mist . . .

The theme is implicit in the short poem 'The Marriage of a Virgin'. A man replaces the sun or the Son, pagan or Christian god, as the virgin's lover. This is the first of the two stanzas:

> Walking alone in a multitude of loves when morning's
>   light
> Surprised in the opening of her nightlong eyes
> His golden yesterday asleep upon the iris
> And this day's sun leapt up the sky out of her thighs
> Was miraculous virginity old as loaves and fishes,
> Though the moment of a miracle is unending lightning
> And the shipyards of Galilee's footprints hide a navy
>   of doves.

John Sweeney has suggested that Thomas may have had in mind a stanza from Marvell's 'The Gallery'; dawn, thighs, manna '(loaves and fishes'), and dove appear in both:

> But, on the other side, th' art drawn
> Like to Aurora in the dawn;
> When in the East she slumb'ring lies,
> And stretches out her milky thighs;
> While all the morning quire does sing,
> And manna falls, and roses spring;
> And, at thy feet, the wooing doves
> Sit perfecting their harmless loves.

The changes he has worked are interesting. It is the mystic who consorts with god, who lives in the 'moment', 'unending' although 'old' in time ('the still point of the turning world' in T. S. Eliot). It is the artist who celebrates without participation, 'alone in a multitude of loves', as Christ with the multitude. This is the second stanza:

> No longer will the vibrations of the sun desire on
> Her deepsea pillow where once she married alone,
> Her heart all ears and eyes, lips catching the avalanche
> Of the golden ghost who ringed with his streams her
> mercury bone,
> Who under the lids of her windows hoisted his golden
> luggage,
> For a man sleeps where fire leapt down and she learns
> through his arm
> That other sun, the jealous coursing of the unrivalled
> blood.

'Alone' is repeated. The imagery suggests to me one method ('her heart all ears and eyes') and the responsibility ('luggage' in its original meaning a heavy burden) of the artist, and the mystic oneness with experience (by implying a reversal of the sexual roles: the ghost 'rings 'her 'mercury bone'; and mercury is a male theosophical symbol). Finally, with the multitude gone, blood is 'unrivalled' (both senses) yet 'jealous'. The shift, then, is not only from god to man, but also from the one to·the one-of-many, from celebration to choice.

Thomas has treated in several poems the theme of the mystic, saint, angel, saviour who has 'fallen'. In most of these, it is an illusory art or faith, and not the vision of process, that has been overcome; but this is irrelevant here. In them, the images that describe life after the fall are very often images of confrontation, conflict, choice:

> Cry joy that this witchlike midwife second . . .
> Makes a with a flick of the thumb and sun
> A thundering bullring of your silent and girl-circled
> island.
>
> . . . To love and labour and kill
> In quick, sweet, cruel light till the locked ground sprout
> out.
>
> Now in the dark there is only yourself and myself.

In Thomas's later poems especially, vision seems not only to celebrate process, but also to inform it. 'Man be my metaphor'. Man, as part of the natural world, is subject to process too, and their resemblance in this allows the poet to speak of external nature in terms of man. But man is Thomas's metaphor in another sense. The consciousness of man shapes the natural world by its awareness of it; man is the metaphor through which the qualities of things find expression:

> O who is glory in the shapeless maps,
> Now make the world of me as I have made
> A merry manshape of your walking circle.

The images of flux are often qualified by adjectival interpreters:

> Am I not all of you by the directed sea
> Where bird and shell are babbling in my tower?

> Your heart is luminous in the watched dark.

> Dust be your saviour under the conjured soil.

In 'Ceremony After a Fire Raid', Thomas laments the death of a child

> Who was priest and servants,
> Word, singers, and tongue
> In the cinder of the little skull,
> Who was the serpent's
> Nightfall and the fruit like a sun,
> Man and woman undone,
> Beginning crumbled back to darkness . . .

The singer is the word; the dancer, as in Yeats, the dance; the garden disappears when the lovers leave it. In 'Vision and Prayer' the life cycle, 'spiral of ascension' (compare Yeats's 'gyre') is transformed from a process in suspense to one weighted with light by 'the happening of saints to their vision', by 'turn[ing] the corner of prayer and burn[ing] /In a blessing of the sudden/ Sun'. Process, the subject of vision, needs man to 'happen' to it to give it life. On another level, Thomas's descriptive imagery is often in the fanciful terms of a consciousness that stays and a world that comes and goes, as in these lines from 'Fern Hill':

> As I rode to sleep the owls were bearing the farm away . . .
> And then to awake, and the farm, like a wanderer white
> With the dew, come back, the cock on his shoulder.

Even in the death of childhood, it is the physical scene that is remiss:

> . . . . the farm forever fled from the childless land.

In 'Poem in October', the transformer is memory:

> Here were fond climates and sweet singers suddenly
> come . . .
> And the blue altered sky
> Streamed again a wonder of summer.

> The following lines are from *Map of Love:* 'Four':

> We lying by seas and, watching yellow
> And the grave sea, mock who deride
> Who follow the red rivers, hollow
> Alcove of words out of cicada shade,
> For in this yellow grave of sand and sea
> A calling for colour calls with the wind
> That's grave and gay as grave and sea
> Sleeping on either hand.
> The lunar silences . . . the dry tide-master
> Ribbed between desert and water storm,
> Should cure our ills of the water
> With a one-coloured calm . . .
> Bound by the sovereign strip, we lie
> Watch yellow, wish for wind to blow away
> The strata of the shore and drown red rock;
> But wishes breed not, neither
> Can we fend off rock arrival,
> Lie watching yellow until the golden weather
> Breaks, O my heart's blood, like a heart and hill.

Much of this is familiar: lovers 'lie'; the way of the lover and the poet is the same (by the circular 'mock who deride who follow . . . [who] hollow'); the moon 'should' cure but does not. The imagery accumulates: the blood, heart, dawn, and calm all partake of the 'red' of river and rock; the day, heart, storm, and strata-hill – as well as the sexual tension – 'break' together. But the theme can, I think, be stated, in the terms I have been using, as the transformation of process by vision. The lovers 'lie watching' (three times repeated) until yellow becomes gold, night becomes day. Process is already the 'sovereign' (golden) strip, joining the water and the rock, in line thirteen. The transformation is effected only when, in the last two lines, vision sees it as such.

To bolster the metaphoric with non-metaphoric props is, as I have tried to suggest, a questionable practice; yet it is interesting to note that the idea that is implicit in *Map of Love:* 'Four' and similar poems of Thomas's, is, generally, an important one in the German philosophers after Kant. To Coleridge, writing under their influence, the best poetry is 'true idealism necessarily perfecting itself in realism, realism refining itself into idealism'. And when Thomas, acknowledging the influence of Freud, speaks of:

> . . . the record of my individual struggle from darkness towards some measure of light . . . To be stripped of darkness is to be clean, to strip of darkness is to make clean . . . My poetry is, or should be, useful to others for its individual recording of that same struggle with which they are necessarily acquainted . . .

he is perhaps moving closer to these men as, with Freud's help, he moves away from Freud. The phrasing recalls that of the idealists: the identification of the 'individual' with the general movement; the 'necessity' of the movement (implicitly contrasted with the 'freedom' which is its end); and the coupling of words for passion and action, for the self and the external ('to be stripped . . . to strip', 'to be . . . to make'). Considering, in the light of

Thomas's statement, the various redemption themes in his later poems, and the gradual shift in imagery discussed above – from the dark, dense, and Freudian images to the clearer, sparser, Christian and mythic images – one may inquire whether his dialectic of composition does not in fact correspond to a dialectic of real movement in his world. It is not impossible to fit the linear 'struggle from darkness towards . . . light' to the 'creative, recreative, destructive, and contradictory nature of the motivating centre' of the earlier quotation. Process, the cyclical return, is not denied by the idea; it requires only that the mind and heart evolve an ever fuller relationship with it.

If Thomas is indeed moving in the direction I have indicated, his next poems may be expected to contain fewer, but more extensive, images; and, within the image itself, an identification, by whatever means, of objects and ideas, of objects and emotions:

> . . . gesture and psalm
> Storm me forever over her grave until
> The stuffed lung of the fox twitch and cry Love
> And the strutting fern lay seeds on the black sill.

There is much in Thomas's poems that I have not treated (I should have enjoyed writing about the sense of humour he displays in some of them). Emotions and sensations are, clearly, as central to his imagery as are ideas, and not finally to be distinguished from them. Abstracted from the world of the poems, the ideas I have considered are meaningless. Criteria that are applicable to them as ideas are inapplicable to them as ideas embodied in images. Yet to trace them is, I think, to say something in answer to critics of Thomas's 'black magical bubblings' (Mr Grigson), and to those of his admirers who damn him with diffuse praise. I have been contending only that Thomas is a poet who, like most poets, thinks before he writes. It seems to me that he deserves to be read as much for his sense – his own kind of sense, admittedly – as for his sound and fury.

One Ring-tailed Roarer to Another[1]

THEODORE ROETHKE

HAS THE RING-TAILED ROARER begun to snore? The limp spirit of a Peruvian prince taken over his wild psyche? Has he shoved down the throttle only to find a ramshackle model of patch-work fancies fluttering to a short cough? What time's the train of his spirit due? To what wonders are we now exposed?

I say: The swish of his tail's wakened another wind. The times he has stood in the white presence, the muse blowing through him with the true fury! Behold him now, a snout in the sun, father and mother imploring! Long may he wallow.

But, ah, where the light is, strange forms of life gather; and what creeps come after him from the cracks, their hard eyes glittering, not lovely like mice, but beetles and toads even God would like to forget: those sea-weevils winding their slimy fingers about him, carrying out his laundry and then hiding it, – May the muse spit in their ears! – those loathly wearers of other men's clothing, those ghleuphs, ouphs, oscars, lewd louies, yahoos and vultures hovering over dead and live horses; hyenas of sensibility; serpentine swallowers of their own slimy tails; dingle-dangle dilly-boys; anglo-saxon apostles of refinement; ageing coy sibylline co-eds; makers of tiny surprises; tweed-coated cliché-masters;

1. Review of *In Country Sleep and Other Poems*, *Poetry*, LXXI (December 1952), 1841–86; appearing over the pseudonym 'Winterset Rothberg', this was written at Thomas's request.

grave senatorial language-swindlers; freak monsters with three frankfurters for toes; sleazy flea-bitten minor mephistoes, playing with the Idea of Good and Evil, – May he blow them all away with a single breath'! And I give them another curse: May they be condemned forever to a perpétual reading of their own works.

What he wants is another Love: the far Son in his eye, not a thick Sunday of white thighs. So he babbles and laughs out of a shrewd mouth, the mournful daughters with him spilling the seed of his soul, praying lovers together in a wordy original song. Holy supposes come out of his mouth and nose. He's bald where it suits the sun; a home-made halo he has in a sour country where at least they love a bard. *And* sing! O the chances he takes with the womanly words as we all wish and cry Never enough of this. Suppose he does beat the last breath from a lively meaning, he never escapes from himself without giving us more than we'd ever dare ask. Was it him I saw step from a cloud, alone as a lark, singing the things we can never know, taking a bird's grace and the breath from us, speaking and thinking with his rude flesh, not a man slowed to a walk, – as if pigs could sing and as God's spy he weeps for us all? Need such a Promethean keeper of fire and secrets look to his meanings, learned and tactful as Wystan? Should we love what we have and not wish for another thing? Here's a great master of sweating who runs and rumbles in and out of his own belly, no staid husband of the dry sad disciplines.

This rare heedless fornicator of language speaks with the voice of angels and ravens, casting us back where the sea leaps and the strudding witch walks by a deep well. May he live forever in those black-and-white dreams, a centaur of something more than he knows, while the white maidens peep from behind the hedges and all the juttiest ends begin talking at once. In a light time the tempter's wrong, – flesh from another dream, ghost on a thorn or a high stone, a wonder a wave out far; a full-blown bladder in love, close to shining, the father and son of a smile.

But I say! In him God is still poor.

Wherefore, mother of fair love and the speckled hen, attend him in this hour. Angel of true serenity, nestle in his nerves. May this motion remind him of rest. His help is still in him, more than a trance of voice or skin. In sleep, in country sleep, he comes to believe.

Dylan Thomas: Yes and No

TWO REVIEWS OF ONE BOOK

CONTROVERSY HAS RAGED like a snowstorm since the early winter in literary and artistic circles. *Collected Poems* 1934–1952, by Dylan Thomas, has been acclaimed the book of the year and awarded the Foyle Prize of £250.

But this seemingly favourable reception has not been unanimous – far from it – and the feeling aroused for and against has led the Editorial Board of the *Poetry Review* to take a unique step in book-reviewing. They have requested two members of the Board, widely divergent in their attitudes to poetry, to contribute reviews, candid – independent – and unknown to each other.

I

The Interior Life

JOHN GRADDON

During a recent evening at Portman Square, Monsieur René Darin, Cultural Counsellor to the French Embassy, remarked in a brilliant commentary on English and French poetry that to a Frenchman there is a clear affinity in all English poetry from Beowulf to Dylan Thomas.

The inability to recognise the inheritance in a modern writer is not only an English characteristic nor peculiar to this age. The grudging and partial recognition of Dylan Thomas as a poet can be compared with the same failure in the case of Ezra Pound. Pound, the scholar with the chilled mathematical rune; Thomas, the Celt, with a song.

The work of Ezra Pound exhibits a structure with calculated beam and stress, the frame filled in with the material of his experience and from prodigious diggings in the mines of forgotten scholarship. There is this unity in all he has written because it flows from an integrated source – the architect is clear as to his purpose.

With Dylan Thomas the work comes from the one person who is many persons, whose work may even prove to reflect all persons. It is the projection of a personality in process of finding universality, not only in many people but in all the strata of consciousness of one human being – the poet himself.

To a great extent he is, of course, unreadable at a first scanning and impenetrable at a first hearing, but the reward is all the greater when repetitive familiarity allows contact to be made. Then comes a close and personal identification, and the living word expresses life.

It is the reader soaked in the traditional English style who finds him the more incomprehensible. Perhaps the reason is that the traditionalist brings into play and relationship only that compartment of his mind labelled 'Poetry'. The uninitiated relate him by association and comparison with personal experience and the word-images often seem to focus astonishingly, obtaining an unmistakable response.

Can Dylan Thomas be fully understood with all the charged meaning of his selected expression? When, biographically, letters and scholarship have had their day with his life and work, there is no doubt that much that is now half-hidden and obscure will be made plain. He is the child of his nation, conditioned, as all of us, by his hereditary equipment and contained within the period of his life. These collected poems are as revealing and rewarding as any

Freudian analytical sheaf, but precisely compressed by an expert in mood; not, be it noted by a moody expert, for he is, essentially, a singer and his writings must be spoken aloud. They are songs of a disquiet world wherein pretence and prettiness, the façade of goodwill, the camouflage of living for to-day, the inherent Micawber-hope for the future, are discounted or discarded; and life as it is for the poet, is sung in complex, intricately-conceived imagery.

He is not imitative, save in the sense of heritage; seldom slipshod unless it is called so when words cannot encompass his full meaning; in all respects honest, for he is none other than himself; a master of his craft, yet sometimes the slave of his wordy invention; as much a reviver of language as Christopher Fry, a Donne to his Marlowe; and achieving so often 'that momentary peace which is a poem'.

To understand that part of his work which is truly difficult, the same intuitive study is required as for any other unusual work of art. The image in a couple of words playing on one's mind may unravel into the images of association and contradiction that went to its making. The vision in a single line, particularly a 'first' line, living for a time in one's life, will inevitably bring the desire to know the second – and then the third:

> 'Altarwise by owl-light in the half-way house';
> 'Where once the waters of your face Spun to my screws . . .';
> 'Hold hard, these ancient minutes in the cuckoo's month';
> 'When all my five and country senses see';
> 'I turn the corner of prayer and burn';
> 'Do not go gentle into that good night';
> 'On almost the incendiary eve';
> 'Never until the mankind making';
> 'A grief ago';

'The force that through the green fuse drives the flower';
'I, in my intricate image, stride in two levels';
'Our eunuch dreams, all seedless in the light'.

For whom does Dylan Thomas write? – 'For the love of man', he avows, 'and in praise of God'.

In my craft or sullen art
Exercised in the still night
When only the moon rages
And the lovers lie abed
With all their griefs in their arms,
I labour by singing light
Not for ambition or bread
Or the strut and trade of charms
On the ivory stages
But for the common wages
Of their most secret heart.

The emotive basis of life remains constant. Beauty, truth, and love have been hymned with lyrical simplicity. Must poetry remain the only art graven in the cere clothes of its past?

The mobile lyricism of water can connote, to a modern mind, the elements capable of devastating a city or animating the industry of a nation. Shall the poet of to-day disdain the prospect of civilisation and culture in eruption and contemplate waterfalls?

Biologically, the theme of love is not for song, but any emotion transmuted by the human mind has its own dignity and beauty. Must it always be disguised in voluminous Victorian petticoats so that the shades of our ancestors will not be affronted?

Must a modern poem be embraced at a glance and its memory loiter for but a thought or two?

It is true, of course, that the unusual or complex art statement may be as phoney as that made by any street-market medicine vendor, but the generalised simplicity is equally unreal and false.

The mind does not consist wholly of Freudian caverns of recessive and repulsive night. The imagination can also play within the fantasies and intricacies of palaces of great beauty and delight.

With their heritage behind them, poets, still alive, will express themselves in the terms of the age in which they live. If they are not read, if no effort is made to understand their message and their song, then we relinquish our destiny and deserve our fate.

II

The Acid Test

GEOFFREY JOHNSON

Much as I value time, I have spent a week of evenings in a sincere attempt to discover why there has been such a chorus of eulogy lavished on this book. After such a whirl of words from poet and panegyrists I could coolly retort, as Nym did to Pistol's hyperboles, 'I am not Barbason: you cannot conjure me'.

But my response, I hope, goes deeper: it is that a poet, however much obscured by rant and bombast, is there right enough in Dylan Thomas, but that he is being done a vicious disservice by flatterers who belaud him to the skies for the wrongest of reasons.

Has there not been an overswing of the pendulum? Poetry-readers, justifiably sick to death of the thin-lipped and intellectualised verse we have had foisted on us, have been too eager to acclaim any sign of its opposite – the sensuous, the sensual, the rhapsodically romantic, in current jargon the visceral, or even the apocalyptic. The dissolution of almost all critical standards by two world wars, and the consequent decadence, hankering for novelty at whatever cost, have contributed further to this over-praise bordering on idolatry. To get away from the fevers of the moment, and to take a sane long look into the future, is this poet likely to release in real achievement his obviously powerful lyrical potential, or will he be, largely as a result of this age's encouragement of his worst verbal excesses, a pathetic warning in some unborn Isaac D'Israeli's *Curiosities of Literature*?

In the first place, his output is not large, nor is it varied. It is monotonously egocentric, and nearly all of it written at the top of the voice; much of it looks backward to childhood, a tendency which in much greater writers like Wordsworth and Barrie is by the same critics vehemently denounced. A hallmark of a major poet is fecundity of ideas, variety of theme, range and vision; the 'I', as in Hardy, is a mask through which the poet speaks, and speaks intelligibly with largeness and nobility of utterance to and for all men; it is never the merely subjective and personal pronoun. Except in a handful of poems, already too much eulogised and anthologised, this major quality seems to be missing. After all the cauls, wombs, processes of parturition and 'I smelt the maggot in my stool', it seems that this writer has discovered two truths, that we all have sexual organs and that we shall most assuredly die.

It certainly cannot be for his matter, over-sexed and death-obsessed as our age is, that he is so belauded; it can only be due to that other disease in modern criticism, its neurotic preoccupation with idiosyncrasy of manner. My contention is that any style which draws attention to itself, to style as such, is bad style, and the less obtrusive it is, as in dress, the better. This extravagant disproportion of idea to the clothing of language, the solemn flamboyance that is entirely humourless, is no new phenomenon. But let the quietly-laughing Prince of Poets (in *Hamlet*, the Players, Act II) speak on the subject:

> Out, out, thou strumpet, Fortune! All you gods,
> In general synod take away her power,
> Break all the spokes and fellies from her wheel
> And bowl the round nave down the hill of heaven
> As low as to the fiends . . .

This tongue-in-the-cheek hyperbole, even at a distance of three centuries and despite the obstacles of language-changes during that time, make, for me at least, more poetic sense than the following, one of many passages composed in all seriousness and in what is or should be in the immediacy of contemporary idiom:

> Altarwise by owl-light in the half-way house
> The gentleman lay graveward with his furies;
> Abaddon in the hangnail cracked from Adam,
> And, from his fork, a dog among the fairies,
> The atlas-eater with a jaw for news,
> Bit out the mandrake with to-morrow's scream . . .

Shakespeare writes bombast and knows it: Mr Thomas writes bombast and doesn't. That is the difference.

To apply the Arnoldian touchstone-passage method further, let us place beside the magical 'When the hounds of Spring are on Winter's traces' of the despised Swinburne, and by no means a favourite poet of mine, any of the writer's rhapsodical nature poems, even 'Over Sir John's Hill', and the descent in quality is obvious. Both poems are born of that fine excess which soars up to the edge and almost tumbles into nonsense, but the first is intellectually controlled and articulated, memorably and inevitably said: the second is a loose association of impassioned words trusting to luck and chance alliteration for psychological linkage with the reader.

Now to our own day. The poet who resembles Dylan Thomas most in rich endowment of awareness to sounds, colours and smells, in fiery impetus and imagistic exuberance, is Roy Campbell, some of whose best work was composed approximately at the same age. Irrespective of traditionalism or any other 'ism', let us judge between poetry in the raw and poetry triumphantly achieved, by comparing two poems of roughly the same length, 'And Death shall have no Dominion' with 'I love to see, when leaves depart'.

Or take Christopher Fry, whose imagery is just as original, often as extravagant, but who contrives to be vastly more intelligible than 'In the White Giant's Thigh'. Just one more example: 'A Refusal to mourn the Death, by Fire, of a Child in London', which has been breathed more than once from the radio as if from Apollo's holy of holies. This poem is certainly much above the ordinary, despite its awkward and affected title, despite its opening broken-backed thirteen lines without a single stop or comma, despite all sorts of uneasiness about what on earth entering 'the round Zion of the waterbead' or sowing 'my salt seed in the least valley of sackcloth' can mean, and above all despite the doubts whether a poet can be truly moved and so elaborately ingenious in verbal artifice at the same time. Let us then turn to 'The Children' from the *Expectant Silence* of William Soutar, a Scotch poet who died in 1943. The first is inadequately realised and vaguely concluded; it is personal and local; the second is beautifully disciplined and without obvious artifice; it is as lucid as running water; it is also impersonal and cosmic; it speaks for all bombed children.

I leave out of account this collection's Dali-esque dither and dazzle, its surrealistic and often nightmarish inconsequence, its usual bag of modernistic tricks – the Owenesque off-rhyme, the internal jingle, the displacement of true rhyme by what is cacophonous and barbarous ('flesh bit', 'ashpit'), the Hopkins-like splutters and explosions, the strained-for perversions of normal speech ('Once below a time'), the naïve device, revived from Apollinaire, of printing verse in the shapes of tiles, lozenges and hatchets; for all these dodges are already on the way to the limbo where they belong. What I am concerned about is my inability to grasp for more than a line or so what really matters, the poet at the core of the welter. A glorious roar of sound intermixed with clashing pebbles of words, with flying foams and spumes of half-sense, is what all genuine poets emotionally experience before authentic creation can begin. But this sensory or visceral excitement, though indispensable, is not enough, not nearly enough. It is in the assembling, the co-ordinating, the giving of significant shape, coherence and beauty to these half-impressions and half-intuitions that the real art of poetry is seen. I am frankly bewildered by this failure of mine to find here this higher quality of the Poet (or Maker). That is, except in those infrequent comparative lulls in the verbal hurricane, where the writer is at his clearest and best, for example, 'The force that through . . .' 'This bread I break', 'The hand that signed the paper'. Hotspur's gibe at this perplexity in not comprehending another's language is witty enough –

I think there is no man speaks better Welsh,

– but it will not do for me. What I honestly want to know is why, as a scholar, as one who is not unacquainted practically with the intricacies and ardours of verse-composition, and after a week of evening readings with a headache at the end, and not a single line of this volume left memorably ringing in my mind, I can get more sense out of an Anglo-Saxon riddle in the Exeter book than I can from scores of passages of which this is a fair example:–

This story's monster has a serpent caul,
Blind in the coil scrams round the blazing outline,
Measures his own length on the garden wall
And breaks his shell in the last shocked beginning;
A crocodile before the chrysalis,
Before the fall from love the flying heartbone,
Winged like a sabbath ass this children's piece
Uncredited blows Jericho on Eden.

Mine is far from being the despairing cry of a paraphrasing fourth-former; for no poem of any worth can be paraphrased. But surely we may ask what the general drift of many a poem in this collection can be? For me at least Mr Thomas's means of communication are almost always ineffective, and communication is the essence and ultimate criterion of art in any form.

Dylan Thomas: Rhetorician in in Mid-Career

CID CORMAN

THAT THOMAS IS A VERY LIMITED POET, despite his birth-(love)-death ambit, is almost a constant self-testimony in his work and particularly in this new book. There is a note of self-pity that is more or less implicit in his previous books and comes to the top more explicitly in poems like 'Lament' and 'Do Not Go Gentle into that Good Night'. He is aware of it, and plays it through a lusty or gentle humour or by carrying his mourning into compassion. The desire for innocence is great. His struggle for 'life' becomes more desperately rhetorical. But particulars are needed.

Most of Thomas's poems are noticeably local in colouring, of the Welsh locale – of course, as by birthright, Carmarthenshire. (His stories, which deserve special consideration, more outrightly so.) He starts from a haunt where music and reverence are companionable and ripe. No one has not noticed his powerful rhetoric, his Biblical breath, and his Anglo-Saxon vocabulary. Lustiness and tenderness confer in his poems. 'When I was a windy boy and a bit / And the black spit of the chapel fold, / (Sighed the old ram rod, dying of women), / I tiptoed shy in the gooseberry wood, / . . . / And on seesaw sunday nights I wooed / Whoever I would with my wicked eyes . . .' Compassion, yes, is the centre of his soul's most conscious development and the point on which his pivot spins. The isolation of the dying body prints lament on the earlier boyish arrogance, which Thomas in interview once remarked a backward envy for. His loneliness is fat with the need of an overbearing love. The dilemma of life as a self bound in body finds its god riding pity. Any man's art is his answer.

I fix this discussion upon what seems to me a crucial poem in Thomas's career, his 'Over Sir John's Hill'. Here the poet is close to home. He is seen at his compassionate most; he grieves, as so many of his verses do, for a world pledged to war, for the weak, the innocent, the many. His hero is inevitably the child, the player and playmate, the boy on the tumbling hill, the girl in the bushes, the sparrows, the bird-breasted, the hunchbacked and aged. The poet is eulogiser of the hot-and-cold inevitable ends. The verses hover and hymn, dramatise with a lyrical break, in much the same way as a choral passage in the *Agamemnon* of Aeschylus about the outbreak of the Trojan War. They are wide with dignity and a sweet care for the language of metaphor, whether in the soft music of 'I open the leaves of the water at a passage, / Of psalms and shadows among the pincered sandcrabs prancing' or the judging incantation and prayer (ah, the paradoxical twinge) of '. . . the led-astray birds whom God, for their breast of whistles, / Have mercy on, / God in his whirlwind silence save, who marks the sparrows hail, / For their souls' song'.

But the poet, in his prayer, is not concerned with either expiration or pity (though he may unintentionally draw on both): he is concerned here with the quality of mercy. And the quality of the poem, and of Thomas basically too, is the quality of his mercy. There is the event of the death of the sparrow, the occurrence of the inevitable depredations of the hawk. Judgment finds the guilt of the sparrow in the sparrow's innocence. The compulsion to compassion moves the poet. He finds his honesty transcending his prayer, his heart's duty in the ceremony of inscription; finds it his hard music to 'grave, / Before the lunge of the night, the notes on this time-shaken / Stone for the sake of the souls of the slain birds sailing'. (Compare Skelton's 'Philip Sparrow'.)

Against this enterprise of the poet, Thomas poses, lets stand, the churchly heron, the calm hungry-but-organized bird, who also stands spectator to the disaster of 'slain birds' and, though itself a member of the tribe, is the formal voice, the liturgy in a late whisper, offering its neighbourly complaint, apart.

Thomas speaks for the poet as the cantor, the incantatory scribe. And yet the tone reaches to an incipient self-lament, the struggle is in the single soul. The involvement is whole. The mask presumes the face.

All the poems of *In Country Sleep* reflect the ritual approach. The poet intones. His is the secular inflection. Faith is the central faith in the sensual fact. His rose is a sexual red. His religion is the Mary-breasted grief-taught love.

Thomas savours his tongue. It is a prime organ with him. Anyone who has heard him read (and who hasn't? and who hasn't, should) remembers the strong syllabic drunkenness (something of an orgy), the craze of sound sometimes running against the flow and the clear sense (something Swinburnian). 'Over Sir John's Hill', typically Thomas, is thoroughly rhymed and thoroughly assonanced and thoroughly reined and pranced. The swash of the lines buckles nicely at the joints.

Having had a chance to study the drafts of a poem by Thomas, I know that his seeming spontaneity is a studied grace. Rhetoric is his controlling artifice; so-called traditional form is not much involved, however invoked. He will rehearse and rehearse a poem to dredge every pun and alliterative emendation. His drafts are many and also the metamorphoses. They testify to a keen critical self-scrutiny and an ear that will not work without the mind.

A poem like 'Over Sir John's Hill', a richly representative piece, very near to an epitaph, proves the capabilities of Thomas's distinctly elemental language. Latin-syllables, the drawn-to-conclusion words, are rare. This precise aversion, or avoidance, is a virtue (to an unexampled and unexpected degree) in his work: it prevents poems of a strong opening cloudiness from being completely overcast and closed. The words are immediate words, the 'spray', as Dr Williams might say, of our life, and they enter, even if not with utter distinctness, with friendliness and frankness and distinction into the listening consciousness. 'Twenty-four years remind the tears of my eyes. / (Bury the dead for fear that they walk to the grave in labour.)'; 'You have kicked from a dark den, leaped up the whinnying light, / And dug your grave in my breast'. As rhetorical as such language may become, as tortured for sense, as cramped for the sake of keeping to form, the very choice of the words, whatever their usage, and the clear-cut heavy rhythms bring a familiarity.

In a poem like 'Over Sir John's Hill' the variety of line-lengths and the shifting of action and the drama inherent tend to intensify and modulate the motion. Thomas reaches his pitch. In contrast, we have to suffer the hemmed and, unfortunately, also hawed structure of 'Do Not Go Gentle into that Good Night', where the set form of the villanelle treads Thomas's feet. The poem endures as simple iteration; it should be compared with (apart from late Yeats) a recent poem of Wallace Stevens, 'Madame La Fleurie', where similar sentiment is more maturely and excellently probed, gaining too by its lack of prefabrication. And Stevens, remember, is the other renowned rhetorician of our day.

Thomas has found his themes at Delphi. He has the choice of going back or going forward and in either case the choice is a necessary illusion, an act desperately trying to be relevant. After the establishment of his reversible (though irreversible) contingency of birth and death, everything he writes is conditioned by it. The sexual act and its aspects reiterate his condition, and, generalising, man's. He rails against the mechanical act, acceptance, resignation, though he has fixed his doom. He reveres the individual soaked in sense. And yet perhaps because he is devoted to the ceremonial, his craft, at the same time he yearns for the convictions of life: '. . . for the lovers, their arms / Round the griefs of the ages, / Who pay no praise of wages / Nor heed my craft or art'. 'Break in the sun till the sun breaks down, / And death shall have no dominion'. 'The sun roars at the prayer's end'.

For all the beauties I have outlined in Thomas's poetry – and they persist through criticism – his verse likes to mimic itself. I suspect that the unusual 'success' he has enjoyed (or possibly not enjoyed) has prodded him to repeat his past performances excessively. He often rides his rhetorical genius too hard and it pants too obviously (as in 'Poem on His Birthday': the celebration is a hog). There is a reluctance to win new ground. Poems like 'Fern Hill' or 'Poem in October' or 'In My Craft or Sullen Art' (some of his most popular pieces) rely on rhetorical devices that sometimes run shallow and use sentimentality to the point where the reader questions sincerity. There is, in these tricks, a sense of self-idolatry that no amount of whimsy or good humour can wholly contradict. The rhythms are heavy and prompt repetitiousness. And even a poem as good as 'Over Sir John's Hill' overplays itself in onomatopœic effects: 'until / The flash the noosed hawk / Crashes, and slowly the fishing holy stalking heron / In the river Towy below bows his tilted headstone'. Exegesis helps this poem by slowing it up in the reading, halts the gabble. Thomas can hypnotize the listener, but there is a loss; Thomas intends more than intonation and the high-pressured phrasing must yield, if the poem is to move with a deep effect.

His peril is the peril of a fixed rhetorical styling that has become such a good seller in the marketplace that it is hard to grow up out of, and into a new event. He has become an established personality, a fixture. He is pinched in by self-definition that occurred at an early age and seems to have considerably limited his potential.

An added taint is the fact that his imitators, who are legion today, have picked up, like most such, all his tricks and so emphasise his weaknesses. His work has little to teach. It is a dead end. Like Eliot. As far as craft goes. He is himself a careful craftsman; he knows the limits of his rhetoric, I believe, though he will indulge it at times. But consider his imitators. You might, for instance, look at the Summer 1952 number of the Beloit Poetry Journal. A poem by a young poet opens:

From heaven my rainy father reigned
more Gabriel than the dawn,
walking how heavy in his top-dollar town
to wear the sun like a derby.

and continues in like fashion. You see the bait swallowed. The slackness it produces, the mask of voice, the mimicry of rhythms without coherence, and the clever combinations. In the same issue, by another new poet, is this opening:

Unanimously from his cowle of flesh
as countries riven,
in tattered grace my frame's five senses break
quickening, wrought buds at civilization's wake.

It is actually possible, if it were worth the effort, to demonstrate almost phrase for phrase, rhythm for rhythm, trick for trick, the influence of Thomas on this poem.

These influencings undoubtedly detract from Thomas's quality. His verve, his crying spirit, his naughtiness, his rhetorical romancing, are wide attractions. It is worth more of our careful consideration as to how deep and insighted are his poems and how superficial and rhetorically blinding, as well as captivating.

The Poetry of Dylan Thomas[1]

ELDER OLSON

THERE IS SOME EVIDENCE that even well-equipped readers have found the poetry of Dylan Thomas difficult; and one would be surprised, considering the nature of his work, if the case were otherwise. It is, in the first place, work characterised by unusually powerful and original conceptions, formulated in symbols difficult in themselves and complex in their interrelations. Secondly, what we may call the 'dramatic presentation' of his poetry – roughly, the whole body of clues by which a reader determines who is speaking in the poem, to whom, of what, in what circumstances – is full of deliberate, even studied, ambiguity. Again, an even greater ambiguity, and even more studied, pervades his language, to a degree where it – the first thing we have to go by, in any literary composition – seems to exploit all the possibilities of the formal enigma. Finally – although this is not a matter of poetic structure but of historical accident – Thomas is working in a tradition not likely to be familiar to his readers.

Much has been said, by Miss Sitwell and others, about the grandeur of Thomas's 'themes'; however, since no artistic work was ever good or bad simply by virtue of its dealing with a certain theme, I presume that what these critics have in mind is the *constituted* theme – what the poet has made of it, not what the theme in itself is – or, in a word, the conception governing the work. The artistic excellence of a work is dependent upon whether the conception itself is of value, and upon whether it has so dominated the

1. Copyright © Elder Olson, 1959.

whole construction of the piece as to be fully realised in it and enhanced by it. When Thomas's power of conception is at its height, when it masters all the elements of the poem, something like sublimity results; when the conception is merely odd, fanciful, or otherwise trivial, or when his handling of it obscures, distorts, or otherwise fails to manifest itself, he fails.

'The Ballad of the Long-Legged Bait', to take one of his best poems as an example, has as its bare theme the notion that salvation must be won through mortification of the flesh. A common enough notion; but in the fiery imagination of Thomas the process of purification becomes the strange voyage of a lone fisherman; the bait is 'A girl alive with his hooks through her lips;' she is 'all the wanting flesh his enemy', 'Sin who had a woman's shape'; and the quarry sought is no less than all that Time and Death have taken, for since Sin brought Time and Death into the world, the abolition of Sin will restore all that has been lost. With the death of the girl, the sea gives up its dead, as foretold in Revelations XX : 13; Eden returns, 'A garden holding to her hand / With birds and animals'; and the sea disappears, accomplishing the prophecy of Revelations XXI : 1 ('and there was no more sea'). In the terrible actuality of the voyage we never guess its essential fantasy; 'the whole / Of the sea is hilly with whales', 'All the fishes were rayed in blood', and most beautifully:

> He saw the storm smoke out to kill
> With fuming bows and ram of ice,
> Fire on starlight, rake Jesu's stream;
> And nothing shone on the water's face
> But the oil and bubble of the moon . . .

As in these last lines the storm is given the menace, the fury and power of a kind of supernatural warship, firing 'on starlight' until nothing shines but 'the oil and bubble of the moon', so the theme of the whole poem is given the emotional power of its legend: the subduing of sensual desire becomes mysterious and cruel as the immolation of the girl, the salvation takes on the beauty and mystery of the resurrection of the dead and the past from the sea.

Similarly, 'Fern Hill' and 'Poem in October', luminous with all the weathers of childhood; 'A Refusal to Mourn the Death, By Fire, Of A Child In London', apprehending the child's death in its relation to the whole universe (all creation is spanned, awesomely, from beginning to end, in the first stanza, and the last carries us back to the 'first dead'); the 'Altarwise By Owl-Light' sonnet-sequence (surely among the greater poems of our century): all these are founded upon conceptions possible, we feel, only to a man of great imagination and feeling. On the other hand, such pieces as 'Shall Gods Be Said To Thump the Clouds', 'Why East Wind Chills', and 'Ears in the Turrets' rest upon trivialities; their themes are conceived with too little imagination, and with too little relation to humanity, to leave us anything but indifferent.

Thomas the poet has much less range than Thomas the prose-writer. The poet is the greater, but the prose-writer assumes far more characters and enters into far more moods and shades of moods. The poet is a single character, and he is a poet only of the most exalted states of mind – the most exalted grief, joy, tenderness, or terror. Such lofty art demands great energy of thought and feeling, and all the accoutrements of lofty style; but when the lofty conception is lacking, energy becomes violence or plain noisiness, the tragic passions become melodramatic or morbid, ecstasy becomes hysteria, and the high style becomes obscure bombast. When the bard is not the bard, the bardic robes may easily be put off; not so the habitual paraphernalia of his art. When Thomas is not master of his tricks, his tricks master him; he is then capable, quite without any artistic point so far as I can see, of calling the dead Christ a 'stiff', of having Jesus say, 'I smelt the maggot in my stool', or of devising such fake nightmares as 'His mother's womb had a tongue that lapped up mud'. In his good work or his bad, his devices remain the same; it is their employment that differs.

The point in employing any literary device is that in the circumstances it discharges its function better than any other. Metaphor and simile, for instance (if we leave aside their instructive function of making the unfamiliar known in terms of the familiar), have two principal functions in poetry: either they isolate a quality or qualities by indicating something else which has them, or they serve as an indication of thought, feeling, or character; and it is thus that poet controls the feelings and ideas of his reader. When Enobarbus says that Cleopatra's barge 'burnt' on the water, its fire-like brilliance is singled out; when Hamlet calls the world 'a rank, unweeded garden' he manifests his state of mind. Both kinds fail, of course, if no real or fancied resemblance can be found to justify the analogy; but the former kind fails in its special function when the qualities isolated are, either in kind or degree, insufficient to produce the idea which might be grasped or the emotion which must be felt; and the latter kind fails in its special function when it fails to identify thought, feeling, or character.

When, in the passage cited earlier, Thomas gives us the storm conceived in all its power, presented in metaphor which discloses fully that conception, he succeeds wonderfully in the first kind; when he makes rain into milk from 'an old god's dugs . . . pressed and pricked', he fails miserably in it. 'In the groin of the natural doorway I crouched like a tailor / Sewing a shroud for a journey' is an excellent simile of the second kind, for it is a sharp index of the frame of mind of one who sees the womb itself as preparation for the grave; but 'my love pulls the pale, nippled air / Prides of tomorrow suckling in her eyes' can hardly be said to identify the state of mind of the lover, or to offer any vision of his beloved with which we might reasonably be expected to be sympathetic.

I have already mentioned Thomas's dramatic and linguistic obscurity. The former is usually a relatively simple matter; for instance, appropriate titles would have made clear that 'Where Once the Waters of Your Face' treats of a sea-channel gone dry, that 'When Once the Twilight Locks No Longer' is the Spirit talking of man's death-dream, that 'Light Breaks Where No Sun Shines', 'Foster the Light', and 'The Force That Through the Green Fuse Drives the Flower' are all variations on the macrocosm-microcosm theme, and that 'If My Head Hurts a Hair's Foot' is a dialogue between an unborn child and its mother. There is no more point in such concealment, I think, than there would be in a dramatist's concealing the characters and the assignment of speeches in a play. Similarly with 'the white giant's thigh'; if, as Thomas is alleged to have said, all is clear to one who knows that the 'thigh' is a landmark on a Welsh hill, the reader should have been informed in a note; any effect which depends upon accidental ignorance can never be permanent, and is not worth trying for.

Yet if these obscurities are faults, those who damn Thomas's and much other contemporary poetry simply on the ground of its obscurity are badly mistaken. This amounts to legislation; whereas the artist is properly bound by no law but the dictates of the individual work. Moreover, it is always necessary for the literary artist, in the simplest lyric or the most extended narrative or play, at times to conceal and at times to disclose, in order to effect surprise and suspense, the subtlest shading of emotion into emotion, and the most delicate or vehement degree of emotion. It is precisely in the manipulation of language to these ends that Thomas, at his best, shows himself a master; consciously or unconsciously, he is in the tradition of the great Welsh enigmatic poets of the fourteenth century, and he seems to have learned or inherited all their art. He is particularly master of the sentence artfully delayed and suspended, through many surprising turns, until its unexpected accomplishment, and also of the mysterious paraphrase which, resolved at its conclusion, illuminates the whole poem. He is at his best in the latter in the magnificent 'Sonnets'; at his worst, perhaps, in 'Because the Pleasure-bird Whistles', but the latter illustrates his procedure more clearly. 'Because the pleasure-bird whistles after the hot wires' means 'Because the song-bird sings more sweetly after being blinded (with red-hot needles or wires)'; 'drug-white shower of nerves and food' means 'snow', snow being seen both as the 'snow of cocaine-addicts and as manna from heaven; 'a wind that plucked a goose' means 'a wind full of feathery snow'; 'the wild tongue breaks its tombs' and the 'red, wagged root' refer to fire; 'bum city' refers to Sodom, 'bum' meaning simultaneously 'bad' and 'given to sodomy'; the 'frozen wife' and 'the salt person' are of course Lot's wife; and so on.

He becomes easier to read if one is aware of his linguistic devices. He is fond of ambiguous syntax, and achieves it sometimes by punctuation, as in 'O miracle of fishes! The long dead bite!' which leads us to think both expressions are phrases, whereas the last is a sentence; sometimes by lack of punctuation, as in the first three lines of 'A Refusal to Mourn', where hyphenation would have clarified everything, thus: 'Never until the mankind-making / Bird-beast – and flower – / Fathering and all-humbling darkness'; sometimes by delaying the complement in phrase or clause, as in the first stanza of 'Poem In October', where many words intervene between 'hearing' and its infinitive object 'beckon', and many again between 'beckon' and its object 'myself'; sometimes by setting up apparent grammatical parallelism where none in fact exists, as in 'tallow-eyed', which is a compound adjective, and 'tallow I', which is adjective modifying personal pronoun. He is not merely fond of puns, but of using them to effect transition; thus in the 'Sonnets' a pun on 'poker' makes the transition from Sonnet IV to the imagery of Sonnet V.

Thomas exhibits astonishing variety in his statement of similitudes. Most commonly he uses compound expressions with metaphorical implications, as in 'lamb white day', (days innocent as a lamb is white) or in 'And a black cap of jack – / Daws Sir John's just hill dons', where the hill capped with jack-daws is seen as a judge donning the black cap for the pronouncement of the death-sentence. He is fond, too, of confusing the reader as to what is metaphorical and what is literal; for example, 'Where once the waters of your face' leads the reader to suppose 'waters' metaphorical and 'face' literal, whereas the reverse is the case. He sometimes offers an apparently impossible statement, whether taken metaphorically or literally, and then indicates its metaphorical meaning much later; for example, in 'Our Eunuch Dreams', 'one-dimensioned ghosts' seems impossible, even though he is talking of images on a movie screen; it is only when he speaks of the photograph's 'one-sided skins' that we understand 'one-dimensioned' to mean a façade merely, something having no farther side. He is much given to various kinds of implied but unstated metaphor: for example, the storm-warship metaphor, where the warship is given only by implication, and again in 'the stations of the breath' where he effects metaphor by substituting 'breath' where we expect 'cross'.

It is difficult to say whether he has progressed much or not. There are extraordinarily fine poems in all his phases; but as he eliminates the faults of one period, he acquires new ones in another. His first poems are sometimes unnecessarily obscure through terseness; his later, sometimes obvious and verbose. In his earlier work the thoughts and emotions are sometimes too complex for lyric treatment; in his later, too simple for the elaboration he gives them. It is difficult, too, to say how he may develop; we must be grateful for the genius already manifest, and for the rest, have faith in the poet, a faith by no means without firm foundation.

* * *

I wrote the above when Dylan Thomas was still a living man. I should like to pay him the tribute of letting it stand exactly as I wrote it; for I meant it as a candid examination of his art which should result in a fuller exhibition of his genius.

The Religious Poet

W. S. MERWIN

APART FROM THE VERSE prologue to his *Collected Poems*, and the poem 'In My Craft or Sullen Art', both of which I mean to discuss later, the two salient remarks that I have known Dylan Thomas to make about his own poetry were one in a letter to Henry Treece where he described the manner in which he wrote poetry, and the prose statement at the beginning of the *Collected Poems* concerning the purpose of his poetry: 'These poems', he says, 'are written for the love of Man and in praise of God'. It is not because I am taking Dylan Thomas at his prose word – a poet may be the last person to be able to speak accurately, in prose, about his own poetry – but because I am trying to take his poems at their word, that I wish to consider Dylan Thomas as a religious poet, and notice some of the means, the craft and language with which he has made his themes.

I think it is safer at this point not to set up a pair of artificial antinomies: as it were, the religious artist and whatever we might call his opposite, but to start by saying that the religious artist is primarily a celebrator. A celebrator in the ritual sense: a maker and performer of a rite. And also a celebrator in the sense of one who participates in the rite, and whom the rite makes joyful. That which he celebrates is creation, and more particularly the human condition. For he will see himself, man, as a metaphor or analogy of the world. The human imagination will be for him the image of the divine imagination; the work of art and the artist will be analogous with the world and its creator. In both man and the world he will perceive a force of love or creation which is more divine than either man or the world, and a force of death or destruction which is more terrible than man or the world. Although his ultimate vision is the tragic one of creation through suffering, his ultimate sense will be of joy. For in the act of love, the central act of creation, he will see the force of love, in man and the world, merge inextricably and mysteriously with the force of death, and yet from this union new creation born through suffering. And his vocation as an individual artist will be to remake in terms of celebration the details of life, to save that which is individual and thereby mortal, by imagining it, making it, in terms of what he conceives to be eternal. The emotion which drives him to this making will be compassion, or better, love of life and the particulars of life.

The poems of Dylan Thomas are peculiarly consistent: as I understand them, they are the work of a religious poet trying, at times desperately, to find and come to grips with his subject, finding it, and making it into a poetry of celebration – into some of the greatest poetry that has been written in our time. How much of this was consciously aimed-at, and how much was at least half-dark necessity, I suspect but do not know; but I think the religious theme as I have described it is the main vein of Dylan Thomas's poetry. He has written a number of genuine personal poems in which the 'I' is overtly the individual poet, but these for the most part are well along in his work, and many of them deal with the religious theme from their particular vantage. In most of the earlier poems the 'I' is 'man' trying to find a means of imagining and thereby redeeming his condition: much of the seemingly baroque and motiveless 'agony' of the earlier poems stems from the desperateness of this need.

The brilliant and powerful first poem in the book, 'I see the boys of summer', presents doom as the final reality in the very moments of man's euphory, and in so far as man ignores or is truly ignorant of this fact about his condition, the poet describes him with contempt. He recommends that the passage of time, and death, be challenged and embraced, but he can give no reason why they should be – birth and death are an endless loveless dull round – and the poem ends in ironic despair. But by the third poem, 'A process in the weather of the heart', which describes the growing of death in life, the natural world and the human body are consistently metaphoric of each other; the heart at the end of the poem is the sea, which 'gives up its dead', though it does so through its own death. In the fourth poem, 'Before I knocked', man is seen as Christ his divine image, and there is an attempt at presenting human life as a continuity by describing the prenatal growth of the consciousness of death, and in the fifth, 'The force that through the green fuse drives the flower', the doom within life is described again, but described because of compassion for things mortal, and the compassion makes the poet at once wish to be able to communicate with all other things that are doomed, to tell them he understands their plight because his own is similar, and makes him feel the depth to which he is inarticulate and painfully unable to do so.

But dumb compassion for mortality, though relieved by this remarkable poem and by the beautiful but hardly more than putative sea-faiths of 'Where once the waters of your face', could not rest content. In the poem, 'If I were tickled by the rub of love', the poet states that if love were real to him he would have the means of facing the fear of death; the poem's remarkable and hopeful conclusion, since the reality of love does not seem attainable, is 'I would be tickled by the rub that is: / Man be my metaphor'. And in the next poem, 'Our Eunuch Dreams', he examines 'reality' and its simulacra in terms of each other, concluding that the world is real, and is an image of man, and the poem ends in faith and joy. The poem, 'Especially when the October wind', takes this development a stage further: here the poet first fully assumes his Orphic role, celebrating a particular day, a particular place, in autumn, offering to *make* it, or aspects of it, and as he names and celebrates them, doing so.

This is moving forward a bit too fast and smooth; (if the poems are not arranged chronologically, then as far as I can see Dylan Thomas has put them in an order admirably suited to present his theme.) For a day in autumn, or even man's condition may to some extent be named and remade and redeemed without love, but personal particular death remains real to the poet. And without the reality of love, the 'Have faith . . . And who remain shall flower as they love', of 'Our Eunuch Dreams', comes to ring hollow to him. The perception of death as the very urge and joy in the act of love, in the poem, 'When like a running grave', makes both sexual love and the love of the world impossible: the poet advocates despair of either and, instead, love of death himself for his devilish ubiquity. And in 'From love's first fever to her plague' Dylan Thomas vainly tried, as a way out, to make a myth of his own physical growth, but concludes that even the creations of the imagination are futile: 'The root of tongues ends in a spent-out cancer'. This poem, reasonably enough if what I am saying makes sense, is one of the few poems of Dylan Thomas's which seems uncompleted, less as if he had not bothered to write it out to an end than as if he had known no end to write it out to.

In the next poem, 'In the beginning', he found what he needed: the poem is about creation, and sees the creation of the world as the metaphor of the creation of man. It sees the individual man through his divine image Christ (it is worth comparing this poem with 'Before I knocked' to see how much surer of his subject Dylan Thomas has become); and it sees imaginative creation and natural creation as one: 'In the beginning was the word, the word / That from the solid bases of the light / Abstracted all the letters of the void'. 'Light breaks where no sun shines' is a further elaboration of the vision of man as a metaphor of the world.

I can see several reasons why the next two poems, 'I fellowed sleep', and 'I dreamed my genesis' should have been written as about dreams. 'I fellowed sleep' is a visionary poem about uncreated ghosts, the dreams of the world which the world climbs always to create. A dream can be a kind of metaphor – as in 'Our Eunuch Dreams' once the imagination has harnessed it; but the *sense* of the subject is not always certain in this poem, which I take to mean that it would have been almost impossible for Dylan Thomas to have approached it more directly – and even St Augustine admitted that our responsibility to dreams is different from our responsibility to the rest of creation. (What it comes down to, of course, is that Dylan Thomas wrote his poems so he could, and the use of dream-subjects helped him get a step closer to what he was trying to say.) 'I dreamed my genesis' describes man's birth through his death, his knowledge of death in his birth, and his passage into the world.

In these earlier poems, as in Dylan Thomas's poetry generally, the language is what is most immediately striking. A language for a poet is always raw even if vitiated; Dylan Thomas's most characteristic twistings of the expected idiom have been mentioned often enough: the puns, the using of one part of speech for another, the manipulation of colloquialisms. He has done violence to the language when it was necessary to his theme – and at times when it was not: even in his later poems he can be vulgar, precious, meretriciously clever. And the style of these earlier poems is often egregious and turgid – a thing is said with devious novelty merely to avoid saying it any other way; as though the words came first and the subject as it could. (And the kind of poetry which he once described himself as writing in a letter to Henry Treece sounded as though it might very well be more a poetry of warring conclusions than of imaginative wholes.) But I think all this is a further indication of the intensity with which Dylan Thomas, with all the means at his disposal, was trying to find and make his subject – but the fact that a poet however gifted may find his subject only with difficulty does not necessarily indicate that he has no subject: it may merely indicate that he has a subject which is difficult to find. It is interesting how many of Dylan Thomas's 'private' recurring words, many of which he uses already in these poems, bear directly on the theme I have been talking about: the constant use of the word 'die' in the sense both of physical death and of sexual climax; 'grain' which is also the dust of the dead; 'grief' to designate the experience of 'death' in the sexual act; 'lock' and 'key' as sexual symbols. Also in these poems one finds already Dylan Thomas's characteristic development of a poem by repetition. There is peculiar to this manner of a live poem's progression a kind of chaste passion and anonymity whatever the subject; at the same time it gives the language and/or emotion of the subject an exceptional range for improvisation. And it presents strikingly, as might a ritual, the difference between the movement of the subject and the moment of the poem.

I have tried to indicate the direction which I think Dylan Thomas's earlier poetry was following, the theme it was trying to make and serve. It would be possible to follow the uses and developments of this theme through many of the succeeding poems, but often less directly, for as his knowledge of the theme deepened and became more comprehensive, the range of experience he was able to handle increased; his skill in his craft at the same time was growing more varied; and in particular he began writing more overtly occasional and personal poems. ('Out of the sighs' is to my reading the first genuinely personal poem in the *Collected Poems*). After 'I dreamed my genesis', there are a group of poems which explore the relationship of love and death, the world as duality, the subject of the continual creation of the world and of the individual. I think the culmination of these particular poems, though it is not the last in the group, is 'I in my intricate image' where the exultant conclusion already has the ring and vision of much of Dylan Thomas's later poetry: 'This was the god of beginning in the intricate seawhirl, / And my images roared and rose on heaven's hill'.

Such a poem as 'Do you not father me' carries both the subject of the individual's continuity in man's continuing creation, which Dylan Thomas had first developed in 'Before I knocked', and the subject of 'The force that through the green fuse drives the flower' a stage further by identifying man the creator-creature with all other mortal creatures. 'A grief ago' explores the theme in terms of the act of love itself, and for the sake of the loved one. The sonnet sequence, 'Altarwise by owl-light' is a glorification of the act of creation, identifying man with that which he conceives as divine. The power and compassion of the personal poems increase; the occasions become more genuinely intense as they become more direct: 'I have longed to move away', 'I make this in a warring absence', 'After the funeral', especially the deeply moving 'A Refusal to Mourn the Death by Fire of a Child in London'.

True personal poetry, where the poet speaks in his own voice directly about his particular experience, is rarer than might seem, particularly among modern poets, and, of course, especially so if it be personal poetry of any stature. Some of Dylan Thomas's personal poems are among the most moving and powerful he has written. And in these poems as well, both the fear, and still more important, the joy, have as their reference the religious artist's vision of the world. The theme of 'Hold hard, these ancient minutes in the cuckoo's mouth' (where we already have the hawk and birds of 'Over Sir John's Hill') becomes more intimate in 'When all my five and country senses see', in 'We lying by seasand', and 'Twenty-four years'; enormously amplified, it is still the background, with the personal fate foremost, in the poem which for me is, until now, the culmination of Dylan Thomas's personal poetry: 'In the White Giant's Thigh'. In this poem it is ancient, desperate barren love which haunts the speaker and lures his creative powers themselves down to death. The poems which bid that death be defied become more actual, more direct with mastery: in the earliest poems the motive for defiance seemed no better than desperation, but in the recent villanelle, 'Do not go gentle into that good night' (which, with Empson's 'Missing Dates' seems to me one of the great poems in this form in English) it is quite clearly love – love at such a pass as to be otherwise helpless against death. And the exultation of such marvellous poems as 'Poem in October', 'Fern Hill', 'Poem on his Birthday', and 'Author's Prologue' is not an exultation proper to the liberal humanist: it is the exuberance of a man drunk with the holiness and wonder of creation, with the reality and terror and ubiquity of death, but with love as God, as more powerful than death.

I think that in general it is the later poems of Dylan Thomas which represent his most important achievement. As love and compassion both have become more sure and comprehensive, so his poetry has become, among other things, increasingly dramatic. I do not find this surprising; I think the work of a religious artist, as his scope and mastery increased, would naturally tend to become more dramatic. For an art which is dramatic cannot burgeon if existence is seen as pointless and fragmentary; but a sense of the reality of love and a sense of the reality of the imagination would seem to me to be two of the most potent means of seeing creation as capable of order (the imagination makes order) and as significantly varied (love embraces details rather than generalities). And as the act of celebration – the metaphor – became more real it would tend to gain a dimension, gain independence of the individual 'lyric' moment (become less 'subjective') and become ritual or dramatic. One can see how a love poem would probably be more dramatic than a generalised statement of private anguish: a case in point, I think, is 'Especially when the October wind', where the *audience*, more explicit than in the earlier poems, may be the reader, but might very well be the beloved; and where the works of the imagination are mentioned 'made' as things with a 'life of their own'. (I should have thought, nevertheless, that his peculiar pitch of language would have precluded his writing poetry that was explicitly dramatic. It would be of immense interest to see what he has done with his hitherto unpublished choral fragment 'The Town That Was Mad'.) As his poetry has grown more dramatic, Dylan Thomas's tragic vision of creation has deepened and grown richer, and with it his power of joy. The faith, sure of itself but not sure why, of 'A grief ago' is a tragic faith; the sense of death is more real and terrible in so magnificent and tender a recent poem as 'In Country Sleep', but the faith is the same, and certain why it is there, and joyful.

'A Winter's Tale' is one of the few narrative poems Dylan Thomas has attempted and I think it is one of the great poems he has written. Its achievement is if anything still more remarkable: for in 'A Winter's Tale' the fact has made myth. I say this without knowing whether or not Dylan Thomas used a known legend for the 'story' of his poem – for several reasons I suspect that he did. It might have run something like this: 'Once in the dead of winter, in the middle of the night, a man who lived alone in a house in the woods saw outside a beautiful she-bird, and all around her it was spring. He ran from the house to find her; she flew ahead of him, and all night he ran and at last she came down and he came to where she was; she put her wings over him and the spring faded back to winter; then she rose and vanished, and when spring came and the snow melted they found his body lying on a hill-top.' (I know of a similar legend among the American Indians.) The main reasons why I suspect that the poem comes from some such legend is that it contains most of the essential elements of a mid-winter ceremony of the re-birth of the year (of the earth, of man). In Wales until the Christian era, and among parts of the population for a long time afterwards, the presiding deity was a goddess; the mid-winter rite was in her praise; she was often represented as a bird; the all-night running of the bride-groom corresponds with the marriage labours in many legends. Also the illusory vision of spring, coming from the land of the dead in Dylan Thomas's poem, and then the reality of winter coming back, might very possibly have come from a confusion of time-sequence such as often happens in legends when their ritual decays – that is, if the poem was based on some such legend, then we might suppose that in the original ritual the real spring came, and that the one-night version was later. But my point is that what I have persistently called Dylan Thomas's 'religious' vision of creation is completely congruous with the vision of life which made the re-birth ritual in the first place. And as poetry comes to be in a manner similar to that in which legend does, Dylan Thomas might very possibly have invented a story whose mythical ramifications were thus comprehensive and deep. He has 'made' the myth whether or not he invented the skeletal story, for it is his own imagination which has given it its immediacy and power, which has seen love-in-death, the 'she-bird', with such certainty as heavenly and all-powerful, which has made articulate within the metaphor itself the triumph of the rite which is life.

In two other major later poems, 'Vision and Prayer' and 'Over Sir John's Hill' the mythology and vision are developed in a different, and dramatic, direction. In these poems the poet, while presenting the condition of creation, intercedes on behalf of mortality. This is a different kind of standing-apart from that of the earlier poems, for there it was the failure to conceive of creation as ordered, and at the same time the overweening preoccupation with personal doom (however generalised), which kept the poet separate. In these poems he bespeaks the tragic order as he sees it, and it is in his very capacity of witness and tongue and celebrator that he stands without as intercessor. In 'Vision and Prayer', because of the vision of man as divine, as love (Christ), of creation as divine and therefore of resurrection as real, he prays that death may die indeed. In 'Over Sir John's Hill' he would redeem mortality itself:

> . . . and I who hear the tune of the slow,
> Wear-willow river, grave,
> Before the lunge of the night, the notes on this time-
> shaken
> Stone for the sake of the souls of the slain birds sailing,'

Dylan Thomas's own sense of his poetic vocation has been

stated more clearly than anywhere else in two poems, 'In my Craft or Sullen Art' and the 'Author's Prologue' to the *Collected Poems*. In the former he states that he writes his poems 'Not for ambition or bread', nor for public acclaim nor for the edification of the self-righteous, nor for the dead, but for the lovers 'With all their griefs in their arms'. If the act of love is conceived as the central holy act of creation, where love, in joy and then in pain and then in joy, overcomes death, it is clear why he should have felt that his poems were so directed. In 'Author's Prologue' as in 'In My Craft or Sullen Art', where he had written 'I labour by singing light', the creative act, in this case the creation of the imagination, is seen as holy:

'. . . song
Is a burning and crested act,
The fire of birds in
The world's turning wood . . .'

It is seen as triumphant over death:

'I build my bellowing ark
To the best of my love
As the flood begins . . .'

and moreover as perpetual, present always, making anew now: 'And the flood flowers now'. This is the office of celebration, it is the reason for the faith and the joy, it is the statement of vocation of a great religious poet. As for the 'craft', Dylan Thomas remains the most skilful maker of verse writing English; the stanzaic forms which he often fashioned for his rhythms are as complex and, for him, unhampering and informative as they seem to have been among the Welsh ollaves. He has 'made' what seems to me to be the major theme to a point of masterful authority, and in the range and intensity of passion which he controlled he surpassed any of his contemporaries. He seems to have assimilated most of his primary influences (though the 'debt' to Joyce in particular was more than verbal – Joyce was prodigiously an artist of celebration – and the 'debt' to Hopkins's 'The Windhover' bore recent fruit in 'Over Sir John's Hill'). He has survived the fads of the thirties, the first wave of fashion and notoriety. He has 'arrived'. How the future will judge him, we cannot tell. We only know that Thomas is a major poet of our century and nobody will be able to ignore him.

Dylan Thomas

GEOFFREY MOORE

Lady P. Lie still, ye thief, and hear the lady sing in Welsh.
Hot. I had rather hear Lady, my brach, howl in Irish.

– *I Henry IV*, Act iii, Sc. 1.

Unable to write in Welsh or reluctant to do so because of the uncommercial nature of the language, [a number of young Welshmen] often give the impression that their writing in English is only a condescension to the influence and ubiquity of a tyrannous foreign tongue. I do not belong to that number.

– *Broadcast by Dylan Thomas: BBC Third Programme*

I TAKE IT there is no need, at this stage, to protest Dylan Thomas's genius. That there is more to him than is implied by the assessments of the thirties (e.g. Stephen Spender's '. . . just poetic stuff with no beginning nor end, or intelligent or intelligible control', or Louis MacNeice's '. . . a series of nonsense images, the cumulative effect of which is usually vital and sometimes even seems to have a message') is now, with the hindsight of nearly twenty years, obvious to most readers. On the other hand, statements such as Philip Toynbee's on the publication of the *Collected Poems* (that Thomas was the greatest living poet) and the almost liturgical repetition of such critical adjectives as 'miraculous', 'beautiful', 'holy' and 'innocent' by his more mystical admirers must be soberly set against the actual details of the poems. Accurate evaluation calls for sympathetic analysis of all the words on all the pages (there are not that many), and the sort of attempt to discern patterns of thought and imagery which characterised Mr Elder Olson's excellent 'The Poetry of Dylan Thomas'. Nevertheless, there is, I believe, another angle of approach which, in the case of Dylan Thomas, can be rewarding. He needs to be *placed*, to be seen both in his local physical and spiritual environment and against the unfolding pattern of modern verse as a whole. This is preliminary; the analysis is central. But precisely because Dylan Thomas was a phenomenon whose significance will, I am convinced, be far clearer to future generations than it yet is to us, one's mind needs to be prepared. In addition to his intrinsic achievement, the kind of thing he represented, as gesture and example, ought not to be lost through seeing it in terms of a tradition other than the one he belonged to. I propose, then, to reserve analysis of the major poems, and to make here some introductory statements about background, local and social, literary and general.

When Dylan Thomas died, on November 9, 1953, a large number of British people discovered that they had a national poet. It was extraordinary, and a great deal of the responsibility for it lay with the BBC; for without the BBC Thomas might have been only as well known to the general public as, say, W. S. Graham is at the moment. But the BBC introduced another Dylan Thomas, not the New Romantic poet appreciated by a small and specialised audience for his *Eighteen Poems*, his *Twenty-five Poems*, his *The Map of Love* and his few stories (his total output at the beginning of the war), but Dylan Thomas the actor, the rich and lively teller of tales, the sonorous, declamatory reader of verse of all kinds, whose voice sounded, as G. S. Fraser once put it, 'like a sea of treacle moving to the beat of a gong'. This BBC patronage had two effects. It not only introduced a vivid histrionic and comic talent to a large and varied audience, it also sent more readers to his own poems. For when Thomas read his work what had seemed to a number of interested but puzzled people merely lively gibberish, became, suddenly, moving and meaningful poetry.

But what is more interesting and, as a comment on Thomas's stature as a poet, more valuable, was the affection and admiration expressed by the youngest generation of poets, would-be poets, and amateurs of poetry. He stood in relation to the literary-minded young of Britain as Graham Sutherland stood in painting and Henry Moore in sculpture. He seemed to be going somewhere in a way that they could feel in their bones was necessary. One must, of course, make some qualification of this statement. There is what might be called the neo-Thomist fringe which does not merely value (as do we all) the immense contribution T. S. Eliot has made to modern verse but feels spiritually in harmony with the grave clarity of Mr Eliot's mystical later mood. There is also the group, born in the early 'twenties, who are Empson-sympathisers, and who write cerebral and neatly-turned verse. But I am talking about the generation of the 'thirties. For a sizeable number of them at least, Dylan Thomas caught the imagination, as poet and as figure. He not only wrote exciting, thought-provoking, highly complicated and sometimes – as in the case of 'A Refusal to Mourn the Death, by Fire, of a Child in London' and 'Fern Hill' – intimately affecting verse, he was also the kind of man one could talk to over a pint in a pub. His wisdom was mixed with a schoolboy sense of fun, and he had a wicked wit and a warmth and love of life which his later verse so vividly communicates. He was a poet of affirmation, where T. S. Eliot was a poet of negation. This appreciation by the youngest generation was expressed in a moving letter from a young Oxford man printed in the February 1954 number of the *London Magazine*, a letter which provoked some tart replies from those whose unrelenting awareness of the high seriousness of literary discussion must leave them little room to enjoy literature itself.

Of course, some of the posthumous brou-ha-ha was spurious.

People who had scarcely read his verse and had once seen John's youthful portrait – the one with the curls and the liquid eyes – spoke as if Adonais was dead. Thomas was no Adonais. But Keats was not, either, come to that. In his love of life, his perky mimicking, his ability to be at one with the sparrow pecking about on the gravel, Thomas might be compared with the Keats of the Letters. But Thomas carried the punning and joking of his life into his poems. He was an earthier character, all through, no piner for Fanny Brawnes, yet no mere pub-crawling bohemian either. Nor was he the Dada-ist or Surrealist he has sometimes been made out to be – although, paradoxically, his verse may be seen as the climax of a process of poetic development which includes these phenomena. In short, a complicated personality, whose verse is a record of his painful progression from 'darkness towards some measure of light', a progression which can also be gauged by the difference between an early statement made to Henry Treece and another made in 1947 to an audience in Rome. In the former he said, 'I hold a beast, an angel, and a madman in me, and my enquiry is as to their working, and my problem is their subjugation and victory, downthrow and upheaval, and my effort is their self-expression.' In the latter he said merely, 'One: I am a Welshman; two: I am a drunkard; three: I am a lover of the human race, especially of women.' One must allow for the difference between private and public statements, for the fact that, where an audience was concerned, Thomas was, as he once said of himself, 'just an old ham'. Nevertheless there is, I think, some indication here of the fact that he had, by 1947, ceased to make brilliant copy out of his psychological problems and was writing poetry of the first order. The man who can make statements like the second is sure of himself, is having his day.

How much emphasis was he placing, in his second statement, on the fact of being a Welshman? Although, as I hope to show, being Welsh affected him in two important respects, the kind of Welshness involved has been much misunderstood. In the first place, the mere fact of being born and brought up in Swansea does not necessarily mean that one can speak Welsh, or even understand much of it. Dylan Thomas went to Swansea Grammar School, where his father was an English master. On both sides of the family he was descended from farming stock of Carmarthenshire, on the bay of which, at Laugharne, below Sir John's Hill, he made his home at the end of his life. The very fact that he was a Grammar School boy had its effect on the objects and the references of his verse, for a Grammar School boy grows up among the people and in the districts that the public school boy knows only from the outside. Dylan Thomas was intimate with the factories, the chapels, the flicks, the 'dogs' and day-excursions that the public school poets of the 'thirties, Auden, Spender, Day Lewis and MacNeice, felt they ought to write about ('August for the people and their favourite islands', 'When clerks and navvies fondle/Beside canals their wenches'). For Thomas these things are casual but nevertheless vital references in poetry which is devoted to another end. He grew up, a grubby, curly, cheeky boy, in depressed South Wales of the between-wars period, and although Swansea was no Merthyr it sent its contingents of unemployed to London too. 'I see the boys of summer in their ruin' is a specific as well as a symbolical observation. He had seen the boys of summer in their ruin. He was one of them. Or rather, he became, spiritually, one of them, for his own childhood and early adolescence were as carefree as those of any independent small boy of the lower middle-class who grows up in a 'crawling, sprawling, slummed, unplanned, jerry-villa'd and smug-suburbed' industrial city. He played in Cwmdonkin Park, with its hunchback, the 'solitary mister', and gazed at the Bristol Channel from the windows of his school above Swansea Bay. But as he grew up, he became aware of the world beyond Cwmdonkin Park, the world, in his own words, of:

> the coal-tips, the dole queues, the stubborn bankrupt villages, the children scrubbing for coal on the slag

> heaps, the colliers' shabby allotments, the cheap-Jack cinema, the whippet races, the disused quarries, the still pit wheels, the gaunt tin-roofed chapels in the soot, the hewers squatting in the cut, the pubs, the Woolworths, the deacons and the Gyppos, silicosis, little Moscow up beyond the hills, sag-roof factory and plumeless stack, stone-grey street, scummed river, the capped and mufflered knots of men outside the grim Employment Exchange and the Public Library.

This awareness did not make him write social verse, however, for his sense of pity was personal and not general. Social verse calls for a generalising imagination. Thomas was committed to the individual, and through the individual to the exploration of profounder themes.

He reported for a time for Swansea's weekly *Herald of Wales*, then left for London, where he stayed in rooms, lived with friends and wrote, living from first to last a hand-to-mouth free-lance literary existence. He might have been an actor, but he was too much of a poet. It was Victor Neuberg of the *Sunday Referee* who was responsible for giving him his start, and from the publication of *Eighteen Poems* in 1934, when he was twenty, to the final Foyle's Literary Luncheon, his career is now fairly well known. He went back to South Wales because his heart was there and because his themes of life and death and love were mostly conceived in terms of the people, the places and the institutions of South Wales. In England he rounded out his Welsh accent until his voice became that curious and fascinating instrument that one may hear at its best in his recording of 'Poem in October', neither English nor Welsh, not exactly artificial but a voice in which there is a great deal of artifice, as there is in his verse.

He was never a professional Welshman. The Swansea or Cardiff boy, living in a city that is as much English as Welsh, is apt to feel that the 'true' Wales, not merely the Wales of coracles and *eisteddfodau*, but the Wales of the Rhondda and the pitted valleys might be real for other Welshmen, but not for him. Of the approximately two and a half million people who live in this rainy, mountainous country half the size of Switzerland, more than half – mainly those who live in the industrial south – do not speak or understand a great deal more Welsh than is implied by learning '*Mae Hen Wlad Fy Nhadau*' at school and singing '*Cwm Rhondda*' at rugger matches. Which is to say, at the most, a phrase-book Welsh. Dylan Thomas, having an educated and a quick mind, knew a little more than the average Southern Welshman, but he took no interest in the language – almost in fact deliberately turned away from it for to him it stood for Welsh Nationalism, and, as he once expressed it, 'F—— Welsh Nationalism!' Yet for all Dylan Thomas's disclaimers and for all that he did not speak or read Welsh, the mere fact of being born in a country so small, so clannish, and so fiercely nationalistic as Wales is meaningful in itself. It is, after all, only comparatively recently that Welsh has declined. My own maternal grandfather, who was born in the 'sixties in a valley north of Newport in Monmouthshire, a county which is not even officially part of Wales, spoke Welsh when he came to London. The national feeling engendered by so many hundreds of years of Welsh-speaking survives now without the actual bond of the language. The harp of Wales sounds in the ears of Welshmen whether they are archdruids from Bangor or boyos from the back streets of Cardiff. Without being hopelessly mystical about race, one can with some confidence assert that both it and environment have an effect on the nature of a people and the art that springs from them. The Welsh are lively, quick-tempered and proud. They talk to you in railway carriages and they sing together spontaneously, musically and unselfconsciously. And if this sounds like *How Green Was My Valley*, it is none the less true. You can find Welshmen who are as phlegmatic-seeming as the average Anglo-Saxon, but get them in an argument, or on a platform, or in a pub, and you will likely as not discover that quality of passion and attack which in the Welsh preacher is called *hwyl.*

In the 'natural' qualities of his poetry – its high emotional charge and sonorous rhetoric, and the lilt and exaggeration of its phrasing – Dylan Thomas reveals himself as a true son of the Cymry. For his subject-matter also he turned to Wales. This is obvious in his stories, and in the later poems with their references to Sir John's Hill and the hawks and herons of Carmarthen Bay, but it is there in the earlier poems too, behind the interest in Freudian and 'new romantic' symbolism. Finally, in his technique Thomas reveals affinities with Welsh poets past and present, and although he preferred detective stories, science fiction, Dickens, or practically anything that might be at hand, to books *about* poetry, it is fairly certain that he must have known something about the manner of the ancient Welsh metres if not their precise form. The metrical tricks and patterns he uses are personal to him and much less complicated than in the Welsh, but they are of the same general type. It has been suggested that he learnt from Hopkins, who made a thorough, scholarly study of Welsh metres and developed in particular the idea of 'consonantal chime' which he got from *cynghanedd.* But Thomas is more tricky than Hopkins. Where Hopkins uses effects of rhyme and alliteration for the sake of more music, Thomas will, when he feels like it, amuse himself with verse patterns which add nothing to the music of the verse at all and, in fact, have only a curiosity-value. For example, the Prologue to the *Collected Poems* is composed in two verses of 51 lines, the first line of the second verse rhyming with the last line of the first verse, the next line of the second rhyming with the penultimate of the first, and so on, outwards. On the other hand, in 'The Conversation of Prayer' he uses the device of internal rhyme and assonance with great musical effect:

1 2
The conversation of prayers about to be said

2 1
By the child going to bed and the man on the stairs
3 4
Who climbs to his dying love in her high room,
4 3
The one not caring to whom in his sleep he will move
1 2
And the other full of tears that she will be dead.

This rhyming/assonance pattern is continued through four stanzas on a groundwork of these four vowel-sounds. It is not *cynghanedd*, but it is in keeping with the idea of it. It is a more meticulous and, in a way, a more wilful patterning than Hopkins allowed himself, and to this extent more Welsh. The fact that Thomas does not seem ever to have used the rhyme schemes of *englynion*, and *cywydd* or *awdl*, or followed any of the three varieties of *cynghanedd* seems to indicate, however, that what he got from the example of his fathers was inspiration rather than specific working patterns. This may have been a result of his temperamental aversion to Welsh, as symbolic of the politically-tinged nationalism he despised. For, although the reverse of scholarly, he worked devotedly at metrical schemes which for some reason caught his fancy (like the villanelle, for example, which he used in 'Do not go gentle into that good night' and the diamond-hourglass early seventeenth century verse-shapes of 'Vision and Prayer'). It may have been partly, also, that the early Welsh metres are too excessively and unnecessarily complicated for even a virtuoso like Thomas to put them into English. For example, of the eight varieties of *englynion*, *englyn penfyr* calls for a stanza of three lines, of ten, seven, and seven syllables, with one main rhyme. As used by the anonymous author of the *Stavell Gyndylan* poem of the *Red Book of Hergest*, the main rhyme is, in the first line, two syllables in from the end of the line (it can be one, two, or three) and these end-syllables are echoed, either by alliteration or rhyme, in the first half of the second line. It can be seen that although this is not exactly the pattern of 'The Conversation of Prayer', it is very much in the spirit of it. In the second form of *cynghanedd*, from which Hopkins took 'consonantal chime', but which also includes 'vowel chime' as well, may be found the strict form of that internal rhyming and assonance which Thomas used in such lines as 'Twenty-four years remind the tears of my eyes', but which he did not continue throughout the whole poem. *Cynghanedd sain* calls for the division of each line into three sections, the first two rhyming, and the second and the third chiming in accordance with the rules of consonantal harmony. The second and third sections may be accented in four possible ways, the most usual of which are that both may end with a stressed syllable or both with an unstressed syllable. In so far as Thomas's verse is in keeping with an attitude to poetry which involved complicated patterns it may be called 'Welsh in feeling'. But it seems to me that the 'Welsh feeling' which came from writing in terms of the life around him was more significant in Thomas's case. It gave his verse its essential flavour, its characteristic suppressed passion and music, its mixture of sex and religion. The Welsh are the only people I know who sing hymns at football matches and in pubs, and the attitude of mind that this reveals is reflected in Dylan Thomas's poetry. Other poets of Welsh birth or parentage who wrote in English – Vaughan, for example, Edward Thomas, W. H. Davies, Wilfred Owen, Alun Lewis – are not like Thomas in style or tone partly because they did not allow themselves to be artistically and emotionally responsive to the natural facts of the Welsh scene, and partly because they wrote in the conventional or pre-Symbolist mode. In their case – even in that of Owen who contributed the idea of assonance to English poetry – the act of composition was a matter of 'writing about' a particular scene, event, or emotion. In Thomas's case, it was living the actual experience through the word, as Hopkins had done. It was carving out words, hewing images that were (there is no other phrase for it but T. S. Eliot's description of Metaphysical imagery) 'felt thought'. It was digging deep. It was recording a spiritual struggle through imagery used in a dramatic and essentially Shakespearean fashion, so that the reader is not *told about* something and thus encouraged to approximate his thought and feeling to the poet's by a process of sympathetic re-creation; he is part of it, he is at one with the poet at the actual moment of impact of the imagery. This conception of poetry has no necessary connection with being Welsh, but it makes the Welshness come out because it implies the unconscious use of whatever is most immediate to the writer's experience. It brings us to what is most significant about Thomas, his uniting of two kinds of poetic communication, the Shakespearean and the post-Symbolist. It is what makes him a 'New Romantic' poet, a description which calls for some clarification.

The term 'New Romantic' has been fairly loosely used over the past fifteen years and the fact that it was appropriated by and falsely identified with the now defunct New Apocalyptic group should make us suspicious of it. However, there is a good reason for using the term to describe Dylan Thomas and to a lesser extent George Barker, W. R. Rodgers and W. S. Graham. The Apocalyptics, gathered under the banner of Henry Treece and J. F. Hendry, were well-meaning but they tried to synthesise verse which would be a defiant challenge to the Object and the Machine. The result read like a cross between Surrealism and imitation-Thomas. This movement, which was an attempt to modify the principles of Surrealism, had a politico-social object and that alone removed it from the spirit of the writers the group professed to admire: Blake, and Lawrence, and Thomas. Poetry was not enough, it must serve a purpose, such as 'reintegrating the personality' or liberating man from the Machine. Myth, said the New Apocalyptics, would be used for this purpose. The result was an extraordinary body of writing published in three anthologies by a very diverse group of people (Henry Treece, J. F. Hendry, Nicholas Moore, Norman McCaig, etc.), with here and there a true and moving poem, by Tom Scott, Vernon Watkins or G. S. Fraser which seemed to have little in common with the self-conscious Apocalypticism of Mr Treece and Mr Hendry. It was fairly clear, from the first, that a movement with such a conscious programme, having no organic centre, might produce verse of a kind, but could not produce poetry. The heterogeneous component elements of the New Apocalypse drifted apart and some of the members, like Vernon Watkins and G. S. Fraser, freed from the burden, developed into excellent independent poets and critics. Dylan Thomas was not connected with this movement except in so far as he unwillingly allowed a story of his to be included in the first anthology. My only object in defining the scope of the New Apocalyptic movement is to bring out the measure of its difference from the art and intention of Dylan Thomas, for in my tracing of a New Romanticism in the present century I wish to be understood as excluding the New Apocalypse – except in so far as the theory of it indicated a desire to express the deep and hidden side of man's nature.

I should like to posit, at this point, two lines of development in poetry over the past hundred and fifty years, my excuse for such an attempted generality being that one such line has already been suggested by Sir Herbert Read, and that it allows no place for Dylan Thomas. Because I do not see Dylan Thomas as an isolated phenomenon but as part of a process in the evolution of modern poetry, it seems to me necessary to trace the strand which I see as running counter to, but contemporaneously with, the one followed by Sir Herbert Read in *The True Voice of Feeling*. Sir Herbert's main point is that the development of modern poetry has been towards a more natural diction and a looser verse structure. This he sees as expressive of what he has called, after Yeats, 'the cult of sincerity'. Freed from the artificiality of conventional patterns and that special attitude of mind encouraged by a poetic diction which is removed from the vitality of ordinary speech, verse has, in Sir Herbert's opinion, moved towards a greater honesty and effectiveness. Although it is better if we do not inquire too closely into this dictum when applied to Shakespeare's or Milton's use of the sonnet-form or Pope's diction and handling of the couplet in, say, 'The Essay on Man', we may feel inclined to agree that in general terms the statement is a reasonable one, and the line he has traced interesting and valid. It includes Coleridge (because of his notion of 'organic form'), Wordsworth (an obvious choice), Keats (a rather more doubtful one), Hopkins, Whitman and Lawrence, Ezra Pound and T. S. Eliot. I begin to balk, however, when Sir Herbert calls this line of development 'romantic'. That would make T. S. Eliot a romantic, and if T. S. Eliot is a romantic, what is Dylan Thomas? Something has happened along the line to lead to this odd result, and I believe it is because Sir Herbert has identified romanticism with Wordsworth, particularly with the Wordsworth of the Preface to the *Lyrical Ballads*. There is another kind of Romanticism, however, and that is the romanticism of 'Kubla Khan'.

I would oppose to Sir Herbert's 'cult of sincerity' some such term as the 'cult of irrationality', for, in looking back over the history of English poetry during the past 350 years, and of English and French poetry taken as a whole during the past 100 years, we can, I think, point to signs of what was to come out into the open at the end of the nineteenth century, the acceptance of the irrational nature of the poetic imagination, and the attempt to express in poetry some of the hidden workings of men's natures. At first this expression took a wild and, in some cases, a deliberately irresponsible and iconoclastic form; but there has been time, during the past fifty years, for the wildness to evaporate and the true nature of this revolution in sensibility to be seen. It can, I think, be seen in its true form in the poetry of Dylan Thomas, who, without knowing it, without ever self-consciously attempting anything like Apocalypticism, was able to draw on the Shakespearean element in English poetry and on the legacy of Symbolism. I refer here not to the use of symbols in the traditional sense, but to the concept of language itself as symbolical which has developed since the experiments of the late nineteenth century French Symbolists and which was given an added impetus by the publication of Hopkins' poems in 1918, of *Ulysses* in 1925, and of the 'Work in Progress' which became *Finnegan's Wake* in 1939. There are two points which perhaps need amplification before we can proceed to the line of romanticism which I oppose to Sir Herbert Read's and which I see as flowering in the art of Dylan Thomas. The first is my use of the word 'irrationality' and the second the linking of Shakespeare's concept of imagery with the symbolical use of language.

'Irrationality' is, in terms of the general development of western culture, a bad word, for the development of reason has always been considered to be one of the chief characteristics which distinguish man from the brutes. Yet we recognise now, in a perfectly respectable and sober way, and in psychological but not specifically Freudian terms, that man does not live by reason alone. I do not wish to press the obvious, but in view of the case I am making it is perhaps better if I attempt some simplified re-statement of what I take to be our present understanding. There is a passage in John MacMurray's *Reason and Emotion* which makes the point very well. 'The nineteenth century', says Mr MacMurray,

> was the climax of a long period of social repression in which the intellectual development of reason was the main effort, and the emotional life was considered chiefly as an intrusive force which prevented the achievement of that calmness which is necessary for the proper functioning of thought. But that development itself brings us back at last to the emotional life. The development of science finally must direct its attention to personality itself; and as soon as it does this it is directed upon the emotional sources of all human activity. It is because it is so difficult for us to

> bring our unconscious motives into consciousness that at last we find ourselves driven to make the attempt.

In the total context of our life and the art which springs from it, the emotional and the intuitive elements have a peculiar force. The revolt against reason has taken many forms since Blake said, 'I assert for myself that I do not behold the outward creation and that for me it is a hindrance'. 'Kubla Khan' and 'The Ancient Mariner' are part of this revolt, and so is the work of the Symbolists. Rimbaud said:

> I accustomed myself to simple hallucination; I saw quite freely a mosque in place of a factory, a school of drums made by the angels.

Those later developments, Dada-ism and Surrealism, are interesting, not so much in themselves as in the role they play in a gradual change of temper. We are now past hallucination and 'thought's dictation in the absence of all control' and we are left with something much more valuable, the idea of language itself as a symbol, by which we can see the possibility of a new art, able to absorb the lessons of the Romantic agony yet not suffer from its excesses, to feel, and through feeling to think, *through* words, and not to regard them as the illustration of thought. As Mr Blackmuir once put it, 'Words bring meanings to birth and themselves contained the meaning as an imminent possibility before the pangs of junction'. Some recent critics, notably Mr Charles Feidelson, have taken this position a stage further and asserted, in contradiction of Edmund Wilson, that the concept of the symbolical use of language has not developed from Romanticism at all, but is something different in kind. The symbolic literary work, Mr Feidelson asserts, is 'autonomous in the sense that it is quite distinct both from the personality of its author and from any world of pure objects'. This viewpoint I cannot find meaningful since it seems to plunge us into a world of cybernetic fantasy. An author's work, however little he might be concerned to clothe in words any hypothetical 'thought', cannot help but be an involuntary expression of something deep-seated in his personality. Dylan Thomas uses language symbolically, he is a carver-out of phrases, but what makes his verse different from the verse of, say, Dryden is not only a completely new concept of literary art but also a difference in personality. Personality helps to form a style; style is expressive of artistic personality. However, be that as it may, my task is now to trace the line I have posited in opposition to Sir Herbert Read's and to justify my statement that Dylan Thomas drew on a sense of imagery which was native to British poetry and fused it with the concept of poetic communication which has developed since the Symbolists.

Sir Herbert calls his line the 'true voice of feeling'. This is for the reader to judge, but I feel that it is rather *a* voice of feeling. The development of a more natural diction, an idea which can, I suppose, be traced to the *Lyrical Ballads*, is dear to our hearts, but it is associated with (one might almost say it leads to, as Sir Herbert seems to indicate by following his line through T. E. Hulme and the Imagists) the idea of imagery as a visual thing. As Hulme said in *Speculations*:

> . . . the effect of rhythm, like that of music, is to produce a kind of hypnotic state. . . . This is for the art of chanting, but the procedure of the new *visual* art is just the contrary.

But this is to deny the verbal magnificence of much English verse. Connotative power and verbal alchemy are at least part of the English poetic genius, even if one argues that they are not basic to it, as Sir Herbert seems to be doing. In fact, if they are not symbolic of the English genius, whose genius are they symbolic of? Visual images, Dantesque lucidity, which T. S. Eliot contrasted with the 'opacity' of Shakespeare – these things are more natural to nations which live in the sun. In the English seasons of mists, such bareness and hardness cannot be felt along the blood. There is a strong strain in British poetry which shouts a sheer delight in words, words which, at their best, make a music equally in the mind and in the ear. Beyond Swinburnian incantation or Kiplingish thumpetythump, there is a deep clear note, which is the note of:

> And pity, like a naked new-born babe,
> Striding the blast, or heaven's cherubim, hors'd
> Upon the sightless couriers of the air,
> Shall blow the horrid deed in every eye,
> That tears shall drown the wind.

of:

> Then glut thy sorrow on a morning rose,
> Or on the rainbow of the salt sand-wave,
> Or on the wealth of globed peonies;
> Or if thy mistress some rich anger shows,
> Emprison her soft hand, and let her rave,
> And feed deep, deep upon her peerless eyes.

and of:

> Never until the mankind making
> Bird beast and flower
> Fathering and all humbling darkness
> Tells with silence the last light breaking
> And the still hour
> Is come of the sea tumbling in harness
>
> And I must enter again the round
> Zion of the water bead
> And the synagogue of the ear of corn
> Shall I let pray the shadow of a sound
> Or sow my salt seed
> In the least valley of sackcloth to mourn
>
> The majesty and burning of the child's death.

This is the other voice of feeling, which is also the voice of Donne, Blake, Hopkins and Yeats, as well as of Shakespeare, Keats and Dylan Thomas. Those who speak with this voice work through a striking imagery, more verbal than visual, towards an indefinable glory of utterance which transcends and yet contains both music and felicitous phrasing. It is a mind-music which they utter; it is artificial in the best sense, and it is one element which I believe can be discerned in Dylan Thomas's poems – in, for example, 'The Ballad of the Long-Legged Bait', 'A Refusal to Mourn' and 'Over Sir John's Hill'. At some points it is connected with, but not exactly identical with, what I have called the 'cult of irrationality', which can be traced from the later Shakespeare, particularly the Shakespeare of *King Lear*, through Blake, the Coleridge of 'Kubla Khan', the signs of *Sehnsucht* and the gothic which precursed Lautréamont, through Baudelaire and the late nineteenth-century French Symbolists, through Surrealism to Dylan Thomas.

I perhaps ought to make one point very clear. I am not saying that Dylan Thomas's verse is *like* any of these aspects of the romantic sensibility; but what I am saying is that they are stages in the development of a concept of literature the present end-product of which is Dylan Thomas. The extent to which Dylan Thomas fused a comprehension of the irrational bases of poetic power with a rigorous intellectual control is fully apparent in his verse, but it is also illustrated in the now famous statement which he made in a letter to Henry Treece:

> I make one image – though 'make' is not the word; I let, perhaps, an image be 'made' emotionally in me and then apply to it what intellectual and critical forces I possess – let it breed another, let that image contradict the first, make, of the third image bred out of the other two together, a fourth contradictory image, and let them all, within my imposed formal limits, conflict.

The phrases I should like to underline in this statement are 'apply to it what intellectual and critical forces I possess' and 'within my imposed formal limits'. In other words, one can let the images come as they will, almost as the Surrealists let them come, provided a poetic-critical intelligence of the first order is operating at the same time. Or, to put it another way, one can be 'organic' and still agree to submit oneself to a control, either of a standard form like the villanelle or of a form of one's own making. One of the false steps in Sir Herbert Read's argument lay, I believe, in his assertion that the development of the 'organic concept' of poetry was bound up with the development of free verse, a belief which led him to say sadly in *Form in Modern Poetry*: 'Why a later generation should have refused to follow where we led is no doubt a phase of history which some devotee of the dialectical method will one day explain'. 'We' refers particularly to Ezra Pound and T. S. Eliot and, more generally, to that group of friends which met in T. E. Hulme's rooms in Frith Street, in Soho. 'Where we led' means, in Sir Herbert's own words, 'in the technique of "free verse" in the original meaning of that phrase'. That cry from the heart was the true voice of Sir Herbert's feeling.

The patterns of development discerned by critics are no more valuable and of course no more definite than the boundaries made by geographers between one vegetation region and another. Lines merge, patterns dissolve before the flux of creation. That this is true, however, does not make the critical attempt any less valid. The achievement of Dylan Thomas is clearer, to me at least, for trying to see him as part of a process which illustrated men's attempts to reveal themselves to themselves. It remains to point out, however, that T. S. Eliot, at the end of Sir Herbert Read's line of more natural diction and visual imagery, has in his own way, been as affected by post-Symbolism as Dylan Thomas. Since he has a different kind of imagination, however, and takes his tone from polite and ironical conversation, the suggestive power of his images is less powerful but more available than Dylan Thomas's. Where T. S. Eliot preserves a level of understandable statement, perfectly acceptable if spoken in an ordinary voice in a drawing-room, Dylan Thomas comes bursting in, throws his head back and spell-binds us. This is embarrassing to the twentieth century Anglo-Saxon temperament, which finds spell-binding all very well when safely removed to the stage, but on the whole prefers the quiet voice and gesture, and the laconic hint. In such a cultural climate the poet of the Hopkins or Thomas type is inclined to be regarded as an exotic. But there are signs that the climate is changing, that we are beginning to feel once more that poetry should sound like poetry and not like the voice of an old man in a dry month. What Hart Crane did in America and what George Barker, W. S. Graham, W. R. Rodgers and Christopher Fry are doing in varying modes and with varying degrees of success in England is not exactly what Dylan Thomas was doing, but it is indicative of a feeling for the music and magnificence of language. It is also indicative of a salutary recognition that artifice is necessary to the poetic art, and that it is only when artifice is uninformed by imaginative power that artificiality and a sense of insincerity are produced. Dylan Thomas was an artificer but he was in no sense 'insincere'. There is, we know, no one right starting point and no one right method, and language itself seems as good a place to start as any. 'Exercises in technique,' as W. H. Auden said in his Preface to W. S. Merwin's first book, 'often end up by being works of art as well.' A feeling for language used in a symbolical and dramatic way and that perception of 'similarity in dissimilars' which is the essence of the Shakespearean metaphor, seem, in fact, a more likely vehicle than bare and Imagist verse to catch that sense of multifariousness which is the legacy of Symbolism. Dylan Thomas, whose work was itself a symbol of this new-old approach to poetry, was able to express the simplicity of the child's vision and the wisdom of the heart and the senses in a more memorable way than any poet since Hopkins. He, too, celebrated man and, in his own way, God, and his affirming spirit was a challenge to those for whom 'the possessors of the inner voice ride ten in a compartment to a football match at Swansea, listening to the inner voice, which breathes the eternal message of vanity, fear, and lust'.

Dylan Thomas

KARL SHAPIRO

THE DEATH OF DYLAN THOMAS a year and a half ago was the cause of the most singular demonstration of suffering in recent literary history. One searches his memory in vain for any parallel to it. At thirty-nine, Thomas had endeared himself to the literary youth of England and America, to most of the poets who were his contemporaries, and to many who were his elders; he was the master of a public which he himself had brought out of nothingness; he was the idol of writers of every description and the darling of the Press. Critics had already told how Thomas became the first poet who was both popular and obscure. In an age when poets are supposed to be born old, everyone looked upon Thomas as the last of the young poets. When he died, it was as if there would never be any more youth in the world. Or so it seemed in the frenzy of his year-long funeral, a funeral which, like one of Thomas's own poems, turned slowly into a satanic celebration and a literary institution.

When Yeats and Valéry died, old and wise and untouchable, there were held, so to speak, the grand state funerals. It was civilisation itself that mourned. When Thomas died, a poet wrote wildly how, to get him up in the morning, he plugged Thomas's mouth with a bottle of beer, – 'this wonderful baby'. All the naughty stories were on everybody's lips; all the wrong things began to be said, and the right things in the wrong way. Someone quoted bitterly: 'Kill him, he's a poet!' and this childishness was the signal for a verbal massacre of the bourgeoisie, reminiscent of the early decades of our century.

The death of a young poet inflicts a psychic wound upon the world and is the cause among poets themselves of frightening babbling and sooth-saying. These doings may be likened to a witches' sabbath, and some have seen in these morbid celebrations the very coming-to-life of Thomas's poems. It is his death as an occasion for literary and psychological insurrection that must interest us today, if we are to understand the meaning of Thomas's poetry and the significance his contemporaries have given it. It is one thing to analyse and interpret poetry and keep it all in a book: it is another to watch that poetry enter an audience and melt it to a single mind. I want to speak about the second thing, the live thing, the thing that touched the raw nerve of the world and that keeps us singing with pain. We want to know what kind of audience that is. The poetry of Thomas is full of the deepest pain; there are few moments of relief. What is the secret of his pain-filled audience? How are we to place Thomas among the great impersonal poets of our time, when this one is so personal, so intimate and so profoundly grieved? Thomas was the first modern romantic you could put your finger on, the first whose journeys and itineraries became part of his own mythology, the first who offered himself up as a public sacrifice. Hence the piercing sacrificial note in his poetry, the uncontainable voice, the drifting almost ectoplasmic character of the man, the desperate clinging to a few drifting spars of literary convention. Hence, too, the universal acclaim for his lyricism, and the mistaken desire to make him an heir to Bohemia or to the high Symbolist tradition.

Writers said of Thomas that he was the greatest lyricist of our time. The saying became a platitude. It was unquestionably true, but what did the word mean? It meant that, aside from the epic pretensions of many of the leading modern poets, there was only one who could be called a singer: Thomas. To call him the best lyric poet of our time was to pay him the highest, the only compliment. Nearly everyone paid him this splendid compliment and everyone knew its implications. But no one, I believe, fully understood that this compliment marked a turning-point in poetry. I doubt that Thomas himself knew how personal poetry might become after him.

During his life there were also the armed camps who made him honorary revolutionary general; and I cannot be sure Thomas refused the home-made epaulets of these border patrols. I rather think he was proud to be taken in. Who were these people? First there are those we can call the Blankety-Blank School of modern poetry, the remnant of Bohemia. These are people who exist in the belief that everyone is dead except themselves. I saw one of these poets lately; he had just come from England and he informed me casually that everyone in England is dead. To change the subject I asked him if he was glad to be home; but it turned out that everyone in America is also dead. Among these poets there is a sincere fascination for all things dead; and it is interesting to speculate upon their adoption of Thomas as a leader and a patron saint. In the same way nearly all critics and lovers of Thomas's poetry have spoken of him in connection with Symbolism. The similarity between the symbolist position and that of the Bohemian remnant is noteworthy. The Remnant poets are clearly materialistic and social revolutionary; the Symbolist critics praise the love of death as the highest order of poetic knowledge. The two positions are really one: one is a vulgarisation of the other.

All the same, this theory of posthumous vitality seems to make sense when we speak of Thomas. How much did Thomas subscribe to official Symbolism? Just enough to provide ammunition for those people. How much did he love death as his major symbol? As much as any poet I know in the English language. These factions have a claim on Thomas which we cannot fully contradict.

Thomas is in somewhat the relation to modern poetry that Hopkins was to Tennyson and the Victorians; this is a relation of anti-magnetism. Thomas resisted the literary traditionalism of the Eliot school; he wanted no part of it. Poetry to him was not a civilising manœuvre, a replanting of the gardens; it was a holocaust, a sowing of the wind. But I do not think we can compare Thomas, say, with Auden, because they are different in kind. Thomas's antithesis to Auden, as to Eliot, and his school is significant. Thomas grew up in a generation which had lost every kind of cultural leadership. The poets who began to write during the Depression, which was worse in Wales than in America, were deprived of every ideal. The favourite poem of this generation was Yeats's 'The Second Coming'. Yeats's poems gave to a generation of prematurely wise young poets an apocalypse, a vision of anti-Christ and a vision of the downfall of civilisation. The theatricality of the Yeats poem was a great convenience to a poet like Thomas who, having nothing of true philosophical or religious substance to fall back upon, could grasp this straw. The acknowledged precedence of Yeats in modern English literature – in world literature perhaps – has been a consolation to all poets. Yeats with his cruel forcing of the imagination – his jimmying of the spirit – is an heroic figure in modern poetry. One thinks of him as brute imagination holding off the forces of speed – the historical speed-up of the spool of film that goes faster and faster and faster and ends up flipping around idiotically on the reel. Like every whole poet he tried to stop this runaway by opening out a more grand and more distant prospect. . . . And this is where Thomas looked in.

The romantic poets who were the new poets of Thomas's generation had one moment of intellectual generalship; to bring about a change of heart, as Auden said, in mankind. The official name of this philosophy: Marxism. But the belief betrayed the believers; and war, always a natural setting for poets, threw down not only the remaining gods but their statues. The poets went leaping through the flames. This was the apocalypse that Yeats prefigured after the first world war; the horror of the second war surpassed the historical imagination; the prescience of the third war paralysed thought. In this atmosphere the poetry of Dylan Thomas was composed.

Thomas suffers from the waifishness imposed upon his generation.

The so-called Apocalyptic poets, which he was supposed to be a member of, never existed. One can see that he plays around with copying the superficies of Vaughan and Herbert and Traherne and maybe David ap Gwilym (who in English is not much better than James Whitcomb Riley) and Yeats and Hopkins. But Thomas was outside the orbit of the English poets who succeeded Eliot and cannot easily be placed in their tradition. He was anti-tradition by nature, by place, by inclination. Certainly Thomas's love for America can also be seen in this light; America is the untraditional place, the Romantic country *par excellence*.

Thomas's technique is deceptive. When you look at it casually you think it is nothing. The metre is banal. It is no better and no worse than that of dozens of other poets of his age. There is no invention and a great deal of imitation. There is no theory. Yeats and Auden and Pound have developed this aspect of English poetry almost single-handed, each for his followers. But despite his lack of originality, the impress of Thomas's idiom on present-day English poetry is incalculable. One critic said not many years ago that Thomas had visited a major affliction on English poetry. This was an unfriendly way of saying that Thomas had captured the young poets, which he certainly had. How did Thomas do this? He did it through the force of emotion. He did it with the personal idiom, the twists of language, the bending of the iron of English. Once he had bent this iron his way everybody else tried it. Thomas has more imitators today than any other poet in the literature. Whether this excitement will last a year or a hundred years, no one can tell. But it is a real excitement. Except Yeats, Eliot, Pound and Auden, and perhaps Stevens, no one else has had this power over the language in our day.

Even when we examine the texture of his language we fail to find anything original. But at the same time, we find something completely distinctive. It is hard to locate the distinctiveness of Thomas's idiom, There are a few tricks of word order, a way of using a sentence, a characteristic vocabulary, an obsessive repetition of phrase, and so on – things common to many lesser poets. Again, if we analyse his images and metaphors, which are much more impressive than the things I have mentioned, we frequently find over-development, blowsiness and euphemism, on the one hand, and brilliant crystallisation on the other. But no system, no poetic, no practice that adds up to anything you can hold on to. The more you examine Thomas as a stylist the less you find.

What does this mean? It means that Thomas is a quite derivative, unoriginal, unintellectual poet, the entire force of whose personality and vitality is jammed into his few difficult half-intelligible poems. To talk about Thomas as a Symbolist is dishonest. Not long ago in Hollywood, Aldous Huxley introduced a Stravinsky composition based on a poem of Thomas. Huxley quoted that line of Mallarmé's which says that poets purify the dialect of the tribe. This, said Huxley, was what Thomas did. Now anybody who has read Thomas knows that he did the exact opposite: Thomas did everything in his power to obscure the dialect of the tribe – whatever that expression may mean. Thomas sometimes attempted to keep people from understanding his poems (which are frequently simple, once you know the dodges). He had a horror of simplicity – or what I consider to be a fear of it. He knew little except what a man knows who has lived forty years, and there was little he wanted to know. There is a fatal pessimism in most of his poems, set off by a few bursts of joy and exuberance. The main symbol is masculine love, driven as hard as Freud drove it. In the background is God, hard to identify but always there, a kind of God who belongs to ones parents rather than to the children, who do not quite accept him.

I went through the *Collected Poems* recently to decide which poems I would keep if I were editing the best poems of Dylan Thomas. Out of about ninety poems I chose more than thirty which I think stand with the best poems of our time. If this seems a small number, we should remember that there are not many more poems upon which the fame of Hopkins rests; of Rimbaud;

or, for that matter, John Donne. And yet we expect a greater volume of work from such an exuberant man. And it is a point with many modern classicists that they have written so little. Thomas's sixty poems that I would exclude are short of his mark: but they are not failures. Even within the past fifteen years the critical consciousness of our time, which is of the most sensitive temper, has noticed the best in Thomas. I would like to name by name those poems which I think belong to the permanent body of any poetry – or most of them anyway:

'I see the boys of summer'; 'A process in the weather of the heart'; 'The force that through the green fuse drives the flower'; 'Especially when the October wind'; 'When like a running grave'; 'Light breaks where no sun shines'; 'Do you not father me'; 'A grief ago'; 'And death shall have no dominion'; 'Then was my neophyte'; 'When all my five and country senses'; 'We lying by seasand'; 'It is the sinner's dust-tongued bell'; 'After the funeral'; 'Not from this anger'; 'How shall my animal'; 'Twenty-four years'; 'A Refusal to Mourn'; 'Poem in October'; 'The Hunchback in the Park'; 'Into her lying-down head'; 'Do not go gentle'; 'A Winter's Tale'; 'The Marriage of a Virgin'; 'When I woke'; 'Among those killed in the dawn raid'; 'Fern Hill'; 'In Country Sleep'; 'Over Sir John's Hill'; and 'Poem on His Birthday'. I leave out the sonnets, which I think are rather forced, and the 'Ballad of the Long-Legged Bait', and the 'Prologue', and many others. My list is probably off here and there but I think it is the substantial list of works by which Thomas will be remembered.

The 'major' poems, that is the more pretentious poems, such as the ten sonnets (called 'Altarwise by Owl-Light'), reveal most of what we know of Thomas's convictions and what we can call his philosophy. He believed in God and Christ; the Fall and death, the end of all things and the day of eternity; while everything living carries in it its own germ of destruction, and one can envisage life as an insane mockery, there will yet be Mercy. This is very conventional religion but Thomas was uncritical about it. Add to this the puritanism which runs through his whole work. And, finally, the forced optimism in the last poems such as 'In Country Sleep', in which, although the whole sequence is unfinished, there is a recognisable affirmation of faith in life. But one feels that these matters are not of paramount importance in the poetry of Thomas. Thomas was not interested in philosophical answers. Religion, such as he knew it, was direct and natural; the symbolism of religion, as he uses it, is poetry, direct knowledge. Religion is not to be used: it is simply part of life, part of himself; it is like a tree; take it or leave it, it is there. In this sense, one might say that Thomas is more religious than Eliot, because Thomas has a natural religious approach to nature and to himself. The language of Thomas is very close to that of Hopkins, not only in obvious ways, but in its very method. Hopkins, however, arrived at his method philosophically, abstractly, as well as through temperament, and the twist of his personality. Thomas, with no equipment for theorising about the forms of nature, sought the 'forms' that Hopkins did. The chief difference between the two poets in terms of their symbols is that Hopkins draws his entire symbology from the God-symbol; Thomas draws his symbology almost entirely from the Sex-symbol. God, in various attributes, is the chief process in Hopkins's view of the world; sex is the chief process in Thomas's view of the world.

Thomas's idea of process is important. The term itself is rather mechanistic, as he intends. He always takes the machine of energy rather than some abstraction, such as spirit or essence. Hence the concreteness of his words and images; obscurity occurs also because of the 'process' of mixing the imagery of the subconscious with biological imagery as in Hopkins. But there is also a deliberate attempt to involve the subconscious as the main process: Thomas's imagination, which is sometimes fantastic, works hard to dredge up the images of fantasy and dreams. Very often the process fails and we are left with heaps of grotesque images that add up to nothing. I would equate the process in Thomas's poetics with his rather startling views of the sexual process. Aside from those poems in which sex is simply sung, much as poets used to write what we called love poems, there are those poems in which sex is used as the instrument of belief and knowledge. I do not know how to make this clearer, but perhaps there is a comparison between Thomas and Baudelaire's description of physical love as a surgical operation. Using the cliché of modern literature that everyone is sick and the whole world is a hospital, Thomas wants to imply that sex will make us (or usually just him) healthy and whole again. And there are suggestions of Druidism (which I know nothing about) and primitive fertility rites, apparently still extant in Wales, all mixed up with Henry Miller, Freud, and American street slang. But sex kills also, as Thomas says a thousand times, as in a dream, and he is not sure of the patient's recovery. In place of love, about which Thomas is almost always profoundly bitter, there is sex, the instrument and the physical process of love. The activity of sex, Thomas hopes in his poems, will somehow lead to love in life and in the cosmos. As he grows older, love recedes and sex becomes a nightmare, a Black Mass.

Thomas moves between sexual revulsion and sexual ecstasy, between puritanism and mysticism, between formalistic ritual (this accounts for his lack of invention) and irresponsibility. In his book one comes, on one page, upon a poem of comparative peace and lucidity, and on the next page, upon a poem of absolute density and darkness. His dissatisfaction with his own lack of stability is reflected in his devices which intend to obscure even the simple poems: he leaves out all indications of explanation – quotation marks, punctuation, titles, connectives, whether logical or grammatical. In addition he uses every extreme device of ambiguity one can think of, from reversing the terms of a figure of speech to ellipsis to over elaboration of images. There is no poetic behind these practices – only an undefined mystique. One is always confused in Thomas by not knowing whether he is using the microscope or the telescope: he switches from one to the other with ease and without warning. It is significant that his joyous poems, which are few, though among his best, are nearly always his simplest. Where the dominant theme of despair obtrudes, the language dives down into the depths: and some of these complex poems of the depths are among the most rewarding, the richest in feeling, and the most difficult to hold to. But, beyond question, there are two minds working in Thomas, the joyous naturally religious mind, and the disturbed, almost pathological mind of the cultural fugitive or clown. On every level of Thomas's work one notices the lack of sophistication and the split in temperament. This is his strength as well as his weakness. But it is a *grave* weakness because it leaves him without defence, without a bridge between himself and the world. Thomas begins in a blind alley with the obsessive statement that birth is the beginning of death: it is the basic poetic statement but it means nothing unless the poet can build a world between. Thomas never really departs from this statement, and his obsession with sex is only the clinical re-statement of the same theme. The idealisation of love, the traditional solution with most poets, good and bad, is never arrived at in Thomas. He skips into the land of love, like somebody else's garden, and skips out again. And he is too good a poet to fake love. He doesn't feel it; he distrusts it; he doesn't believe it. He falls back on the love-process, the assault, the defeat, the shame, the despair. Over and over again he repeats the ritualistic formulas for love, always doubting its success. The process is despised because it doesn't really work. The brief introduction to the collected poems sounds a note of bravado which asserts that his poems 'are written for the love of Man and in praise of God'. One wishes they were; one is grateful for the acknowledgment to God and Man, but in the poems we find neither faith nor humanism. What we find is something that fits Thomas into the age: the satanism, the vomitous horror, the self-elected crucifixion of the artist.

In the last few years of his life Thomas was beginning to find an audience. No one, I think, was more surprised than he at this phenomenon, because most of the poems which the audience liked had been in books for five or ten years already. Thomas was the one modern poet who by his presence created an audience. His audience was the impossible one: a general audience for a barely understandable poet. His way of meeting this audience, at the end, was no solution for Thomas as a poet. He became a dramatist, a writer of scenarios, a producer. What he wrote in this phase was not negligible by any means; but it was probably not what he wanted and not what his audience wanted. His audience wanted the poetry; they wanted the agony of the process. The frenzy that attended Dylan Thomas's death was a frenzy of frustration. Many times, in his stories and letters and his talk, Thomas tried to leap over this frustration into a Rabelaisian faith; but it never rang true enough. After the gaiety came the hangover, the horrible fundamentalist remorse. Yet through the obscurity of the poetry everyone could feel the scream of desperation: not a cry of desire; on the contrary, it was the opposite; it was the cry of the trapped animal; the thing wanting to be man; the man wanting to be spirit.

He is a self-limited poet; and an exasperating one. He runs beyond your reach after he has beckoned you to follow; he arouses you and then slumps into a heap. He knows, more than his readers, that he has no bridge between life and death, between self and the world; his poetry is absolutely literal (as he himself insisted all the time). But its literalness is the challenge to literature which is always significant. Thomas sought to keep poetry in his hand, like a boy who has captured a bird. Sometimes the bird is squeezed to death. He is too honest to rhapsodise or to intone over the great symbols: rather he growls or rages or more often hypnotises himself by the minute object, which he is likely to crush in his anger. Unlike Hopkins, he has no vision of nature and cannot break open the forms of nature; he cannot break open words. He focuses madly on the object, but it will not yield. He calls a weathercock a bow-and-arrow bird. Metaphor won't come and he resorts to riddle, the opposite of metaphor. A good half of his poetry is the poetry of rage: not rage at the world of society or politics or art or anything except self. He is impatient for a method and the impatience early turns into desperation, the desperation into clowning. Consider the enormous patience of Yeats or Pound or Stevens in stalking their prey: these are great hunters of the word. Thomas falls off his elephant and ends up by thinking it funny. But not really. Because he was not a member of the hunting party in the first place; he just happened to wander that way. He was not the kind of poet who knew what was meant by the tradition; he was another *naïf*, like Rimbaud, a countryman, who having left the country wanders over the face of the earth seeking a vision. He is running away from his fame, which he does not feel equal to. He is running away from the vision of self, or keeping the integrity of self by fleeing from the foci of tradition. I interpret the life and work of Thomas this way: the young poet of natural genius and expansive personality who recoils from the ritual of literary tradition and who feels himself drawn into it as into a den of iniquity. (This is both the puritanism and the provincialism of Thomas). Such a man can never acquire the wisdom of the world which is called worldliness, and he turns to the only form of behaviour, literary and otherwise, permissible both to society and to self. That is buffoonery. All the literary world loves a buffoon: the French make a saint of the clown. But folklore always says the clown dies in the dressing-room.

It is the most certain mark of Thomas's genius that he did not give way to any vision but his own, the one authentic source of knowledge he had – himself. And it is the most certain mark of his weakness that he could not shield himself from the various literary preceptors who buzzed around his head like a helmet of bees. He became immobile, I think, out of pure fright. He wrote personal letters (which are now being published) apparently meant for publication, in which he adopted the modern clichés about modern life. He pretended to be horrified by the electric toaster (or maybe really was).

The doctrinaire impersonality of our poetry demands allegiance to a tradition: any tradition, even one you rig up for yourself. Thomas represents the extreme narrowness of the individual genius, the basic animal (one of his favourite symbols) in man. The animal to Thomas is everything and we listen because he calls it animal, not spirit or essence or potentiality or something else. It is the authentic symbol for a poet who believes in the greatness of the individual and the sacredness of the masses. It is Whitman's symbol when he says he thinks he could turn and live with animals: because they are natural and belong to nature and do not try to twist nature out of its socket. They do not try to believe anything contrary to their condition.

But Thomas is drawn away from his animal; he becomes brute. And this he knows. In the brute phase of his poetry (which is the phase loved by the modernists who picked up his scent) the poetry is a relentless cutting down to the quick, surgery, butchery and worse. And as Thomas is the one and only subject of his poems, we know what is being destroyed.

It is some of the saddest poetry we have. It leaves us finally with grief. The pathos of Thomas is that he is not diabolical, not mystical, not possessed; he has not the expansive imagination of Blake nor the fanatical self-control of Yeats, nor the suicidal gaiety of the accursed poet. He is the poet of genius unable to face life. Like D. H. Lawrence he is always hurling himself back into childhood, and the childhood of the world. Everyone speaks of Thomas as a child. He became a child.

It is easy to dismiss him but he will not be dismissed. He was a tremendous talent who stung himself into insensibility because he could not face the obligations of intellectual life. He could not take the consequences of his own natural beliefs; and he could not temporise; there was no transition, no growth, only the two states of natural joy and intellectual despair, love of trees and fascination of the brute process. He said everything he had to say: it had little to do with wars and cities and art galleries. What he said was that man is a child thrust into the power of self; an animal becoming an angel. But becoming an angel he becomes more a beast. There is no peace, no rest, and death itself is only another kind of disgusting sex. Yet man must not believe so little. He must invent a belief in love, even if it doesn't exist. – For Thomas it did not exist. Other writers knew that here was his Achilles heel.

But something happened. Somehow the spark escaped; it leapt out of the hands of literature and set a fire. Thomas, I think, did the impossible in modern poetry. He made a jump to an audience which, we have been taught to believe, does not exist. It is an audience that understands him even when they cannot understand his poetry. It is probably the first non-funereal poetry audience in fifty years, and an audience that has been deprived of poetry by fiat. It bears certain characteristics to the mob – but that, under the circumstances, is also understandable. The audience understands Thomas instinctively. They know he is reaching out to them but doesn't quite know how to effect the meeting. The reaching ends in a tantalising excitement, a frenzy. It is not a literary frenzy, the kind that ends in a riot with the police defending Edith Sitwell after a reading of *Façade*. On the contrary, it is the muttering of awakening, a slow realisation about poetry, a totally unexpected apocalypse. This audience sees Thomas as a male Edna St Vincent Millay, or perhaps a Charlie Chaplin; they hear the extraordinary vibrato, a voice of elation and anguish singing over their heads like a wind that tears all the blossoms off the trees. They know this is poetry and they know it is for them.

He is like the old cliché of vaudeville in which a tragi-comic figure engaged in some private act (such as keeping his pants from falling down) wanders on to a stage where a highly formal cultural something is in progress. Naturally the embarrassed clown steals the show. One must remember Thomas's own story about himself – there are many variations – the story in which he gets his finger stuck in a beer bottle and can't get it out. He goes from place to place, beer bottle and all, meeting new people. The beer bottle becomes Thomas's symbol of his natural self: it is his passport from the common people to the literary life, and back again. It is both his symbol of self and his symbol of other-self. But to Thomas it is mainly a horror symbol. It is the key to no-man's-Land. Because Thomas is an uncivilisable puritan and a hardshell fundamentalist of some undefinable kind, the puritanism sets up the tension in his poetry – a tension based upon love and fear of love – the basic sexual tension, the basic theological tension. The greatness of Thomas is that he recognises the equation; and the weakness of Thomas is that he takes to his heels when he tries to grapple with it.

Everything I have said can be said better in the little poem by Thomas that takes nine lines. The last line of the poem is so much like a line of Whitman's that I have searched through Whitman's poems to find it. I am sure it is there and yet I know it isn't. The line reads: 'I advance for as long as forever is'.

> Twenty-four years remind the tears of my eyes.
> (Bury the dead for fear that they walk to the grave in labour)
> In the groin of the natural doorway I crouched like a tailor
> Sewing a shroud for a journey
> By the light of the meat-eating sun.
> Dressed to die, the sensual strut begun,
> With my red veins full of money,
> In the final direction of the elementary town
> I advance for as long as forever is.